THE
BREACH

THE

THE UNTOLD STORY OF THE
INVESTIGATION INTO JANUARY 6TH

BREACH

DENVER RIGGLEMAN

with HUNTER WALKER

Henry Holt and Company

New York

Henry Holt and Company
Publishers since 1866
120 Broadway
New York, New York 10271
www.henryholt.com

Henry Holt® and Ⓗ® are registered trademarks of Macmillan Publishing Group, LLC.

Library of Congress Cataloging-in-Publication Data is available.

ISBN: 9781250866769

Our books may be purchased in bulk for promotional, educational, or business use. Please contact your local bookseller or the Macmillan Corporate and Premium Sales Department at (800) 221-7945, extension 5442, or by e-mail at MacmillanSpecialMarkets@macmillan.com.

First Edition 2022

Designed by Meryl Sussman Levavi

Printed in the United States of America

10 9 8 7 6 5 4 3 2 1

To my wife, Christine, my daughters,
and my granddaughters

CONTENTS

AUTHORS' NOTE

This book is not the January 6th committee report. While I played a part in the investigation, I was not aware of every aspect of the committee's work. I do not mean to present this book as a complete account of that day. Instead, I hope to build on the public's knowledge of what happened when the Capitol was attacked. I also hope to add to the conversation about January 6th. It's something we can't look away from.

While this is just one man's story, I do believe my time advising the committee and my own life experience, including decades of military intelligence work and two years spent as a Republican member of Congress, give me a unique vantage point and insight into how our country went down this dark road—and how we might prevent something like January 6th from happening ever again.

I had to pick and choose how to explain complex topics in a way that's understandable to anyone reading this book. It was impossible to include every person and contingency. I also left out sensitive data that could affect the January 6th committee. I ask all open-source intelligence researchers and others who are studying January 6th extensively to please forgive me for excluding certain individuals and events.

This book makes a simple case. There is a growing militant, far-right, Christian nationalist movement that is being fueled by online disinformation. That movement now constitutes an extremist wing of the Republican Party—the party that I once belonged to—and it poses a serious danger to our democracy. Fringe movements of any political stripe can turn violent. The Left is not immune and certainly not blameless. However, at the moment, the Far Right is more organized and more militant. My story lays out the concrete proof and data showing the scope of this threat and what I hope is the beginning of a blueprint for how we can confront it.

Memory is only human. I described the events and recounted the conversations in this book to the best of my abilities. Whenever possible, I augmented my own recollections with original records, video footage, news coverage, and official reports. This book includes many text messages. No alterations were made to their content apart from some capitalization at the beginning of quotes, inserting bracketed ellipses to indicate where they have been shortened for readability, and adding some periods at their ends.

The text messages from former White House chief of staff Mark Meadows's phones that are included in this book weren't given to us with the names of the people who sent and received them attached. As I'll explain in more detail in the chapters to come, part of the work I oversaw on the committee was the painstaking process of matching phone numbers to names, utilizing powerful law enforcement databases and other clues as we could find them. While my team maintained rigorous standards and made attributions only where there was a very high degree of certainty—and while I have the highest confidence in our work—we can't entirely exclude the possibility that this identification process could have introduced unintended errors because of an undiscovered flaw in our source data or our methods. Moreover, we also can't rule out the fairly rare circumstance when a message is sent by a person from a phone number they don't ordinarily use—such as when the phone is shared or borrowed—and we don't detect it. Although this was a possibility, all these texts were sent to the phone number of the White House chief of staff, all of the texts in this book were part of the evidence considered by the Select Committee to Investigate the January 6th Attack on the United States Capitol, and many of them were introduced in the committee's public hearings.

I am an intelligence officer by training. There is nothing more valuable than raw data. I tried my best to get out of its way. I am not asking you to like me or even to trust me. I want to let the data do the talking. Through countless ones and zeroes, it paints a clear and disturbing picture.

THE
BREACH

CHAPTER 1

THE DARK TIME

As the United States Capitol was attacked on January 6, 2021, the White House went dark for seven hours and thirty-seven minutes. It was my job to turn the lights on.

One year after the siege, the National Archives turned over more than seven hundred pages of White House records requested by the investigators of the US House of Representatives Select Committee to Investigate the January 6th Attack on the United States Capitol. I was one of those investigators. And embedded in those pages were the call diaries for the former president Donald J. Trump.

Here's what the call logs showed: According to those records, on January 6, 2021, there were no phone calls in or out of the White House from 11:17 a.m. through 6:54 p.m.

I'm a former air force intelligence officer and National Security Agency consultant. I have extensive training in analyzing military operations, counterterrorism tactics, cyber warfare, and generally finding secrets my enemies don't want found. But it didn't take an intelligence genius to look at that call diary and know something was off. The Oval Office never goes quiet that long. That void also happened to overlap with the hours when Trump supporters brawled with police, smashed windows, and rampaged through Congress as Trump's election loss to Joe Biden was being certified. This was a hell of a coincidence.

The White House is technically required to keep track of the commander in chief's calls, thanks to the Presidential Records Act, which was enacted in the wake of Watergate. But like so many of our campaign finance and ethics regulations, the PRA is essentially toothless. The regulations require the West Wing to preserve records, but it leaves it up to the president and their staff to determine what exactly that means—and how to do it. This leaves a lot of room for negligence, carelessness, and, sometimes, deliberate misconduct.

I didn't know why the White House went dark and I didn't really care. As an intelligence officer, you learn not to make assumptions. It might have been an innocent mistake; it could have been a cover-up. What mattered to me—as the senior technical advisor to the committee and as an American—was why they stopped tracking the calls, and what happened next.

I had signed on to the select committee six months earlier, and had put together a top-notch team of telecommunications analysts and intelligence researchers, some of whom had worked on counterterrorism with the NSA and a whole host of secretive three-letter agencies. Our mission was simple: get the data.

The stakes were clear. Anyone with a screen could see our democracy was in peril. And the rift between Trump's wing of the Republican Party and objective reality didn't begin with the election. There had been an explosion of far-right conspiracy theories during the Trump years: QAnon, Pizzagate, and anti-vaccine pandemic paranoia. They spread like wildfire as social media algorithms ensured that susceptible audiences received a steady dose of them. This digital outrage cycle also presented an opportunity for all kinds of hustlers, who fueled the fire while generating cash through clicks and selling all manner of merchandise from T-shirts to questionable vitamin supplements.

The January 6th attack made clear that online lies could fuel directed political violence against targets the American public believes are sacrosanct. The moment the barricades of the Capitol came down, we all went into the breach. And the information my team would find in our analysis of the dark time in Trump's call diary would make clear just how far we'd fallen.

* * *

I am intimately familiar with the inflammatory climate on the Far Right. I joined the January 6th committee just a few months after leaving Washington, where I spent two years as a card-carrying Republican member of Congress in the conservative House Freedom Caucus. I was also one of the earliest and loudest critics of QAnon dogma and other increasingly violent and, frankly, unhinged far-right rhetoric. I became convinced this apocalyptic ideology was akin to a cult, that social media was spreading it like a digital virus, and that it posed an existential threat to our republic.

"It takes leadership from the top to stand up against extreme ideas like QAnon," I declared from the House floor. "We should not be playing with fire. I've been in the intelligence business. I know the power of information operations and false information."

You can't say I managed to rally the troops. I fought a lonely fight, one which led to vile insults, threats, and even a terrifying incident where someone sabotaged my truck. My term in Congress up, I left DC three days before the breach, disappointed and disturbed by the direction of our country.

January 6th brought me back.

I thought the attack could be a wake-up call—it needed to be. Our fellow Americans were being radicalized to believe in twisted fantasies and conspiracies. We had to make the rest of the country understand we were now engaged in a new war, whether the battles were immediately visible or not. Welcome to our new forever war: the Information War.

Data and algorithms got us into this mess—but they also might hold the key to bringing us back out. I knew how the committee could obtain intelligence on the individuals involved in the events of January 6th. This would help paint a clear picture of what happened that day. With data analysis we would be able to draw lines between people, called logical links, and trace how memes and conspiracies evolved into an organized, militarized assault. In a link analysis chart, people are called "nodes." Logical links between groups and individuals identify connections that can indicate coordination between those nodes. I was damn sure those networks spread far and wide.

This committee was the best—and maybe the last—chance to make the public fully aware of the growing threat of extremist thinking. And to truly take it on, we would have to go all the way to the top. It was already apparent that Trump and his inner circle led the push to subvert the results of the election. With the former president and his media machine vehemently denying he did anything wrong, we had to show the world exactly what they did and how they did it. We needed to see into the dark.

* * *

My committee office space was in the O'Neill House Office Building, named after late former Speaker of the House Thomas P. "Tip" O'Neill. It is one of those massive, marbled buildings, and my office was down in the basement. It looked like a converted equipment closet, about three hundred square feet of space with no windows and four desks. Private and cramped, even COVID didn't want to visit down there. That was exactly how I wanted it. This was early 2022, peak paranoia and Omicron season in a sharply divided DC.

Republican members and staffers who worked to challenge the election walked the halls. Eavesdropping was an obvious risk. I also heard rumors from a former colleague that some were planning to storm our offices, as they had during the second impeachment hearings. My files included information on thousands of sensitive texts, language for subpoenas and preservation requests, as well as technical plans and documents related to advanced analysis. They needed to be kept safe.

The committee had other fears too: leaks. We were obsessed with them, and the fear of leaks led the committee to compartmentalize the various teams of investigators. Save for weekly meetings, we were kept in our own silos, each group handling evidence in secrecy. I wondered sometimes if there was an overabundance of caution—whether in the desire to thwart the press, we deprived the overall investigation of coordinated information. Was that a necessary trade-off?

In any case, although the committee obtained Trump's call diaries on January 21, 2022, I did not get to see them until Tim Heaphy, the committee's chief investigator, summoned me out of the basement, up to the fourth floor, on February 9 to take a look.

At a borrowed desk, I pored over Trump's calls, tapping out notes on my phone. When I finished, I handed my copy of the diary to a staffer for shredding and headed out to brief Heaphy, emailing him my notes as I walked. Heaphy already had vivid experience with the growing dangers of far-right extremism. As a US Attorney, he'd helped draft the report on the 2017 tiki torch white supremacist riot in Charlottesville, Virginia. Charlottesville had been in my district. We both knew the threat too well.

I had a data-driven plan of attack. The backbone of my team's work consisted of documents called "CDRs"—call detail records. A CDR is the basic record of an individual's telecommunications transactions as maintained by a service provider. It's a chronology of your incoming and outgoing calls and messages. Depending on the network or company involved, the CDR can also include geolocation data. While it will show when short message service (SMS)—standard text messages—or multimedia messaging service (MMS)—content like photos—were sent and received, CDRs do not usually include the content of those written messages unless requested within a given period of time. Phone companies do not keep texts for long. Your messages are far harder for law enforcement to get than you might think, unless they act very quickly.

Breaking through the seven-hour blackout was not going to be easy. Searching through hundreds of CDRs while merging data formats and simultaneously narrowing the scope of the search to specific periods—or what us analyst types call "time hacks"—is extremely labor intensive. With a tall order like this, expertise and technical acumen are the only way to cut through the static.

My data analysis team was led by Glenn Bard, a former soldier, state trooper, and amateur kickboxer who ran his own forensics firm. He was a tough nut with almost three decades of experience in computer forensics and telephony analysis. Glenn was so good he impressed spooks at the NSA. That's how I'd come to hear about him.

Even for someone as experienced as Glenn, we were doing unprecedented work. Our team analyzed phone numbers that belonged to those in the Trump family, rallygoers, rally planners, influencers like Flynn, Stone, and Bannon; and many others. We were dealing with spoofed numbers, difficult registrations, and intense court fights. As seasoned as Glenn was, the surprising connections we found were about to floor him.

The scope of this investigation was beyond anything any of us had experienced before. A homicide case typically has just a few sets of records to analyze. Even foreign adversary networks I had mapped in my past couldn't match the volume of records we had to ingest and merge. Standard criminal conspiracies also involve a limited universe of suspects. January 6th was different.

According to the George Washington University Program on Extremism, which has been tracking the rioters' court cases, over eight hundred people have faced federal charges related to the attack on the Capitol. Our work encompassed all of these rioters, far-right activists who planned the protests that drew them to Washington to fight the electoral certification, and the officials who were leading the formal objection to the vote in the halls of Congress.

We had to not only gather but parse a massive amount of data. That meant devising procedures to combine all of the evidence and work with it effectively.

* * *

The first White House phone number was installed almost 150 years ago. Numbered "1," it reached a line in the telegraph room of the Executive Mansion. It was put in by President Rutherford B. Hayes in 1877. Now, of course, there are seven key digits in every phone number: the area code; the exchange, which is the next three numbers; and the final four, which make up the individual line.

In going through CDRs received via subpoena for DOJ-charged defendants, planners, and senior influencers, we had already spotted several phones that connected with White House phone numbers. This included some numbers known to the public, such as the general White House switchboard line. Others were not readily obtainable. We found those through leveraging sources and our own deep dives into the data.

While we have moved past the era of manual switchboards, when all the numbers in a given organization's headquarters would be on the same exchange, service providers still tend to grant large entities like the White House blocks of extensions. When my technical team went through phone records, we spotted a few key exchanges that, in combination with the DC area code, were associated with the West Wing. The general number for the executive office of the president, 202-395-0000, came up quite a bit in our analysis, as did the White House switchboard number, 202-456-1414. Others seemed likely to be individual executive branch extensions. White House cell phones typically started with 202–881-XXXX.

As we received phone records, we also did reverse lookups, checking individual numbers against our robust registration database to tie them to their owners. 202–881-XXXX numbers were simply registered to "U.S. government." No name attached. My team dubbed these area code and exchange combinations that were associated with the White House "root numbers."

After I got a look at Trump's logs, we began scanning all our CDRs for these White House landline and cell phone numbers. We kept a particular eye on calls made during the January 6th dark time. It became a part of the workflow. At first, when we looked for White House calls during the blackout, we saw what we expected to see: the president's attorneys, family members, allies, and top political advisers all calling out to or receiving calls from West Wing root numbers. It was easy to see that, contrary to the call logs, White House lines were active during the attack on the Capitol. Still, there was a lot we didn't know—including who made or received each call. Communication managers employed by federal, state, or local government organizations, as well as by private companies, can selectively mask sensitive extensions based on a government or company policy. It's really quite simple. As noted above, White House cell phones, while they use individual numbers, trace back to an opaque US government registration. The team attempted to tie these mobile phones to their individual users, but we didn't have much success. Why? Requesting root number extensions from the White House proved difficult. I'm not quite sure why the committee could not procure a listing of which White House extension or mobile number belonged to whom. It would seem that a request to the White House Communications Agency (WHCA) should suffice. Never happened as far as I know, although I begged for it.

This seems like a good time to say flat out that there are some things I just don't know. That said, I had a senior position on the committee and I had the data: I saw plenty. Witness testimony can be fallible or even faked. Digital data doesn't lie. Our analysis of phone records and text messages allowed us to see the Trump inner circle during the attack through their own eyes. I had unique access and a unique perspective. I was on the inside. And because, just before the attack, I had been on the House floor with the same lawmakers who were now appearing in my evidence files, I knew what they were after and how they operated.

* * *

I was making the three-hour drive from the committee offices in DC to my home in the Virginia woods when my phone rang. It was Glenn Bard.

"I hope you're sitting down," he said.

Glenn was not prone to exaggeration, and he'd been knee-deep in the data. I pulled into a gas station on Route 29.

"We got it," Glenn said.

My team had been running the White House root numbers through every new CDR that came in, including the records for individuals listed as DOJ-charged defendants, some convicted and some still in process. We had a hit.

It was a critical discovery.

Even if part of me expected it, seeing the raw numbers on the page was chilling. At 1634 hours on January 6th, roughly four hours after the first windows were smashed and in the thick of the dark time in the call diary, it seems someone attached to the White House dialed out to one of the rioters through the White House switchboard. Not an incoming call from a charged defendant, mind you, where an argument could be made that a crazy person simply dialed a publicly available number. The call was outgoing to an individual rioter as the violence played out. And the DOJ-charged defendant answered the call.

In CDRs, there is a data line called "seizure time." Seizure time indicates if a phone call is answered or not, and if answered it even shows how long the phone rang before pickup. We can see the pickup and duration of the call. Connection happened. This isn't like the television show 24. We can't "tap in" and listen to conversations. But analysts damn sure can determine who is doing the talking.

Department prosecutors had photos of this person inside the Capitol. They pleaded guilty to a charge related to the riot. I can't tell you the person's name because, as of this moment, it hasn't been made public. Even if I revealed it, it's unlikely it would ring a bell. But the point is this: during a period when the White House supposedly went dark, someone there connected to a rioter's personal cell phone.

* * *

There are a few things you should know about me. I am a full-blooded redneck. My father's side came from a rambling ravine in the mountains of West Virginia. Mom's people were from Northern Virginia and the Pennsylvania woods. The combo was pure Appalachian—with all the problems that come along with it.

Somehow, those wild-country roots put me on a path to Congress and high-level intelligence work. Through a combination of hardheadedness and sheer dumb luck I ended up with a unique set of skills that are essential for investigating a modern criminal conspiracy. The road I took also gave me a deep understanding of the people who attacked Capitol Hill. I've known them all my life. In fact, if it weren't for a few turns, I might have been one of them.

January 6th was one of the most dangerous days in the modern history of our republic. Nine deaths—including the loss of five police officers—were connected to the demonstrations and unrest at the Capitol, according to a bipartisan senate report and subsequent newspaper reporting. But it could have been so much worse. There were so many lucky bounces. The bombs placed outside the Republican and Democratic National Committees didn't go off. Capitol police and DC Metro largely held their fire. Contrary to what some of my former colleagues would later claim, some of those in the mob carried concealed weapons. In the desperate hours of hand-to-hand combat on the Capitol steps, even just one more shot could have provoked a deadly firefight or stampede.

As a society, we have to reckon with what took place on January 6th. It was the first time in our history that the peaceful transfer of power, the bedrock of any thriving democracy, failed. A large portion of our fellow countrymen, over one hundred members of Congress, a slew of top officials, and the president were all willing to subvert our core values based on twisted fantasies. If former vice president Mike Pence and a firewall of judges, local officials, and key folks in the West Wing hadn't stuck to their principles, we could have tumbled over the edge.

My time in the GOP and as a member of the January 6th committee team has left me convinced that the only way we can turn the tide is through an open and honest dialogue. This book is my effort to contribute to that conversation.

Our work on the January 6th committee was done on behalf of the public. I can't in good conscience hold back the things I have seen. It's especially important since Trump and his Republican allies have been dedicated to denying the severity of what took place at the Capitol. I won't let them do it, and I have data to back me up.

I firmly believe the American people need to know as much as I do about what happened that day. Data can confirm so much. Speed is critical in such a short investigative cycle. By the time you read this book, most of the findings about January 6th will have been made public by the committee. Some mysteries will remain, however. How the committee's analysis happened and what that process looks like is pretty damn cool, and this committee had to create novel ways of investigating a massive data ecosystem. There's still more to learn. Every person in this country deserves to know the who, how, and why of January 6th immediately. Data and the accompanying analysis are the new superheroes in fighting conspiratorial threats and weaponized disinformation. Ones and zeros are the new polygraph against digital shysters and provocateurs. The committee understands that.

The committee's work and its hearings have been compelling, expert, and fact-based. I am proud to have played a part. My hope is that I can highlight some key findings and share the story of what it looked like behind the scenes, warts and all. I also feel compelled to alert the public to this new information war, a fight rooted in data, algorithms, and distortions.

We have a new enemy. This is how we combat it head-on.

CHAPTER 2

THE CROWN JEWELS

We never received a CDR for Mark Meadows, Trump's chief of staff, but the telephone texts he turned over to the committee became the Rosetta Stone for the January 6th investigation. They provided a staggering amount of information.

There were 2,319 of them, incoming and outgoing. Meadows defied many aspects of the committee's subpoenas by claiming executive privilege. He failed to show up for depositions and battled in court to avoid providing his CDRs or the full contents of his phones. But he must have saved or uploaded his own data to the cloud or another storage device. And then he, and his legal team, willingly turned over this extraordinary number of messages to the committee. And in doing so, Meadows gave us the keys to the kingdom. We called them the "crown jewels."

What we found in the texts was a road map to an insurrection fueled by apocalyptic propaganda flying over 3G, 4G, and 5G connections and livestreams. It was a toxic stew of old-school zealotry and internet authoritarianism. In my mind, some of the messages also provided irrefutable, time-stamped proof of a comprehensive plot—at all levels of government—to overturn the election.

Everyone texted Meadows: the president's family, top White House aides, Trump's cabinet, members of Congress, big donors, political operatives, state officials, the army of lawyers whose election lawsuits were tossed out of courts all over the land. He engaged with activists directly involved in planning the rallies that culminated in the siege. He made plans with advisers who presented militarized plans for troops to seize the voting machines and stop the election.

The tranche of texts was filled with messianic and frequently hysterical conspiracy theories, accompanied by video and links dredged from fringe sites and foreign forums. Incredibly powerful people wrote him, trafficking in bizarre paranoia and violent Christian nationalism. Some were my friends.

Reading through the texts was like staring into the mouth of madness.

For three days straight after the phone team completed the "first edition" of the spreadsheet that broke down Meadows's texts, I sat in front of my computer going through each message. It was time-consuming work. We had merged the data into an analyzable format. Each line of data—who was on the chat; whether it was incoming or outgoing from Meadows's phone; the date the messages were exchanged; extracted text; attached link—had to be reviewed to understand how the conversations fit together. It was a contextual puzzle time-stamped in an Excel spreadsheet. As I scanned the rows and columns, I kept shaking my head. This was crazy stuff. Some of the messages were so extreme.

When Wyoming congresswoman Liz Cheney, one of two Republican members of the committee, first read them, she was floored.

"This is an amazing document," Cheney said.

And it was stunning. Along with the shocking content of the texts, there was the central riddle they presented. Why had Meadows turned them over? What the hell was he thinking? Here, right here, the messages made clear—or appeared to, at least—that there was a grand plan to overturn the 2020 election. The texts suggested intense coordination in executing the Stop the Steal plan through legal, executive, and legislative means. Meadows was smack in the middle of it.

Some of the world's greatest mysteries are why people do stupid things. Months later, I would still catch myself scratching my head, wondering what had possessed Meadows to deliver incriminating evidence right into the hands of congressional investigators. Did he simply have an awful legal team? Were the texts provided by mistake? Could he have actually wanted to assist our work? Or was Meadows trying to play some kind of chess game with the select committee? Did he figure he could appear to be cooperating or maybe even make some sort of deal while not handing over anything useful?

I tend to think it was the latter. There were multiple indications that—despite how much he turned over to the committee—Meadows was trying to keep information from us.

I can't confirm that Meadows even delivered all the texts that he didn't try to argue were privileged. While the text logs were incredibly revealing, they hinted at just how much we still don't know. If this was what Meadows was willing to turn over, I can't imagine how bad it got in the messages he didn't want the committee to read. The sprawling spreadsheet left me with an uneasy feeling that everything the messages were telling us about extremism and authoritarianism in the Trump-era Republican Party was just the tip of the iceberg.

*　*　*

As I've said, Meadows handed over the logs in formats that were frustrating to parse. The texts he provided were initially in an Excel spreadsheet, presumably in chronological order but lacking timestamps. Different lines showed who was in the conversation, whether Meadows sent or received the message, and what it said. Meadows and whatever staff helped him prepare the document didn't include names anywhere—just numbers. There were hundreds of unidentified phone numbers; we needed to figure out their owners. Meadows's legal team also separated out the timeline of the messages and sent it along much later, in a different format. I'm not sure if this maneuver was intended to annoy or to buy time.

Regardless, we learned many things from Meadows's texts. Most essentially, the messages revealed that the Far Right was much more organized and well-connected than we'd ever imagined. They had a robust organizational and messaging plan to create constitutional chaos based on a conspiratorial fantasy.

We homed in on the most extreme texts. Basically, with Meadows's help, we built an essential tip sheet or, as we military types like to say, a "Prioritized Integrated Target List," or "PITL." Many of the key players were there, racked and stacked. By cross-referencing Meadows's text log with other CDRs, we created a robust map of communications and relationships across the far-right ecosystem, exposing the intent and scope of the events of January 6th—from initial thoughts about and legal strategies for overturning the election, through the recruitment phase for lawyers and influencers, to rally planning and funding, and then through to January 6th itself and the aftermath. QAnon conspiracy theories were littered throughout the conversations.

* * *

Meadows's messages made clear that, even before the polls closed, efforts to contest the election and declare Trump's loss fraudulent had begun.

The first text he provided to the committee came from David Bossie, a top Trump adviser who was the former president's deputy campaign manager in 2016. Bossie messaged Meadows on the morning of November 3, 2020, as voters headed to the ballot box. He was already spoiling for a fight and advised Meadows to prepare for "the potential legal battle we are facing."

On the evening of the vote, Meadows was also hearing from well-wishers. A Trump supporter who operates an airfield in the southwest sent a message about an election-night party to a group chat that included Meadows and Jim DeMint, the former South Carolina senator and ex-president of the Heritage Foundation.

> "So a small group of us right wing conspirators have gathered to watch the returns, Nancy fixed the spread, and we'll enjoy our white privilege . . . Every bit of it hard earned," they wrote.

Emojis and other images in the messages were not visible in the logs provided to the committee. They showed up as question marks, and some punctuation dropped off. Apart from these issues, I have done all I can to quote these texts as they were written, including spelling and grammatical errors. I believe there is a compelling public interest in sharing these messages because they show, more clearly than anything else I can think of, the full scope of the effort to discredit and overturn the vote that culminated in the attack on the Capitol. Whether we like it or not, this is part of our history.

The first whiff of potential election fraud in the text logs came on election night from a person close to Meadows. That person, without providing any evidence, warned Meadows of problems with the vote in the Atlanta area.

> "Hey keep your eye on Fulton county ga for potential interference," they wrote.
> "I will [. . .] Thanks so much," said Meadows.

About twenty minutes later, they messaged again, this time with a question about Pennsylvania, a key swing state.

> "Why has Pennsylvania stopped counting?" they asked.
> "Trying to suppress the vote," Meadows said.

Over the next twenty-four hours, as the vote was still being counted in key states, Meadows received allegations about individual votes being "cancelled." One woman sent him a frenetic message:

> "Mark, THEY ARE CHEATING! I KNOW EXACTLY HOW! DON'T MISS THIS! SO IMPORTANT! [. . .] Voting Equipment is how they are winning these states. [. . .] They have inverted cellular modems in the tabulators!" she wrote. "This is not a singular incident and now with the forensic evidence we know this is happening across the country."

Her text went on to suggest the issues with voting machines were somehow connected to human trafficking, a central fear for believers in the QAnon conspiracy theory. It was a striking example of how Q was blending with Stop the Steal.

> "We could find all of the trafficking rings, we can track all the money in minutes," the woman continued. "I really wanna be part of this. I am available my kids are all grown I'm ready to put my whole heart and full time exposing this just fraud in Jesus name."

These were the true believers.

I am not naming the woman because she's not a public figure. While I think it's vital the public knows what people in power did in the leadup to January 6th, I'm not in the business of publicly shaming ordinary American citizens. That said, the woman's text is worth pointing out because it is indicative of the type of alarming content that was pouring into Meadows's phone. It was deeply troubling to see such crazed rhetoric reaching a man who was, at the time, White House chief of staff. If all the conspiracy allegations had not already seeped into the White House, they were there now.

A former cabinet official was the first one in the text logs to write Meadows about a plan to have Republican state legislatures appoint alternate slates of electors who would declare Trump the winner in the event of a Biden victory. On November 4, while the votes were still being counted, Rick Perry, Trump's former secretary of energy, wrote Meadows about his "AGRESSIVE STRATEGY."

"Why can't the states of GA NC PENN and other R controlled state houses declare this is BS [. . .] and just send their own electors to vote," Perry mused.

Perry sent the message to a group chat that included Meadows and two people who were still part of Trump's cabinet at the time: Secretary of Housing and Urban Development Ben Carson and Secretary of Agriculture George Ervin "Sonny" Perdue III.

"Interesting," Carson wrote.

Alternate electors were a central element of various plots to overturn Trump's loss that were cooked up by his allies in the weeks after the election. There were basically five states that mattered in the 2020 presidential race: Arizona, Pennsylvania, Michigan, Georgia, and Wisconsin. The rest of the results were predictable. It was all coming down to the margin in those swing states. Of course, presidential elections aren't technically decided in the states. They are won with votes in the electoral college and, really, when those votes are certified in Congress at a ceremony presided over by the sitting vice president. If any one of the big swing states didn't go Trump's way, the proponents of this plot wanted to use Republican officials in those states to appoint alternate electors who were loyal to Trump and would back him regardless of how the state voted. On January 6th, when the vote was set to be certified, they theorized that Vice President Mike Pence could use objections from Republican members of Congress based on fact-free accusations of fraud to reject the results in key states and either count Trump electors, who had not been certified by their states, in the vote instead of the official electors or refer the matter back to the state legislatures. It was all very logically—and legally—dubious.

As the weekend after the election approached, the votes were still being counted and the race still had not been called, but things had begun to turn for Biden. Meadows was also in touch with members of Trump's family. Ivanka Trump, the former president's daughter and adviser, sent a message on November 5, two days after the election, to a group chat that included Meadows and several top aides from Trump's campaign and the West Wing: her husband, Jared Kushner; Trump's longtime right-hand woman Hope Hicks; the former president's social media guy Dan Scavino; Bill Stepien, Trump's campaign manager; and Jason Miller, a senior adviser on the campaign.

"You are all WARRIORS of epic proportions! Keep the faith and the fight!" Ivanka wrote.

Don Jr., Trump's oldest son, was the first in the text logs to explicitly mention January 6th, which was the day the election was set to be certified by Congress. He framed it as the moment congressional Republicans could deliver victory for Trump.

"This is what we need to do please read it and please get it to everyone that needs to see it because I'm not sure we're doing it," he wrote to Meadows, adding, "It's very simple If through our lawsuits and recounts the Secretary of States on each state cannot certify that states vote the State Assemblies can step in and vote to put forward the electoral slate Republicans control Pennsylvania, Wisconsin,

Michigan, North Carolina etc [. . .] we get Trump electors There is a Safe Harbor on 8 December if for whatever reason you miss that the Electors then cannot meet in the individual state Capitols on 14 December So we either have a vote WE control and WE win OR it gets kicked to Congress 6 January 2021 the House meets to vote-by state party delegation 1 vote per state California 1; Montana 1 Republicans control 28 states Democrats 22 states Once again Trump wins Senate votes for VP Pence wins [. . .]."

Through his various typos, Don Jr. seemed to be articulating a variation of the alternate electors strategy.

Rules for the electoral college say that electors must meet and vote on the Monday after the second Wednesday in December following a presidential election. US code specifies that all election-related disputes must be resolved six days before that vote, a date referred to as the "safe harbor."

Don Jr. seemed to be suggesting that, if Biden won a key state where Republicans controlled the legislature, they could deliberately avoid accepting the result by the safe harbor deadline. His logic appeared to be that this would either allow alternate electors to vote on December 14 or that undetermined state results would allow Congress to name a winner when it certified the election on January 6, 2021.

Several aspects of this theory were questionable, at best. With no real evidence of fraud, state legislatures had no basis to overturn their results, and despite some working behind the scenes, none ultimately did so. Exactly 147 Republicans in Congress ended up objecting to the election in some fashion, but even if the entire GOP conference had voted in lockstep, they still wouldn't have had enough votes to stop the elector certification. The objectors were essentially trying to pressure Pence and offer him political cover to toss out millions of Americans' votes. Pence had no real power to ignore or reject the results, but if he had tried to, the country would have been plunged into an unprecedented constitutional crisis. The plan might have seemed like a farcical fantasy, but if the vice president had gone along with it, the effects could have been terrifyingly real.

Trump allies had good reason to want the election resolved on Capitol Hill rather than in the swing states where polls showed voters split between him and Biden. The Twelfth Amendment of the US Constitution specifies that, in the event of an electoral college tie or disputed result, the House of Representatives will elect the president. This so-called "contingent election" is voted on by state delegations rather than the individual House members. In 2021, Democrats had a majority of individual House lawmakers, but the GOP controlled twenty-seven state delegations outright, more than enough for a majority of the fifty states. Even if Liz Cheney, Wyoming's sole House representative, broke ranks, it still would have been a two-vote win. Other scenarios—including counting the electoral votes after the contested votes were disallowed, or coupling delay tactics with instituting martial law and applying the Insurrection Act, as well as combinations thereof—made the rounds with those close to Trump. If Pence was willing to seat enough Trump electors to make it an electoral college tie or electors were jettisoned based on disputes about a "stolen" presidential race, a vote on the House floor could have kept Trump in office.

Don Jr.'s message to Meadows wasn't exactly coherent, but it indicated he was aware of the GOP's advantage in a contingent election on the House floor.

> "We have multiple paths We control them all We have operational control Total leverage," Don Jr. said.

Based on the text logs, Meadows did not initially respond to Don Jr. On the morning of November 6, nearly a day after his first messages, Don Jr. wrote again to make sure Meadows had seen his idea.

"You see this and what do you think?" Don Jr. asked.

"Much of this had merit," Meadows belatedly replied. "Working on this for pa, ga and nc already."

* * *

The texts showed Meadows eagerly searching for examples of fraud to provide a basis for challenging the result. He didn't seem to care how questionable the source was or how thin the evidence was. It was all-hands-on-deck and Meadows wanted anything that could be used to question the vote.

On the morning of November 5, two days after the election, he texted Trump's campaign manager, Bill Stepien, a link to a website that argued the "fix was in" based on reported vote totals in Milwaukee.

"Have someone look at this," Meadows wrote.

The site Meadows was reading, NOQ Report was filled with pro-Trump propaganda and wild, apocalyptic advertising. Rambling articles alleging the election was hacked appeared alongside advertisements for doomsday food supplies and "Z-DTOX" dietary pills.

As I clicked on the various links Meadows received, I was truly astounded that some of our government officials were getting their information from such far-out sources. Republican Arizona congressman Paul Gosar sent Meadows several texts between November and December 2020 warning about "dead voters" and Dominion, the voting machines destined to become a lightning rod in the months to come. (It was a line of inquiry that even Meadows repeatedly indicated he doubted in emails to other associates.) One of Gosar's texts included a link to a movie about "cyber warfare" and voting machines from an anti-vaccine conspiracy blog called *Some Bitch Told Me*. Republicans in Washington mined briefings from very dubious sources.

Along with members of Trump's family and cabinet, the text logs showed Meadows discussing efforts to challenge the election with multiple members of Congress. In total, the text logs showed Meadows communicated with thirty-nine sitting Republican House members (staffers and former congressional members were also quite active) and five sitting Republican senators in the period from election day until January 20, the day of Biden's inauguration.

Messages in the days immediately after the election, even before the result was declared, indicated multiple House Republicans were eagerly reaching out to the White House and Trump campaign looking for talking points so they could publicly question the validity of the election.

At about 8 a.m. on November 5, Texas congressman Chip Roy wrote Meadows to ask for guidance on how to challenge the integrity of the vote. He indicated other Republicans were eager to join the fight.

> "We have no tools / data / information to go out and fight RE: election / fraud. If you need / want it, we all need to know what's going on," Roy wrote.
>
> "Thanks so much. Working on it for surrogates briefing. Congratulations btw," Meadows replied, hinting at his search for evidence.

An hour later, another Texas congressman, Brian Babin, sent a similar message asking for direction on how to challenge the election.

> "Many of us as Republican House members want to help the President in any way we can to prevent the outright theft of this presidential election," Babin said, adding, "We need some guidance as to what we should be saying and doing. Please let some of us know what you would suggest. In earnest prayer for POTUS and our Republic."

Strikingly, some of the members reaching out to Meadows were willing to cast doubt on the election before they had any details.

> "Any help on message appreciated. We're all just making generic statements," Roy said to Meadows on November 5.

That evening, another Texas congressman, Louie Gohmert, wrote in. He offered to start a "fuss" in Pennsylvania and touted his experience as an attorney, asking to join the Trump advisers at the White House.

> "I'm in DC. Thinking I'll head to Philadelphia to fuss. Would love to be there for at WH to be ear for discussions & advice if asked. Handled massive fraud case vs Texas biggest utility," Gohmert wrote before rattling off highlights from his work as an attorney. "So some legal experience. May I come over?"
>
> Meadows responded, "Most of this is being handled at the campaign. Would love your help and would love you going on TV."
>
> Babin sent another message that shed light on the reason for his desire to interfere with the election—devotion to Trump above all else: "Mark, When we lose Trump we lose our Republic. Fight like hell and find a way. We're with you down here in Texas and refuse to live under a corrupt Marxist dictatorship. Liberty!"

Even in those early days, the effort to overturn the election involved officials from all levels of government. Along with congressional Republicans, Meadows received messages from state and local officials who wanted to help Trump stay in office.

Midday on November 5, Tommy Long, the Republican commissioner in Haywood County, North Carolina, texted thoughts on how to challenge the election.

"Yes, the election is being stolen right before our eyes. So, what would I recommend to President Trump I'm no expert but here are some good ideas: (1) challenge the late-night 'finds' in the courts; (2) hold rallies in contested states; (3) urge GOP officials in close states to expose shenanigans and, if necessary, to refuse to seat Biden electors in the event of a fake count; (4) mount a campaign to marshal grassroots public opinion in the president's favor."

Long's message contained no proof of his claim the vote was being hijacked. What it did have was clear echoes of the Stop the Steal movement that was growing online as far-right activists whipped up opposition to a potential Biden victory.

"Convince the people that if in fact the election is in the process of being stolen, the president and his allies are going to fight the steal on their behalf," Long wrote. "If middle America wants to prevent this election from being stolen, it will have to be willing to act now."

Shortly before midnight on that same day, Ginni Thomas, wife of Supreme Court justice Clarence Thomas, made her first appearance in the text logs. It included a link to a seven-minute conspiracy-filled YouTube video and several lines of Ginni Thomas's barely intelligible paranoid ranting in which she predicted a wave of violence and repression if Biden took office.

"The QFS blockchain watermarked ballots in over 12 states have been part of a huge Trump & military white hat sting operation in 12 key battleground states where 20,000+ natl guard were deployed," Thomas wrote. "Biden crime family & ballot fraud co-conspirators (elected officials, bureaucrats, social media censorship mongers, fake stream media reporters, etc) are being arrested & detained for ballot fraud right now & over coming days, & will be living in barges off GITMO to face military tribunals for sedition."

The wife of the senior justice on the Supreme Court envisioned the Democratic candidate for president being charged with sedition and thrown into the brig, with his family, off Guantanamo Bay.

I didn't know if I was dazed or horrified. More like validated and yet still horrified. I knew QAnon had infiltrated every level of the GOP by this time . . . but damn!

This was a lot to absorb. I felt fear—anger too. I couldn't believe this was happening in my country. The chief of staff was being counseled by people who believed babies were being harvested for adrenochrome; and people like the wife of a Supreme Court justice seemed on board with this insanity.

The vote was still being counted four days later. It was clear that it was close and would come down to a handful of crucial swing states. Then, on Saturday, November 7, 2020, at 11:24 a.m., CNN took the lead and announced that Biden was projected to win Pennsylvania's electoral vote, thereby winning the election. Within seconds, NBC, CBS, MSNBC, and ABC followed suit. The Associated Press weighed in at 11:26. And at 11:40, Fox News projected Biden's win. The election was over. In theory.

Meadows's messages took a dark turn.

Less than an hour later, Rick Perry sent a text to the group chat that included Meadows, Secretary of Housing and Urban Development Ben Carson, and Secretary of Agriculture Sonny Perdue. Perry wanted Trump to dispute the call based on unspecified "data."

"POTUS Line should be: Biden says hes president . America will see what big data says," Perry wrote. "This sets the stage for what we're about to prove."

Carson took a more cautious line.

"We will see what the evidence shows," he countered.

Based on the words of his text, Perdue was far less concerned about seeing proof.

"No quit!" he wrote.

Members of Trump's cabinet were detaching from the reality of election results and spoiling for a fight. In the hours after Pennsylvania was called, Republican House members began streaming into Meadows's phone. Paul Gosar reached out with another one of his strategies to run the clock and call the vote into question: hand recounts of the ballots.

"Could you or the VP call me," he texted Meadows. "It is about a
possible full hand audit in AZ and the obstacles we need to clear.
There's one I need some immediate help with."

He followed that with a link that he said summarized the "risk" posed by Dominion, the voting machine company that would both feature prominently in election conspiracy theories and file several subsequent defamation suits.

Based on the log, Meadows didn't reply to Gosar.

To be sure, there are things we couldn't see in Meadows's texts. Without Meadows's CDRs, there's no way to tell who he spoke with on the phone. We only had the text messages his legal team released to the committee. Maybe someone texted him and he replied with a call? Or with an encrypted app? There was no way for us to know. We could see that, over time, Meadows and his correspondents came to prefer moving their communications to more secure channels. On four separate occasions, Pennsylvania congressman Scott Perry, who texted Meadows fifty-seven times in the logs, asked that they switch to Signal, an encrypted messaging app that Meadows and other Trump administration officials regularly used.

Still, the text logs still offered a startling look at a Republican Party willing to defy the will of the people to keep their man in the Oval Office.

Three hours after the election was called, South Carolina congressman Ralph Norman reached out to Meadows.

> "What our delegation is doing in SC is gathering on the statehouse steps on Tuesday to advocate for standing with our president and other arguments/options that are at our disposal," Norman wrote. "I will go anywhere anytime to help our cause. Bottom line, it's time we FIGHT FOR THE ONE PERSON WHO HAS CHANGED THIS COUNTRY!! WAY TOO SOON TO GIVE IN NOW!!"

Through the texts, one could watch the Stop the Steal movement growing. And one could track the efforts by several Republican members to embrace it and enforce it.

In the months after my team decoded the texts, messages were selectively read to the public or leaked to the press. Several of those leaks enraged me. Here's why: In snippets, it was easy to misread the intention of the texts. Wrongdoers could come off as downright, well, if not saintly, decent. Utah senator Mike Lee and Texas congressman Chip Roy were quoted as souring on their colleagues' efforts to keep Trump in power. They received kudos in the press for their apparent reasonableness during unreasonable times. Meanwhile, these were guys who had actively worked to undermine the will of the people.

What other texts revealed was that on November 7, 2020, when the election was called for Biden, Mike Lee wrote Meadows asking that attorney Sidney Powell be brought into the White House. Powell

had a difficult-to-define role in the postelection period. She dubbed
the evidence of election fraud that she said she'd gathered, and eventually herself, as "the Kraken," a reference to a legendary Scandina-
vian sea monster—a colossal octopus—that is released from captivity
to fight for the gods in the movie *Clash of the Titans*. For a time, she
was a member of the Trump campaign's legal team and one of Trump's
personal lawyers, and she appeared in those roles at a notorious press
conference alongside Rudy Giuliani. A few days later, she was publicly
booted from them both, which Meadows's texts suggest happened in
part due to her inability to make her #StopTheSteal Kraken hum with
any kind of momentum or facts-based proof. After her ouster, Powell
kept going on her own. She filed lawsuits in four states questioning their
election results based on dubious evidence and crackpot theories. She
lost those cases and was formally sanctioned by a federal court in Michigan. By mid-December, she was back in the Oval Office with Lt. Gen.
Mike Flynn at her side for a dramatic showdown with the White House
counsel in front of Trump, but it ultimately didn't go her way. Powell
is currently fighting disbarment in her home state of Texas, where the
state bar insists that she broke ethics rules by filing frivolous claims.

Even Trump's own staff tried to keep Powell at arm's length, but she
had a friend in Lee and, according to him, Trump.

> "Sydney Powell is saying that she needs to get in to see the president,
> but she's being kept away from him. Apparently she has a strategy to
> keep things alive and put several states back in play. Can you help
> her get in?" Lee asked Meadows, adding, "It was at the president's
> request that Sydney has been working on a strategy and has been
> trying to get in to see him. But she's being kept out."

Lee followed up with Powell's contact information about fifteen minutes later.

There was no response from Meadows in the log, but in mid-November 2020, he sent a message to a White House number that said:

"Let me review anything coming from sydnee for potus. Apparently there is some crazy things being passed around. I will take the heat."

Distancing himself—and the president—from Powell is one moment in the text logs where it seemed like Meadows might have been a moderating influence. It didn't stop Powell from introducing plans to overturn the election late into December 2020. There were also plenty of exchanges where Meadows almost drowned in the Kool-Aid. One November 24 conversation between Meadows and Ginni Thomas seemed to show he was a true believer in the Great Trump Tribulation.

"The fracturing now. The stabbing in the back of anyone daring to still say there seemed to be fraud. All the Rs congratulating Biden," said Thomas. "Your/his loyalists can't take this. It is so evil. Thank you for being in my choir then too!!"

"This is a fight of good verses evil. Evil always looks like the victor until the King of Kings triumphs," Meadows replied. "Do not grow weary in well doing. The fight continues. I have staked my career on it. Well at least my time in DC on it."

As November rolled on, the efforts to overturn the election became more organized—in Congress and on the streets. And those efforts all seemed to revolve around Meadows.

* * *

On the evening of November 9, Mike Lee sent Meadows a text saying he and other "Republican senators" had held a meeting with Powell at the Conservative Partnership Institute.

"We had steering executive meeting at CPI tonight, with Sidney Powell as our guest speaker," wrote Lee. "You have in us a group of ready and loyal advocates who will go to bat for him, but I fear this could prove short-lived unless you hire the right legal team and set them loose immediately."

The Conservative Partnership Institute (CPI) is a little-known charity clubhouse for congressional conservatives. Founded by former senator Jim DeMint in 2017, CPI is located just a short walk from the Capitol in a three-story redbrick row house with bay windows and a leafy patio tucked behind the Library of Congress. When I was a member of the Freedom Caucus, we had our meetings there. "Our Conservative Partnership Center provides a home base and a networking hub for conservatives," the institute's website boasts. "Nearly every day of the week, you'll find our facilities filled with conservatives connecting with one another, recharging, and getting back out to win." Meadows's texts show CPI also hosted Republican lawmakers on multiple occasions in 2020 as they strategized on how to overturn the election, including the Republican senators' early encounter with Powell. After Trump left the White House, Meadows joined the group as a "senior partner." In late 2021, as Meadows was engaged in his legal battles with the January 6th investigators, Trump's political action committee donated $1 million to CPI.

Texts from Scott Perry indicated he and Meadows spoke about supposed whistleblowers making allegations about the vote. Perry also passed along messages from "one of the state representatives in PA" presenting ideas for questioning the results based on wild and debunked theories about dead people voting. He also urged Meadows to have intelligence agencies investigate Dominion based on an even more deranged version of the algorithm theory.

"Was china malware involved?" Perry asked.

Trump himself made a handful of appearances in Meadows's messages, even though we never saw a text from him. In one message that was sent on November 13, Meadows suggested Trump had told him to ask Republican National Committee chairwoman Ronna McDaniel if there were any "illegal" votes cast. McDaniel replied that she had no proof of that. Meadows was in touch with Arizona Republican Party chairwoman Kelli Ward, who had been consistently sending Meadows allegations about the vote—including in her text from November 10:

> "This is from our AZGOP attorney. Are we going to allow the Dems to claim victory when no such victory exists? We cannot allow Democrat threats to push us out of court."

Days later, she wrote Meadows about speaking with Trump:

> "Just talked to POTUS [. . .] There are potential issues with Dominion systems that MUST be adjudicated before certification should ever be considered," she texted.

Meadows was also in touch with one of the activists who was leading protests against the election all around the country. Amy Kremer, the chairwoman of the pro-Trump organization Women For America First, reached out to Meadows on November 13 about the nationwide March For Trump bus tour that the group sponsored to protest Biden's victory. Kremer, who made her name as an activist during the Tea Party wave, spent the months after the election on board the bus, traveling between rallies where activists associated with the tour baselessly questioned the vote and, at times, explicitly called for violence. Witnesses who spoke to the committee subsequently accused Kremer and her daughter, Kylie, of using money from the tour for lavish hotels, drinks, and meals. Such accusations haven't been proven, but they raised an interesting question in my mind: Was Kremer aiming for a coup by way of the luxury suite? She was hopeful that Trump himself would attend a March For Trump rally in DC the following day.

> "If you find out POTUS is coming to our rally here in DC, can you please let me know for logistical purposes?" Kremer asked.
>
> "If we did. It will be last minute due to security," Meadows replied. "But nothing planned currently."

Trump ended up treating the various groups who gathered in DC that day to a drive-by in his motorcade. That night, people who came to the city for the rallies—including members of the far-right "Proud Boys"— brawled in the streets of Washington.

Kremer's organization went on to host the main rally at the White House Ellipse on January 6th. Before that, she held a rally in Washington on December 12. Ahead of that event, she wrote to Meadows and asked for help securing a place to park her bus, which was emblazoned with March For Trump logos.

> "We will be staying at the Willard and I'm very fearful or destruction by Antifa," Kremer wrote.

Paranoia was high for MAGA supporters. As upsetting as the messages were, there were a few ridiculous moments like that where I just had to laugh.

Along with her terror, there might have been something else behind Kremer's parking request. She wanted a photo op connecting her bus tour with Trump and his White House.

> "Hey Mark. I wanted to circle back with you on this . . . Is it possible to bring the buses to the south lawn WH driveway to take a picture

of them in front of the WH? Would be incredible to have the President come out with them too?" Kremer asked ten days later, after
the rally was over. "We would be so grateful and it would give the
millions feeling disenfranchised to keep the faith while we continue
with the buses rallying the base while the legal process plays out."

Based on the text logs, Meadows did not respond. It's unclear if he
helped with that request, but on the day itself, he delivered an even
more high-profile favor for Kremer. Trump flew over the December 12
rally in Marine One, the presidential helicopter.

"Thank you for the flyover! POTUS made the people so happy
today!!!! Truly, what a blessing. God bless you and thank you!"
Kremer gushed in a text to Meadows that evening.

"That is what friends are for. It was the best I could arrange,"
Meadows responded, adding, "I was waving the entire time."

* * *

Throughout December and the early days of January, Meadows continued to text with members of Congress, top Trump campaign aides, and
other allies who shared encouragement, advice, and absurd, unfounded
allegations about the vote.

On December 1, 2020, Texas congressman Brian Babin sent Meadows an approximately hour-long clip from a YouTube broadcaster named
Brannon Howse, who has written a book dedicated to "exposing the sinister influences sweeping the world toward a Satanic global empire." In
the clip, Howse described the election as a "c war" backed by America's
enemies abroad.

Meadows also received a text on December 20, 2020, from Mike
Lindell, a mustachioed, self-described former crack addict who'd made a
fortune as CEO of the bedding company My Pillow. Lindell, who was an

infomercial star, major Trump rally fixture, and financial backer of various protests against the former president's loss, implored Meadows to have federal agents seize voting machines in key states. He was famous for wearing a large cross necklace and his message was an overheated blend of Christian prayer and internet insanity.

> "Hey Mark, I felt I was suppose to text you this message . . . You being a man a faith and on the front line of the decisions that are going to be historical! I would ask that you pray for wisdom and discernment from God! You are one of the people the president trusts the most. That being said I want to add my input. . . . Everything Sidney has said is true!" Lindell wrote. "We have to get the machines and everything we already have proves the President won by millions of votes! I have read and not validated yet that you and others talked him out of seizing them . . . If true . I pray it is part of a bigger plan . . . I am grateful that on the night of the election the algorithms of the corrupt machines broke and they realized our president would win in spite of the historical fraud! I look for deviations every day in my business . . . when I find one I investigate relentlessly until I know why it happened and how it happened . . . (this is my gift from God that has made my business so successful) From 11:15 pm on the night of the election I have spent all my time running impossible deviations and numbers from this election . . . I also was blessed to be able to get info and help Sidney Lin General Flynn and everyone else out there gathering all the massive evidence! I have been sickened by politicians (especially republicans) judges, the media not wanting to see truth (no matter what the truth would be!) This is the biggest cover up of one of the worst crimes in history! I have spent over a million$to help uncover this fraud and used my platform so people can get the word not to give up! The people on both sides have to see the truth and when they do. . . . There will not be

no civil war, people (including politicians!) are fearing! The only thing any of us should fear is fear of the Lord! Every person on this planet needs to know the truth and see the evidence!!! Mark . God has his hand in all of this and has put you on the front line . . . I will continue praying for you to have great wisdom and discernment! Blessings Mike."

Meadows seemed grateful for Lindell's input.

"Thanks brother," he replied. "Pray for a miracle."

*　*　*

Meadows continued to receive advice and aid from Republican politicians in Washington and around the country.

North Dakota senator Kevin Cramer forwarded Meadows a note from that state's US attorney, Drew Wrigley, who felt "the Trump legal team has made a joke of this whole thing" and had his own idea for a "last ditch effort" in crucial states.

> "Demand state wide recount of absentee /mail-in ballots in line with pre-existing state law with regard to signature comparisons. Legislative leaders could pledge to abide by the results, no matter what. If state officials refuse that recount, the legislature would then act under the constitution, selecting the slate of electors," Wrigley explained.

Wrigley suggested a rejection of the demand for a recount would "call into question the vote itself" and lend "credibility" to any alternate electors.

On Capitol Hill, throughout December 2020, the plan to object to the electoral certification on the House floor was coming together.

Alabama congressman Mo Brooks sent Meadows a text on December 6 that he felt should be delivered widely to all House members and senators:

"Mark. Mo Brooks here. Thank you for ALL you do. You are a GREAT patriot! Please help inspire everyone you can reach across America to send the following message, or one similar to it, to their Congressmen & Senators. Thanks! 'America's survival as a Republic is at stake. This year, Socialist Democrats exploited numerous systemic election system flaws to engage in massive voter fraud and election theft on an unprecedented scale! Knowing Democrats enacted laws making it ILLEGAL for voter registrars to require proof of citizenship from illegal aliens when they demand to be registered to vote, Joe Biden at the Nashville presidential debate promised over ELEVEN-PLUS MILLION illegal aliens amnesty & citizenship as a reward for voting for Biden. Despite the Constitution's Elections Clause that empowers Congress to set ONE DAY (November 3), with very minor exceptions, as the election day on which to vote (NOT an election week an election month or an election season), Socialist Democrats pushed on an unsuspecting public illegal mass ballot mailing schemes that both clearly violate federal election day law and open up a Pandora's Box of election theft opportunity. 2020 voter fraud examples and election theft schemes are compelling and so overwhelming and numerous as to not be able to itemize them here. I ask, no, I demand, that you, on January 6, formally object to, and vote to reject, the electoral college vote submissions of Nevada, Georgia, Pennsylvania and every other state whose election system flaws render their reported electoral college vote submissions unworthy of support. If you do not join this fight to save America from Socialism, I pledge to you that I will NEVER again vote for you in any primary or general election. If you won't fight for America, I will fight you.'"

Brooks's idea that Meadows would "inspire everyone you can reach across America to send the following message, or one similar to it, to their Congressmen & Senators" is interesting. In other words, Brooks hoped the White House would use Trump's bully pulpit to prompt millions of Americans to send this threatening message (or one similar to it) to their congressmen and congresswomen, not simply that Meadows or the White House send an email distribution to Congress.

> Two days later, an activist wrote to Meadows asking if he had "anyone working to tie together all the efforts of the various state legislators challenging the elections?"
>
> "Yes. Have a team on it," Meadows wrote.

On December 19, Republican Georgia congressman Jody Hice wrote in to say he would be "leading" his state's "electoral college objection on Jan 6." He said that Marjorie Taylor Greene, a far-right Republican who had just been elected to a House seat in Georgia but had yet to be sworn in, "spoke" with Trump about the election and believed the then-president was interested in meeting with the House Freedom Caucus and the Peach State members about it.

> "Hope this can happen ... I think it's important that all the states work together strategically to make the effort as strong as possible," said Hice.

Meadows initially set the meeting for the next Monday, December 20. Subsequent messages from Babin to Meadows show it ultimately took place on December 21.

Nine days later, Babin wrote to say "objectors" would be getting together at CPI for a strategy session. Greene also texted Meadows and described being at CPI on the last day of 2020.

"Good morning Mark, I'm here in DC," wrote Greene, who was sworn in on January 3, 2021. "We have to get organized for the 6th. [. . .] We are getting a lot of members on board."

As the plans for the objection came together, Meadows was also texting with former Trump campaign adviser Katrina Pierson, who was coordinating with Kremer's Save America Ellipse rally. In a series of messages to Meadows on January 2 and January 3, Pierson warned that things had "gotten crazy" with the event. Pierson claimed Caroline Wren, a Trump fundraiser, was planning to have a "psycho list" of speakers and that it had "apparently" been approved by White House aide Dan Scavino. She specifically objected to the inclusion of far-right activists Ali Alexander and Scott Presler.

"These are the grifter fringe of the right. [. . .] The crazies," Pierson said.

"Talk it over with Scavino," answered Meadows.

On January 5, Meadows sent Pierson a message saying Ohio congressman Jim Jordan would not be able to speak at the Ellipse rally because he was "prepping" the electoral objection. The next morning, Meadows wrote Mo Brooks to say he was being tapped for the event.

"You are speaking this am," Meadows wrote. "Are you aware."

Brooks checked in with Meadows when he left the stage of the Ellipse rally.

"Did it in 10m. Thanks!" Brooks said. "Crowd roaring."

Brooks, who was reportedly wearing body armor, closed his speech by declaring, "The fight begins today!" Trump took the stage about two hours and forty minutes later. His words ended with a similar call to arms—and to the Capitol.

"And we fight. We fight like hell. And if you don't fight like hell, you're not going to have a country anymore," Trump said, before adding, "So we're going to, we're going to walk down Pennsylvania Avenue. I love Pennsylvania Avenue. And we're going to the Capitol."

The mob charged through the first barricade while Trump was still speaking. Meadows's phone exploded.

"It's really bad up here on the hill," Georgia congressman Barry Loudermilk wrote Meadows. "They have breached the Capitol."

Greene, newly sworn in and fresh off her own work on the election objection, also sent a worried text to Meadows.

"Mark I was just told there is an active shooter on the first floor of the Capitol," she wrote. "Please tell the President to calm people This isn't the way to solve anything."

I don't give Greene too much credit for sending one responsible message in the middle of the violence as Trump supporters raged at the Capitol police. She did plenty to get us to that point. It's hard not to see this as a degree of ass covering. It's all fun and games until you're actually in a brawl. Besides, near four o'clock, before the crowds had been cleared, she was already making excuses and building a new big lie.

"Mark we don't think these attackers are our people. We think they are Antifa. Dressed like Trump supporters," Greene claimed.

Trump campaign senior adviser Jason Miller sent Meadows a similar idea a few minutes before Greene. He suggested it might be a smart move for Trump to blast out a tweet blaming the Left.

> "Call me crazy, but ideas for two tweets from POTUS: 1) Bad apples, likely ANTIFA or other crazed leftists, infiltrated todays peaceful protest over the fraudulent vote count. Violence is never acceptable! MAGA supporters embrace our police and the rule of law and should leave the Capitol now! 2) The fake news media who encouraged this summers violent and radical riots are now trying to blame peaceful and innocent MAGA supporters for violent actions. This isnt who we are! Our people should head home and let the criminals suffer the consequences!" Miller wrote.

Of course, Trump—despite the entreaties of multiple advisers and even Fox News hosts who texted Meadows—didn't issue any public statements telling the rioters to "go home" until 4:17 p.m., hours after the Capitol breach. And well over a year later there has not been a single shred of evidence that there was any large-scale left-wing presence in the January 6th crowd. The idea was half deflecting blame and half genuine delusion.

The antifa theory rocketed through the Far Right in the hours after the riot. An article posted by the conservative *Washington Times* declared that a "software firm" used facial recognition software to identify prominent antifa activists in the crowd. Florida congressman Matt Gaetz was among the politicians and activists who quickly promoted the story. The company, XRVision, subsequently informed the paper that—while they did use their software on footage of the riots—it did not identify any leftist activists. A major correction was appended to the piece noting the company "did not identify any Antifa members" and the newspaper referred to its own reporting as erroneous. As of this writing, Gaetz's tweet remains up and uncorrected.

Meadows clearly bought in to the fantasy. That night, as the smell of tear gas still hung in the air at the Capitol, a man texted the White House chief and said, "These are antifa."

"I agree," answered Meadows.

Two days later, with less than two weeks until Biden's inauguration, Louie Gohmert wrote in. He wanted federal agents to pin the attack on the Left.

"Constitutional loyal DOJ personnel have 11 days to prove the truth: Antifa led the breach of the Capitol," Gohmert said. "It was a brilliant leftist op, but it's got to be exposed by DOJ quick."

Almost before the press could say "antifa," other conspiracy theories bloomed in the far-right troll farms. Those theories hit believers right in the amygdala. That's their superpower. Logical inconsistencies are a feature, not a bug.

Something else was brewing out in the extremist wilderness. As the January 6th rioters faced public condemnation and FBI sweeps, their rage and fear only grew. Four days after the attack, Marjorie Taylor Greene sent Meadows an ominous text that landed somewhere between a warning and a threat.

"Hey I need to talk with President Trump. People are freaking out. The messages I'm getting show extreme fear of what is about to happen," Greene wrote. "I think some of their fears are warranted. However these extreme fears could lead to out of control actions. Some one call me."

Meadows—and the others in his phone—had awakened something. That anger isn't going anywhere.

CHAPTER 3

AMONG THE BELIEVERS

I grew up in a world of true believers.

I was born on March 17, 1970. St. Patrick's Day. My parents were teenagers.

Their marriage didn't last long. My father left my mother when I was around three and my sister was a year younger. Mom worked a series of jobs until she met my stepfather, who made a housewife out of her. Our new nuclear family ended up in Manassas, a Northern Virginia backwater about thirty miles out of DC. My stepdad commuted into the district for a gig at the sewage plant. He jokingly referred to himself as a "turd herder."

We moved into a tiny two-bedroom apartment in a complex called Coverstone, which was just a bunch of squat brick buildings around a dirt patch. Still, it was a place to call our own. The complex is there to this day. They've tried to gussy it up a bit over the decades, but it's still the familiar and well-worn shithole I remember.

Our place was on the ground floor, apartment A1. One day, a pair of Mormon missionaries came by and rapped on the door. The Church of

Jesus Christ of Latter-day Saints never left. Indeed, it ended up defining the first few decades of my life.

For better or worse, my mom and stepdad had been free spirits. They raised us with long hair, incense, and hand-me-down bell bottoms. The arrival of those missionaries meant a new, clean-cut, all-encompassing reality. The church was a constant presence for me—but not as some kind of loving spiritual connection. My religious experience was mostly a gnawing fear of going straight to hell for any infraction that went against the teachings inscribed in the Book of Mormon. I needed to be a warrior for God.

Now, don't get me wrong. A lot of Mormons are decent, charitable, and absolutely lovely people. During my military career, generous church members supported and cared for my family. But for me, the Mormon religion was a destructive force. It nearly tore my wife and me apart. It pains me to say, but I truly believe that—despite the kindness of many members—the LDS church, like many other religions, has elements that function as a cult.

Cults are all about programming your mind. That's how they reel you in and that's what Mormonism was for me: mental manipulation. The whole *going to hell* thing is strong stuff. Fear of death is one of the most basic elements of the human condition. And appealing to that full-on terror of the eternal dirt nap is one of the best ways to rock a person to their core. It makes us vulnerable, malleable.

Another key ingredient of cult programming is saturation. If you beat people over the head with an ideology and make them live it 24–7, they don't have any time to question little things like inconsistencies in the doctrine. My Mormon life was total saturation. During my high school years, I attended seminary every morning at 5:00 a.m. and went off to church functions or youth activities for priesthood holders—in the LDS church, men and boys twelve and over are ordained in the lower order of the church's priesthood as a matter of course—almost every weeknight. On Sundays, church was an all-day event, with televisions staying off and me slouching around with forced humility.

I needed years of deprogramming to break the religion's hold on me. It took the love of a great woman and military training for me to learn to think for myself. Once I did that, I realized the extent to which the LDS church had controlled my life through regimented teachings and insular community activities. And when I saw my fellow Republicans worshiping at the altar of QAnon and Donald Trump, I recognized the same cultish behavior I had been running from or fighting my whole life.

For better or worse, I was raised to be a fighter. My own upbringing was intense and devout, but I still managed to get in my fair share of misbehavior and general delinquency. My folks were working all the time or taking care of their rapidly growing number of children. It was the Mormon way. I was completely free to run around Coverstone, especially at night. Since it was pretty rough around the edges, that meant a lot of run-ins with bullies.

When I was about eight years old, I burst into the house and breathlessly told my stepdad some older boys were chasing me. His response was, "You just got to fight." The best compliment he ever paid me was that I "wasn't a crier." My biological father also believed in letting his fists do the talking. However, they had two very different philosophies on when to engage. My stepdad thought you should never swing until the opponent hit you first. My father counseled me to always take the first shot if a fight was brewing; I was smaller than most, so I followed his advice more often than not. Those early role models and scraps at Coverstone instilled in me a deep hatred of bullies. I can't stand anyone who uses their power to take advantage of people weaker than them.

I measure those early years in Manassas by the number of children and by square footage. There always seemed to be too much of one and not enough of the other. As I said, our first apartment in Coverstone was tiny. By 1979, we had graduated to three bedrooms. However, by that point, I had a sister, two half-siblings, and a third was on the way. A fourth kid would soon follow. Finally, in 1980, my grandfather sold his house, my mom's childhood home, to my mother and stepfather. Built in the 1950s on a slab, the Cape Cod—although extravagant next to our claustrophobic apartment—still presented challenges because the family kept growing. By the time I was sixteen, my sister Shelly had a kid of her own. There were nine of us living in a fifteen-hundred-square-foot house with one working bathroom.

I would escape the crowded quarters and pressures of the church with books. I was a voracious reader who devoured fantasies, sci-fi, and thrillers. Athletics were also a big deal for me. I lost myself in sports and reading. On the football field, I started out as a quarterback and then moved to running back because I never grew over five feet eight. When it came to baseball, I had a hell of an arm, but it wasn't that accurate. I was a good athlete with a real gun, I just couldn't hit the target half the damn time.

Growing up in the South meant a steady dose of right-wing politics. Everyone around us was some type of Evangelical, strict Catholic, or Mormon. My school, Stonewall Jackson High, was named for the Confederate general. When I took the field, I was one of Stonewall Jackson's Raiders. Virginia was the borderline between South and North and we knew exactly which side of the Potomac we lived on.

In my family, my mom and stepdad were the only ones who converted to the LDS church. The rest worshiped Southern Baptist style. They lived by a conservative code that made allowances for booze, but otherwise dreaded hellfire. My relatives were all what we called "old school," which meant being to the right of Genghis Khan. All of us thumped some type of Bible and, even though no one in the family was in the Klan or the League of the South, we were all on board with the general program and completely convinced of the superiority of our race and culture.

It was validating, which is another key part of cult programming. I was proud of the Confederate flag. Taught to love it. To me, it signified heritage, Southern born and bred, a Virginia boy. I never questioned any of it. Why would I? While pride isn't a truly Christian value, it felt darn good. Retrograde views on race were like religion, part of the culture, background noise like the hum of the cicadas.

Insularity is another one of the ways that cults work on you. If you are surrounded by your fellow true believers, you're immersed. It's an environment where no one gives you cause to question your belief system, and breaking free of the pack often means being ostracized or shunned. The growing far-right media ecosystem is one of these unicast echo chambers. And it provides all of the ideal ingredients for cult programming: insularity, saturation, fear of a common enemy. While the Far Right may not technically qualify as a religious cult, it often behaves like one, and its direct appeal to evangelical Christians shouldn't be surprising. Yes, Trump, with his love of gilded luxury and his philandering, would seem like a hard sell for any "real" Christian. But he has been embraced as an "imperfect vessel" brought by God to help the evangelical movement achieve broader policy goals in the culture war and on issues like abortion. I have family members who believe this; it is painful.

Trump's cult of personality was built on a blend of social media and old-time religion—as was the cult of QAnon. QAnon may have sprouted up on internet forums, but its mythology is riddled with religious elements instantly recognizable to those of us raised in fundamentalist traditions. Satan and Satanists are everywhere. Even operating pedophile rings out of the basement of your local pizza parlor. It is the calling of the righteous few to take on evil. At its heart, QAnon is a story about an apocalyptic struggle against the Devil, or what they call "The Storm." It's Judgment Day.

There's a reason this fable has endured and inspired zealots for so many centuries. It's all about our most basic fear: death. Q adherents are motivated by this same fundamental terror. These people genuinely believe someone they love could end up murdered in some sick ritual slaughter in tunnels underneath the halls of Congress. And they find confirmation in broadcasts, social media, memes, rallies. Far-right extremist programming has hit saturation level. Anyone can visit the digital church or chatroom of their choice on the internet and mainline conspiracies that confirm their worst fears.

Both Trump and QAnon promoters stoke fear to provoke a religious level of devotion. And the most extreme elements of the Far Right have come to believe they are warriors for God doing battle against the liberal modern society. They've plunged us all deep into their holy war. The fight has begun even if many of us don't realize we're in it. And January 6th was the First Crusade.

* * *

After having the Mormon religion steadily drummed into me, my deprogramming process essentially began when I met Christine.

It was late July 1986 and one of the guys, Ron, gave me the rundown. Christine was just about to turn sixteen. I was a couple months older. She had just broken up with her boyfriend and her picture knocked me out. Best of all she was working at the Boot and Belt World and we could go see her!

A few days later, I walked into the store and saw my very own teenage dream behind the counter. Christine had feathered blond hair with red tints, blue eyes, and dancer's legs that went on for days. The photo didn't do her justice.

Somehow, I managed to convince her to go out with me. I didn't have my own car, so Ron and his girlfriend took us to Wendy's. It was a Friday night and Manassas was hopping as everyone cruised the strip.

Playing sports meant I was a fairly popular kid, but the years of LDS teaching emphasized the sinfulness of premarital relations, not romance. I had no idea what to do with a girl or how to go about dating. For the first three months of our relationship, I was so terrified of going to hell that I kept her out of bed. Then, I stopped worrying.

Even with my newfound love, guilt wracked me. I prayed for forgiveness almost every day.

Christine was a member of the Church of the Brethren. To my Mormon mom and stepdad, that made her an outsider. They saw her as being sent from Satan to test me and lead me astray.

I did my best to try and bring my new girlfriend into our Mormon life. When I turned eighteen, I was given the power to baptize and I formally inducted Christine into my family's religion. Another major milestone in the LDS church is the mission, where nineteen-year-olds spend two years spreading the Mormon faith in an area of the world that's supposedly chosen by God just for them. When my time came, I was called to Lisbon, Portugal. I dutifully headed off to the Missionary Training Center in Provo, Utah, the Mormon motherland, to prepare.

Now, before one leaves on a mission assignment, all sins must be confessed to the bishop of the local ward. Fornication is frowned upon in the LDS church, to put it mildly. And since the ripe young age of sixteen, I had broken that rule quite frequently. Being with Christine sure felt heavenly, but part of me was ashamed and felt certain it could send me to hell. When my time before the bishop came, I initially lied and pretended to be pure.

At Mormon churches, they have what is called a Fast and Testimony Sunday once each month. Everyone skips food before church service.

During Fast and Testimony meetings, church leaders encourage every member to publicly share. I was something of a star pupil at the MTC. I picked up my Portuguese lessons quickly and still had that cachet from the football field. A few weeks into the training program, when Fast and Testimony Sunday rolled around, it felt like a lot of people in the room wanted me to speak.

Along with peer pressure, there was something else that compelled me to deliver a testimony. I was longing to feel some type of spiritual connection, to cleanse the nagging sense that I was in the wrong place. The rules I broke to be with Christine weighed on me. Suddenly, on this hungry Sunday, I thought testifying to my fellow trainees would bring me back to the church and help me *feel the spirit*. It did the exact opposite.

I took the stage and started to deliver my own version of the script that was drilled into us each day. Joseph Smith was the one true prophet and we were holy warriors girded with the armor of God ready to go out into the world and deliver salvation to the sinful.

The other boys in the room were moved by my words. I was surrounded by a sea of weeping nineteen-year-olds. They felt the spirit. I felt nothing.

It shook me. Why wasn't I having the same reaction as my fellow future missionaries? Why didn't I share their connection with God? I became convinced that Jesus himself had removed the spirit from me because I was a sinner and had failed to confess.

I decided to visit the stake president, an older man who volunteered at the training center, and unburden myself. He listened intently and even asked for an exact count of how many times I had sinned with Christine. I was so haunted by the gravity of my transgressions that I knew the number. Three hundred and sixty-four acts of lust in about three years. The stake president was disappointed, but kind. After a stern rebuke, he told me my sins would be forgiven by God. I felt an instant, immense sense of relief. It didn't last.

Little did I know, the staff at the training center called my church at home in Manassas. I had just baptized Christine and, based on my confession, the local church ward leadership felt spiritually compelled to disfellowship her. She was essentially blacklisted for an undetermined period. Christine could no longer take the sacrament and sat in the rear of the church during services. It was degrading, cruel, and unfair. We both messed up, but she was the one who paid the price.

To this day, it still angers me. She endured the humiliation because she loved me. Hell, she didn't care about the LDS church. She was only in it for me. I couldn't imagine a God that would punish Christine, who was so kindhearted and good. I began to see the Mormon church as another bully. For the first time, I felt myself questioning the authority of the church.

Seeing Christine disfellowshipped also made me deeply afraid of losing her. With the local ward essentially shunning her and me prepping to jet off for two years in Portugal, I feared there was no way she'd be waiting there when I came home. My love for her forced me to look at my church programming critically. I made a cold calculation. I chose Christine.

I was able to make my getaway because Christine's parents loaned us the money for a plane ticket. But there was still the matter of escaping the training center. The Church of Jesus Christ of Latter-day Saints is serious about maintaining its insular bubble. There was a man guarding the MTC compound. As dawn was breaking, I ran up to the gate and breathlessly told him my mother was sick and needed me to race home. He fell for it. I rushed into a taxi and flew home to Virginia. I didn't look back.

When my best friend and Christine picked me up at the airport, they both gasped. Amid all the stress about our potential damnation, I had lost forty pounds.

When I got home, my parents refused to allow me in. The three words my mother said when she answered the door rang in my ears:

"Satan got you."

I spent that first night back sleeping in my grandfather's Chevette.

* * *

Though Christine's parents weren't Mormon, they were plenty religious. Her father gave us an ultimatum; we could not live in their home together unless we married. I immediately put together a civil wedding. We were now both disfellowshipped but the bishop of the ward kindly allowed us to use the chapel and the gym for our wedding.

That gesture strikes me as an example of the charity and community that are the Mormon religion at its best. A key hallmark of cults is the damage they cause their followers. They break up families and turn on outsiders. This is not to say that Christianity, Mormonism, and other major religions are inherently destructive. Jesus's teachings explicitly call for forgiveness and kindness. Yet, in my experience, evangelical Christians too often forgo the merciful God and focus instead on heavenly wrath. Rather than redemptive love, it's the gospel of my-way-or-the-highway. This type of preaching leads to tribalism and anger—the precise conditions a truly destructive cult like QAnon needs to flourish.

About six weeks after my exodus from the Missionary Training Center, on October 27, 1989, Christine and I were married in front of about one hundred people in Manassas. I didn't talk much to my mother or stepfather for quite some time after I ditched my mission, but they did attend our wedding, and they helped with the venue. Their good standing in the church made it possible for Christine and me to spend only $1,500 on the entire ceremony. At the end of the reception, my stepdad handed me a hundred-dollar bill and said, "I hope it works out for you." Nobody thought we would make it.

We moved into the basement of Christine's parents' modest home. Her dad sold cars and her mother was an administrative assistant. We were going to have to make our own way out of there.

For those first few years, I didn't have much to contribute. I was a shithead, a powerlifter who spent much more time focusing on my muscles than any real ambition. I bounced between different jobs, working construction, waiting tables, and earning awful grades at a local community college.

Around Christmas in 1991, Christine got pregnant. Six months into it, she gave me an ultimatum.

"Either you've got to take care of us or I have to leave and take care of us myself," she said. "We can't go on like this."

Two days later, I enlisted in the US Air Force.

* * *

For a guy who has spent his whole life in institutions, I sure do love to take them on.

My early fights at Coverstone infused me with a desire to stand up for myself. Clashing with the church only hardened that resolve. It was an independent streak that led me to question LDS and, later on, the Republican Party. Weirdly, it also helped me succeed in those organizations. I wanted to prove myself by meeting any challenge they had, to beat any test they could give me. That drive made me a star missionary trainee and helped me climb the ladder in the air force. I was the top-ranked airman in my basic training flight and received top scores on aptitude testing.

I was also driven by a deep anger that intensified when Christine was cast out from the Mormon church. I hated where I came from. I hated that people looked down on me. I hated that I was a Mormon. I hated that I left my mission. I hated how I let everyone down. Most of all, I hated that God hated me. I wanted to show them all.

I had my eye on the skies. I wanted to become a fighter pilot. And I almost made it too.

Through a program called SOAR, which stood for Scholarships to Outstanding Airmen for ROTC, I managed to complete my college education at the University of Virginia. At first it was fucking incredible to be there. Denver Riggleman, little Denny the redneck from Coverstone was now a UVA Wahoo. I was walking the lawn!

That shine wore off quickly. Those twenty-four months at UVA were an absolutely brutal run. By that point, Christine and I had two little girls. I was putting myself through school by bouncing for $100 a night at my dad's bar about a two-hour drive away in Petersburg, West Virginia. We were broke, on Medicaid and food stamps, and driving a car that barely had brakes.

When the time came to graduate, my grades were good enough to pick my next move in the air force—except there was one hitch. At twenty-eight, I was six months too old to fly, and they wouldn't grant me a waiver. I was devastated.

I "settled" for my second choice—becoming an intelligence officer—intent on showing the commanding officers who'd kept me grounded what a mistake they had made. I was going to be the best damn intelligence officer they had.

The mid-nineties were a tense time on the world stage. The collapse of the Soviet Union led to a cascade of conflicts, particularly in the former Yugoslavia. I wanted to be in the hot zone and had focused my UVA studies on the Yugoslav republics. That decision paid off.

When I got to intelligence training as a brand-new second lieutenant, I gave the brass a briefing on Yugoslavia. It blew them away. Ten months later, I found myself fifty miles from the Serbian border in Romania with the 726th Air Control Squadron.

Our mission involved operating a mobile radar post to monitor threats from Russia and their Serbian allies. It was all very exciting stuff. We landed at night, lights out in a C130 on an Eastern Bloc runway that was totally pitted. It was supposedly a classified mission. When we stepped off the cargo plane, there were hundreds of Romanians cheering and waving. It wasn't that top secret after all.

We were the first American troops officially deployed to Romania since 1946. The spotlight was on us and it was my job to protect the servicemen and -women. The Romanians hadn't permitted us to bring weapons and we were stationed in Craiova, which had a thriving underworld full of Romanian mobsters and houses of ill repute. I handed over cash for protection. There were rolling blackouts and, at night, much of the city went dark. In my first twenty-four hours, we had to track down a GI who went missing in one of the seedier sectors. The streets were filled with shadows, gangsters, and secret police.

The radar post featured a TPS 75, a portable system that we used to track Russian jets and weapons systems. It painted targets and conducted route surveys to track potential threats from Serbia. With my background in avionics, I knew how the radar worked. With time, they started using me to track the larger threats outside along with the potential trouble for my GIs in the city.

In the intelligence world, we break down information into two main categories. There's human intelligence, or HUMINT, which is gathered from human sources, including targets, informants, and allies. Then there's signals intelligence, or SIGINT, which is all the information you can gather from electronics like radar or by tracking communications.

The work I did in Romania, where I made assessments based on technical data while also looking at human behavior and building relationships on the ground, was the first time I blended the two types of intelligence. I spent the rest of my military career combining disparate forms of data for analysis. It became the foundation of my approach to investigating QAnon and January 6th.

I left Craiova with glowing reviews and, in subsequent missions, I was read into tactical programs where the air force was working alongside the secretive National Security Agency. These were major mission-planning cell operations where we coordinated F-15s, F-16s, and B-1 bombers. We merged the data from the NSA's massive surveillance apparatus with tactical data to enhance targeting capabilities for multiple air platforms. In other words, we analyzed intelligence to help tell the planes where to hit and what threats might jeopardize their lives and airframes.

Working with the jets also meant I finally was able to fly. As we studied the armed targeting systems, I got my hand on the stick of B-1s and the F-16. Living the dream.

Rising through the ranks helped me get over the pain and guilt I carried from the church. I was a damned good intelligence officer. Here was something I could do. My family was taken care of. We were happy. Maybe God wasn't punishing me after all.

Being an intelligence officer also let me see the world. After Romania, I spent time in Oman training their air mission–planning intelligence officers to work with F-16s. I developed real friendships with people from religions my community condemned.

Still, in the years after my escape from missionary training, the LDS church maintained a hold on me. After being disfellowshipped, both Christine and I were eventually let back in. We were even married for time and eternity in the DC temple five years after our civil ceremony in the gymnasium. But as I served and our life experiences broadened, our appearances in church became fewer and farther between. One warm night at Mountain Home Air Force Base, I realized I was out.

"Fuck it," I told Christine. "I'm done. Let's have a drink."

That night I went from beer to whiskey to passing out in our backyard. It was glorious.

* * *

Ending the Mormon church's sway over me took more than two decades, an unjust slap in the face to my future wife, and a few trips around the world. This long, tortured journey is something I have thought about a lot while investigating QAnon, January 6th, and the various pro-Trump fever swamps. Deprogramming is not easy. I have no doubt that if I hadn't been lucky enough to get an education and some of the opportunities I found in the air force, I could have fallen in line behind Trump. After all, many of my friends and family have fallen down far-right rabbit holes in recent years. I am not that different from them and I know it took a lot to put me on a different course.

My first wild summer out of the church was followed by the harshest fall of them all. It was 2001. After September 11th, I was deployed to a small island base in the British Indian Ocean Territory halfway between Tanzania and Indonesia. There, in Diego Garcia, our joint team mission planned some of the first B-1 bombing runs into Afghanistan.

As that invasion turned into the Global War on Terror, I found myself detailed to the NSA. I was a uniformed air force officer, but I worked inside the agency's headquarters in Fort Meade, Maryland, a secure compound full of hulking office towers carved from blacked-out glass. That posting would be my last as a commissioned officer. In 2003, just as the US was charging toward Iraq, my military career came to a screeching halt.

I loved the air force and was planning to retire in uniform. All of that changed when I was diagnosed with asthma. They told me I would be non-deployable and that this would limit my chances for advancement. I seemed set to go from the tip of the spear to the back office, or what we derisively called "flying" the D-7—a desk with seven drawers. After months of trying to battle the military medical bureaucracy, I knew it was a lost cause. I was done.

As I walked out of the complex for what I thought was the last time, I passed by a smoking area. A voice called out to me.

"Hey, buddy!"

It was Marty Kurdys, an ex-navy guy who was a program manager for Science Applications International Corporation, or SAIC. It's a multibillion-dollar contracting company that provides staff, technology, and services for the Pentagon and the various three-letter agencies that require security clearances. Marty was a recruiter who helped the NSA put butts in seats and ensured they had the talent they needed for highly specialized and sensitive positions.

Marty was a fast talker and a chain smoker. His pitch came out between puffs.

"I heard you're really good at your job. I heard you got every clearance. Hey, how would you like to be a contractor?"

"I'm finished for a while," I replied.

Leaving the air force was hard on me. If I wasn't going to be able to do the work I loved, I couldn't imagine watching it. Fort Meade was the last place I wanted to be.

"What would it take for you to stay?" Marty asked.

"Man, it would take six figures," I answered.

It was 2003. That went a long way then. I thought there was no way they could pay that kind of cash.

Marty grinned at me with his tobacco-stained teeth.

"You can start tomorrow," he said and gave my hand a shake.

I was out of uniform, but the air force let me keep my clearance. I continued to blend NSA surveillance data with tactical data to assist operations on the ground. But now, I was doing it at an even more advanced level because I was putting together development and analysis teams and leading them. Soon enough, I got the call from Big Safari, a program that the air force describes as their "rapid procurement force." Our specialty was quickly designing, building, and deploying advanced systems using multiple intelligence and operational disciplines. We used various technologies and platforms to create fused weapons systems that could prosecute targets and deliver enhanced situational awareness. Put simply, we mixed intelligence, manpower, arms, and cyber elements to help the air force stay bigger, faster, and more lethal.

Counterterrorism work needed quick-reaction capabilities. Big Safari knew how to build the plane while flying it. I learned contracts and funding lines. There was no time or reason for competitive bidding since we knew the universe of people who had the clearances and experience required for this highly specialized work. Big Safari had what they called a "black budget" and "sole source authority." We were exempt from those traditional procurement rules. People called us when they needed something done fast.

The NSA also schooled me in telephony analysis, which is the construction, operation, and analysis of telecommunications networks. I rode in surveillance vans and learned to exploit phones, read their metadata, and other tricks of the trade like spoofing numbers and playing tricks with cell towers.

I also began learning about new threats. Even as the War on Terror heated up, I stayed dual-hatted and kept one eye on Moscow. I tracked advanced Russian radar and armaments. I also learned to watch Al Qaeda terrorists, Iranian operatives, and Taliban militants. I studied their weapons systems—from homemade bombs to Toyota pickups kitted out with machine guns—and their methods. I saw how they radicalized new recruits. I analyzed how they attacked and how they covered their tracks.

Years later, as I followed the radicals who sought to overturn the election for President Trump, I recognized some of the same techniques, tactics, and procedures. The command and control structures were similar. Trump's holy warriors and the jihadists both changed strategies in real time if they believed law enforcement was looking for them. They tried to hide communications by going dark through encrypted apps.

I see these patterns faster than most people. I've been trained to do it, but I never imagined I would put these skills to use against a massive threat in my own country.

CHAPTER 4

FRINGE SOUP

As you can tell, I pride myself on my intelligence skills. But I have to admit, I was slow to grasp the reach and impact of QAnon. It seemed bizarre that anyone would believe such a toxic stew of conspiracy theories. A secretive Satan-worshipping, child-killing global cabal that included Democrats, celebrities, and the media? Yeah, sure; tell me about it.

For those of you uninitiated in the darker corners of the internet, QAnon officially began in late 2017 on 4chan, a notorious imageboard. Imageboards are based on forums that were popular in Japan, particularly for discussing anime and manga. The format encourages anonymity. English-language imageboards, the most popular of which was 4chan, became hotbeds of gore, revenge porn, and the neo-Nazi memes that helped popularize the Trump-era "alt-right."

The writer behind the "Q" persona used something called a trip-code, which allowed 4chan users to see that their posts came from an individual author. They claimed to be a deep government insider with a "Q" level security clearance. According to their posts, which became known as "Q drops" among the faithful, President Trump was leading a group of patriots who were trying to take the government back from this aforementioned cabal. This was supposedly a real-time record of a heroic struggle—and the writer was turning to random internet users as their primary reinforcements. The writings were dark warnings. They suggested Trump and his allies were preparing for "The Storm," a massive, final confrontation against this dark new world order.

The posts spread like wildfire, eventually migrating to multiple other forums and authors.

Trump and the members of his inner circle helped fan the flames. Some Trump allies became full-on QAnon promoters. Media outlets have linked Trump's former national security advisor Michael Flynn to QAnon. Other insiders—like top White House aide Dan Scavino and the president's two sons—seemed to wink at the conspiracy theories by making social media posts with blatant QAnon imagery. "Q" symbols became a staple at Trump's rallies. In 2018, Trump invited "Lionel," an influential QAnon voice and talk show host, to the White House. By 2020, as Trump ran for re-election, there were days when Trump retweeted QAnon accounts multiple times. These gestures were not missed by the eager online devotees who parsed the "Q drops" and posts from Trump for anything that might validate their beliefs.

I began to detect QAnon's prevalence in 2018, when I ran for Congress. My district was the Fifth Congressional District of Virginia, which covers an area bigger than six US states, and includes Charlottesville.

As I campaigned around Virginia, more and more QAnon paraphernalia began turning up at my events. Older evangelical women were the first ones I noticed. They wore necklaces and shiny brooches decked out with the letter "Q." At first, I figured it was some kind of new custom Christian jewelry. After seeing it enough, I asked one woman with a jeweled "Q" pin what it stood for.

"It represents what I believe in," she said.

At one event, a kind, elderly lady approached me to declare that she couldn't vote for me if I didn't read the Bible every night. Another older woman informed me that if I couldn't quote a certain book of scripture, she'd know God had not ordained me for public office. It was stunning to see true born-again holy rollers lining up behind Trump, a man who shunned church and had already been caught on camera bragging about grabbing women "by the pussy." None of this mattered to his evangelical base. Trump had hands laid on him by "Holy Men." A network of extremist preachers promoted the narrative that Trump, flawed though he might be, was an instrument of the Lord.

* * *

I was an accidental congressman. My path to politics began with a fight over whiskey.

In 2007, I started my own intelligence company that supported the NSA, air force, and other government agencies. It was the continuation of my Big Safari work, but I had gone from contractor to CEO and directed rapid-response teams that supported military operations and conducted predictive analysis tracking traditional threats and cyberattacks. Five years later, I sold the business for a nice chunk of change.

Christine had been following me from base to base over the years. She had put her own career aside to support mine and raise our three daughters. I told her it was her turn. We'd use the windfall to fund her dream job—distilling.

Christine got bitten by the whiskey bug on a trip to Ben Nevis distillery in Scotland. She was completely drawn in by the complexity of the mash, grains, cooking protocols, and the aging process. It's in her blood; her great-aunts are famous inside their family for making bathtub gin during Prohibition. Christine clearly inherited their skills. She was blessed with an incredible palate that helped her concoct blends that have gone on to rack up a slew of awards.

We incorporated in spring 2013, and by August 2014 we had set up shop and opened Silverback Distillery along the Rockfish River in the lush woods by the Blue Ridge Mountains. The calm of our idyllic distillery dream was suddenly interrupted when we found ourselves at war with the Virginia Alcoholic Beverage Control Authority.

The Commonwealth of Virginia has a state-run system for selling hard liquor. It's basically a Prohibition-era relic designed to limit the flow of the "devil's water" in a state that stretches from the fairly progressive Washington suburbs to the deeply conservative edge of the Bible belt.

In more recent decades, the ABC has become big business for the state. It brings in over $1 billion in revenue each year. But while the officials clearly had no problem profiting off of alcohol, they also put limitations on hard liquor distillers that didn't apply to beer- and winemakers. I came to learn this wasn't so much a political stance against whiskey and gin or the result of a modern temperance movement, it was the work of aggressive beer and wine lobbies that perpetuated their advantage over distilleries by pouring cash into the political arena. I set my sights on them.

Hard liquor purveyors paid higher taxes and had strict limits on the amount of product they could sell. I saw it as an outgrowth of decades of backslapping and backroom deals between lobbyists and their buddies in Richmond. Christine and I helped set up a distillers' guild to compete with the beer and wine lobbies.

At the same time, a surveyor showed up at our house and said they were there to map out a pipeline for Dominion Energy. Our little corner of the Blue Ridge was right along the route of a six-hundred-mile pipeline proposal that would take gas from the shale in West Virginia all the way down to North Carolina. It cut straight through Virginia's valleys and the Appalachian Trail. The state intended to take our property via eminent domain.

I saw these two issues—the beer lobbying and the pipeline proposal—as linked. They were both examples of a government based on cronyism. By default, a politics based on connections, fundraising, and favor-trading will stiff the little guy. If you know me by now, then you know I hate bullies and love a challenge. It was time to fight the system.

I ran for governor; failed. I ran for Congress; won.

Both races offered inklings of what the Republican Party had become. I encountered lots of crazy, and I was not prepared for it at all. At local party events and meetings in Virginia, particularly the more rural districts, I noticed the party morphing into one made in Trump's image. There was growing anger about the "deep state," shadowy forces embedded in the government working to sabotage Trump. New administrations always have to deal with holdovers from the old guard. Our federal government rightly doesn't require any kind of loyalty test and is filled with career functionaries of all stripes. This kind of ideological diversity in the unelected portions of our government is a feature of democracy, but Trump and his allies weaponized it. They openly promoted the idea of a dark deep state as he faced investigations into his own questionable conduct. His paranoid political attack harmonized with the rapid rise of QAnon.

Along with the deep state madness, I witnessed the racism that was now flourishing openly in certain circles. One of my rivals in the GOP's gubernatorial primary was Corey Stewart, a local official who openly campaigned with Confederate symbols and allies who were linked to organizers of the neo-Nazi, white supremacist rally that turned deadly in Charlottesville in 2017. Stewart went out of his way to base his bid on defending "our heritage" in spite of the fact he was born in Minnesota.

For me, the governor's run highlighted how much Republicans were falling in line behind Trump. Activists attacked me for a Facebook post I wrote during the 2016 election where I quipped that both Trump and his Democratic Party rival, Hillary Clinton, were awful choices. Vicious rants came at me from multiple platforms. It was all a heavy dose of Trump's new brand of Republican politics: conspiracy-driven, angry, and demanding absolute loyalty.

This was a far cry from the organization I thought I belonged to. When I jumped into the race, I didn't question for a second which party I would run in. My family and I were all lifelong Republicans. To me, the GOP signified appreciation for small government, which meant personal freedom. A party of liberty should stay out of peoples' private lives and not interfere with their businesses.

The increasingly radicalized religious element of the party quickly made itself known during those first months of Trump's presidency. Growing up in Manassas, I certainly saw the evangelical base of the Republican Party. However, as a kid, the people I knew respected a line between church and state. Trump's party was veering more and more into Christian nationalism, where they demonized Democrats as having an unholy agenda.

* * *

None of this fringe soup seemed to bother the Fifth District Republican committee.

My campaign for Congress began when a sitting House member abruptly decided not to run for re-election. I became his last-minute replacement after a five-day frenzy and a vote by a few dozen members of that local committee.

I was only able to secure the support of the committee thanks to a promise to join the conservative Freedom Caucus in Congress should I win. Since I had criticized Trump, some of the committee members were wary that I would be sufficiently conservative. My consultant told me the way to ease their fears and earn their support was by vowing to go all in.

So, I did.

The Freedom Caucus was founded in 2015 by Tea Partiers including North Carolina's Mark Meadows and Ohio's Jim Jordan. It was ostensibly dedicated to advancing conservative policies and played a key role in ousting House Speaker John Boehner in favor of Paul Ryan.

However, by 2018, like so many other Republican organizations, the caucus was becoming laser focused in support of Trump. Two prominent members—Mick Mulvaney and Meadows—would go on to serve as his chiefs of staff and many of the others (notably Jim Jordan) were known for mounting increasingly over-the-top defenses of Trump as he faced a growing list of scandals.

In my heart, I knew the caucus was not for me. I was turned off by how Jordan and his ilk bent over backward to make excuses for Trump. I also didn't appreciate how much they injected religion into politics. However, my consultant convinced me the caucus was all about free-flowing conversations on politics. He also suggested that compromising myself would be in service of a greater good—beating the competition.

I made the deal, and once I won the primary, I turned to my campaign consultant with a big grin on my face.

"It's a new day. Every decision we make in this race has to be about integrity," I declared.

"You already broke that rule," he replied. "You joined the Freedom Caucus even though you didn't want to. You did it to win. Congratulations. That was your first major political decision."

＊ ＊ ＊

As hard as this might be to believe, after winning the primary, my general election race devolved into a battle over Bigfoot. That's right, I am talking about the mythical Sasquatch. When I studied radicalization as part of my air force work, I came upon the Bigfoot community. There's a whole subculture of people who are obsessed with the possibility of great apes hidden in the American wilderness. True believers range from conspiracists who think the government has a secret collection of Bigfoot bones in the Smithsonian to spiritualists who are devoted to Native American lore. They're all people who passionately believe in something with scant and questionable evidence—and there's a whole ecosystem of hucksters and grifters eager to take advantage of their faith. I came to see it as the perfect low-stakes example of how cults and fantastical belief systems can take hold. Bigfoot became my go-to case study when trying to explain these concepts over drinks.

I got it into my head to write a book based on the idea. Among my drinking buddies and former military colleagues, it all became a running joke. We particularly enjoyed mocking the Bigfoot fetish community—yes, that's a real thing too. As my birthday approached in 2018, one of my friends made a crude photoshop of my face on Bigfoot's body. It had a big black bar censoring its nether regions. I thought the whole thing was a hoot and put it on my Instagram along with a note that jokingly promised I would be releasing a book called *The Mating Habits of Bigfoot and Why Women Want Him.*

It was an obvious gag. My Instagram post noted that the silly picture was a birthday tease from my buddies. The only thing it proved was that I wasn't a polished enough politician to realize I could no longer kid around on social media and that I should have cleaned up my old posts. However, my opponent, Democrat Leslie Cockburn, seized on the picture. She tweeted it out along with a note that described it as part of my "Bigfoot erotica collection." I had to Google that term, but it's actually a real thing. Right now, if you skim through Amazon, you'll find over 150 titles that feature protagonists in love with a Sasquatch monster, such as *Seduced by Bigfoot and Ravaged by the Yeti.* My silly post was nothing of the sort. Democrats can dabble in disinformation too. Politics is a dirty business. All of her effort dragging me through the mud got Cockburn a nearly seven-point loss on Election Day.

* * *

When I came to Washington in 2019, the GOP's flexible ethics were on full display at our private orientation for congressional freshmen. The events for new members included a speech by House Minority Leader Kevin McCarthy that culminated with a simple declaration.

"Winners make history," McCarthy said.

How do you win? By appealing to your base. You need their votes and, most especially, their donations. Polls can show you where the base is on a given issue. Polls can also show what gets the base riled up. Those are the messages most effective for fundraising, the ones that provoke outrage. And an endless outrage cycle leaves little room for compromise or genuine integrity.

A lot of my Republican colleagues were like me when it came to Trump. We thought he was a buffoon and a good number of us even publicly opposed him in 2016. By a year or so later, when Trump was firmly in power and dominating polls of our base, we all just hoped to secure his endorsement and avoid his wrath.

While some of us held our noses as we followed the leader, others were true believers. This became abundantly clear to the world on January 6, 2021, when, directly after the violence inspired by Trump's lies that the election was stolen from him, 147 Republicans objected to the vote. But it was just as clear earlier than that. In the Freedom Caucus meetings, I began to understand that some of my colleagues had fully bought into even the more unhinged conspiracy theories I had been seeing out on the campaign trail. I went to a meeting where Texas congressman Louie Gohmert promoted a conspiracy theory related to master algorithms. He suspected there was a secret technology shadow-banning conservatives across all platforms. As he spoke, others in the room nodded along.

Of course, that's crazy. And I said something to that effect during the meeting. While trying to be as diplomatic as possible, I suggested the idea was a very difficult thing to square for the same reason the conspiracies about election-stealing algorithms didn't hold up. There's basically no way for one program to function on multiple social media platforms with different operating systems. It's technically impossible. My explanation was met with an uncomfortable silence.

In subsequent Freedom Caucus meetings, which typically took place at the Conservative Partnership Institute (CPI), I would come to see that Gohmert was one of a few colleagues who had gone deep down the rabbit hole. Scott Perry, Jody Hice, Randy Weber, and the caucus chairman, Andy Biggs, all said things that stunned me. Gohmert and Arizona congressman Paul Gosar seemed to be joined at the brain stem when it came to their eagerness to believe wild, dramatic fantasies about Democrats, the media, and Big Tech. I came to believe Gosar and Gohmert may have had serious cognitive issues.

Gosar also—along with former Iowa congressman Steve King— seemed to be a blatant white supremacist. In mid-2019, Biggs led a delegation that included members of the Freedom Caucus down to the southern border. I went along for the ride. One night around the barbecue table, Gosar and King dove into a conversation about how they felt white people had really created superior civilizations. In their view, it was absurd anyone would question that. They were making a case for white supremacy over pulled pork and ribs.

It was unbelievable. I had always bristled when I'd hear Democrats dismiss Republicans as "racists." To me, it seemed like an easy insult that dodged policy discussions. Now, here I was behind the curtain, seeing that some of my colleagues really seemed to hold these awful views.

I left the table. While I was horrified by what Gosar and King were saying, I didn't confront them. I just got out of there. Part of me regrets keeping quiet. The other part tries to comfort myself by rationalizing that they were too far gone; they wouldn't have cared about my pushback. While that's clearly true, as much as it pains me to say it, I also did a lot of going along to get along early in my congressional stint. I knew extremism was rising in the party. I honestly tricked myself into thinking I could change it. My plan was to show the world I could be a "new kind of Republican."

I am certainly no Democrat. Too often their solution is to simply tax and spend. I believe in removing unnecessary regulations to allow small businesses to grow and entrepreneurs to succeed. I'm a strong Second Amendment guy. At the same time, I support gay marriage and legalizing marijuana. My line was that "I didn't want a party small enough to fit in anyone's bedroom." While I lean pro-life, I believe in the right to abortion early on in a pregnancy and am adamant about exceptions for victims of rape or incest, or for when the mother's health is at stake.

In my view, a lot of these positions fit with the traditional Republican ideal of liberty. And in keeping with this value, I also figured my fellow Republicans would be able to tolerate some differences of opinion. Boy, was that wrong.

I am haunted by a vote I cast in May 2019. Along with the majority of my colleagues, I voted against the Equality Act, a measure that would have made it illegal under federal law to discriminate against people based on their sexuality or gender identity.

There were certainly technical aspects to the Equality Act that I disagreed with; no bill is perfect. However, enhancing federal protections against discrimination was something I wanted to support. But going into the vote, I received directions from the conference to be a "team player." In my first weeks in office, I had voted to reopen the government after the Republicans pushed a shutdown in a strong-arm effort to help Trump secure border-wall funding. To those supporting the values of the Freedom Caucus, that meant I had already started my nascent political career on shaky ground. I did what I was told.

In hindsight, that vote was a turning point for me. After that, I couldn't any longer compromise myself for the party. Soon after, two men who had volunteered on my campaign, Alex Pisciarino and Anthony "Rek"

LeCounte, asked me to officiate their wedding. They were my good friends and fantastic people. And it is a great honor when someone asks you to preside over their nuptials. I didn't hesitate.

Christine knew I was in trouble.

"Honey, now you've done it," she said, shaking her head. "I'm proud of you."

She knew we were in for a fight.

I knew the ceremony would cause an issue. I still held out hope that people would see the ceremony and start to warm to the idea of a Republican Party that welcomed people of all stripes.

Hardly.

The backlash was beyond anything I could have ever imagined.

I received official censures from multiple local Republican organizations and, at events around the Fifth District—particularly in the southern stretch near the Carolina border—I faced the ire of our base. In Halifax County, I went to a public meeting where some guy in a "Make America Great Again" cap charged up to me.

"You're the general of the Sodomite armies!" he shouted, veins bulging and face as red as his hat. "You're evil! You are a tool of the Antichrist!"

Others accused me of wanting to change the sexual orientation of children.

While I was in session in DC, my oldest daughter offered to take my GMC Canyon into the shop for an oil change. On the way over, the truck wobbled a bit, but she thought little of it. A few hours later, a friend who ran the shop called my wife in tears. Checking over the truck, one of their mechanics noticed that the lug nuts on one of the front tires had been loosened to their final thread. The caps had been carefully placed back so we wouldn't notice. It was unmistakably clear: this was a deliberate act.

If I ever find the individual responsible, God help that person.

They also worked to take me out politically and, on that front, they were more successful. Roughly two months after the wedding, the local GOP committee chose a Republican challenger. His name was Bob Good. He was a staffer at Jerry Falwell Jr.'s evangelical Liberty University. Good described himself as a "biblical conservative," suggested COVID was a hoax, and stressed that, unlike me, he didn't even support abortion in case of rape.

My district made its hard turn right: QAnon and Christian nationalism were not just ascendant but, for now, invincible. I had literally nothing left to lose. I was going to be a one-term congressman.

* * *

I never back down from a fight. The QAnon wing of the party had pushed me out of my seat. I was going to dedicate my remaining time in office to taking them on. On October 2, 2020, less than one hundred days before the attack on the US Capitol, I stood on the House floor and warned that we were at "a pivotal moment in our nation's history and a moment of reckoning in our national discourse."

The speech was part of my effort to co-sponsor a resolution officially condemning the QAnon conspiracy theory. In my remarks, I noted that QAnon had already inspired terrifying real-world violence. The partial litany of outrages included at least one murder, a bomb threat at the Illinois State Capitol, and death threats against my colleague, the resolution's co-sponsor Tom Malinowski, a New Jersey Democrat who was falsely accused by QAnon fanatics of lobbying to protect sexual predators.

I was speaking to a half-empty room. While a good number of Democrats were in the audience, almost all of my Republican colleagues skipped the session. Even the two other Republican co-sponsors, Adam Kinzinger of Illinois and Brian Fitzpatrick of Pennsylvania, voted in absentia. I was alone out there. Our resolution passed, but seventeen Republicans voted against it and another thirty-five avoided voting one way or the other.

One of the House members who opposed the resolution was Drew Ferguson, a Georgia Republican whom I had come to think of as a mentor since my own election one year earlier. Ferguson was walking in as I came off the floor. He pulled me aside.

"I don't think you should be doing this," Ferguson said with a kind smile, as he patted my shoulder. "You want to keep the big man happy."

The warning didn't concern me. The Far Right had already taken me out.

* * *

Two years in the House Freedom Caucus; I was the canary in the coal mine. I had been attacked, threatened, and, ultimately, pushed out of office by digitally radicalized zealots.

It was harrowing. I feel like I aged ten years during the two I spent on Capitol Hill.

On December 10, 2020, less than a month before the Capitol attack, I delivered a farewell address where I railed against disinformation and "super-spreader digital viruses that create a fever of nonsense."

As I made my case, I turned to the first representative of Virginia's Fifth District, James Madison, who once wrote that "knowledge will forever govern ignorance: And a people who mean to be their own Governors, must arm themselves with the power which knowledge gives." Knowledge and a well-instructed people were clear pillars of our nation as Madison and the founding fathers envisioned it. I warned my colleagues that "those pillars are now being assaulted by disinformation and outlandish theories surrounding this presidential election."

After invoking the founders, I leaned on my own two decades of experience in intelligence and counterterrorism. I noted how QAnon promoters were linked with both the conspiracists who questioned the COVID pandemic and Trump's Stop the Steal movement to overturn the election. I used technical terms to show how these disinformation operations attacked "specific pillars of democracy at strategic moments, from belief in democratic elections to trust in public health and public institutions." I explained that these influence operations used "combinations of bot-like networks and synchronous mass posting behavior termed 'coordinated inauthentic behavior' . . . with great success to hijack the national conversation."

I said: "Just like creating a vaccine to eradicate COVID-19 we must work together to inoculate against the social contagion of disinformation conspiracies, anti-Semitism, dehumanization, racism, deep state cabal nonsense cults, and those grifters posing as servants of the people." I added, "Radicalization through disinformation has no place in the United States and, in this fight, I will not relent."

Based on what I had been seeing, I warned that we were heading down a very dark road. No one listened. I figured—hoped?—some of my colleagues would understand the urgency and rise to the occasion. None took up the call.

On January 5, the night before the election was set to be certified, with the far-right message boards I was tracking raging and Trump supporters descending on DC, I posted an even more explicit warning on Twitter referencing the far-right violence that had erupted in Charlottesville, Virginia, in 2017.

"Charlottesville is in my district," I wrote. "All the indicators are there. A 'Charlottesville' in DC could be catastrophic."

I fully expected some degree of violence as Trump's loss was certified that day. Nevertheless, what happened next shocked me. Sometimes I beat myself up for being too naive. As bad as I thought things were, the chaos of January 6th eclipsed my worst predictions for where we were as a country. Thousands of people—including at every level of the government—were willing to attack the Capitol and topple the core institutions of our republic.

Worst of all, their rage was based on twisted fictions that were being hammered into their minds. Many people in the mob that broke into the Capitol and brawled with law enforcement bore "Q" symbols and pictures of the alt-right's cartoon mascot, Pepe the Frog. They waved flags for "Kekistan," the fictional nation where the far-right frog is worshipped as a god. Banners also bore the QAnon slogan "WWG1WGA," or "Where We Go One, We Go All." There was no mistaking it, the digital fever swamps had been crawling with insurgents, and they were now marching on Washington.

The people storming the building were doing real damage based on a complete fantasy.

CHAPTER 5

OPS AND OPTICS

I was sure the committee didn't want me. For nearly a week after I made my pitch to Pelosi's staff members and members of chairman Bennie G. Thompson's team, there'd been radio silence.

I chewed over the presentation again and again in my head. Where had I gone wrong?

During my brief, I showed the team various types of data we could mine and I'd outlined strategies for combining that evidence to not only paint a complete picture of what happened on January 6th but uncover who was behind it.

It seemed so clear to me, and I thought my résumé spoke for itself: I was the guy to get it done.

Yet even after being invited to interview and presenting what I thought was a compelling plan, I began to worry the committee might not let me on board. As a former House member, I knew exactly what this kind of delay meant after an interview: politics.

Someone on the team had concerns about me. I had been afraid of that. As a former congressman I knew the "R" after my name could cause a problem. The committee members and staffers were almost all Democrats, and there I was, a Republican who had been part of the Freedom Caucus just a few months before. Trust was in short supply.

* * *

I was invited in by Liz Cheney, the Wyoming congresswoman. Like me, Cheney had a solid conservative voting record that was in line with Trump over 90 percent of the time. And like me, she wasn't willing to excuse the president's behavior because she appreciated his policy on taxes. We both still believed in a pre-Trump vision for the party.

Cheney was one of the few Republicans who came up to me after my first floor speech on QAnon. She'd wanted to know more. Afterward, I sent her the report I had compiled with the Network Contagion Research Institute in the weeks before the Capitol attack. Now, Cheney had a request: "Can we find out exactly who was behind this?"

At the time, members of Congress were debating how to respond to the violence—including mounting an investigation or removing Trump during his final weeks in office. Cheney didn't say it, but it was clear to me that she wanted evidence as she tried to persuade our fellow Republicans to act against Trump. I thought what she was doing was brave.

Cheney wanted the evidence quickly. Working with the NCRI team, I was able to put together a quick-turn report on the attack that was delivered privately to her in about ninety-six hours. The NCRI researchers have a unique set of skills that enable them to collect and analyze an extraordinary amount of data in short order. Our initial report, the one published about three weeks before January 6th, had demonstrated how QAnon's myths fueled an insular online social group that was increasingly becoming a real-world threat.

QAnon and the alt-right bloomed from internet imageboards where neo-Nazi ideology and crazed conspiracies were peddled alongside jokes and cartoons. Since everything was cloaked in anonymity and irony, the purveyors of these dark memes could operate in plain sight and have some degree of plausible deniability when confronted. They reveled in their reputation as "edgelords" who pushed the boundaries of good taste. The new digital extremism was cast as joking, mocking, and trolling. Experts termed this "memetic warfare." It metastasized online and mixed ridiculous fantasies with real threats. The dynamic made it easy to dismiss it all as a fantastical joke.

Now, after January 6th showed the world just how deadly serious these far-right deep-web subcultures were, we described in our report to Cheney how the Stop the Steal anti-election propaganda flowed from that toxic fountain and evolved into calls for Trump supporters to converge on the Capitol. Not only that: the institute, with its massive amount of data, could identify key drivers and participants in the deep-web radicalization pipeline.

Cheney was impressed. She told me she hoped I would be part of any investigation into the attack that came out of Congress. It goes without saying that, after having already dedicated myself to the fight against extremist disinformation, I was in.

I was also adamant that time was of the essence. There's an old adage that everything you put on the internet is forever. It's a good rule to live by, but the truth is online content is permanent only if someone saves it in time. Digital information can be ethereal. Nothing is permanent in the world of pixels. Texts, emails, and posts can all be deleted. Phone companies store records for limited periods of time. Other corroborating evidence like surveillance footage also has a limited shelf life. And, of course, when bad actors get the sense their crimes are being investigated, they work to cover their tracks. What's more, social media companies, feeling the heat over how they may have enabled the violence, were scrubbing their tracks. Facebook, Twitter, YouTube, and others had hosted content that included false claims of election fraud and specific plans for converging on the Capitol. Silicon Valley was now responding to the breach with a mass deletion.

This was potentially an investigative disaster. We had to get moving. If we didn't get on the ball, even more data was going to disappear.

* * *

It took more than six months for the House committee to formally get started. Partisan wrangling and games were the order of the day.

Republican leadership killed a proposal for an independent commission that would have been modeled after the one that investigated September 11th. In his remarks opposing the commission, GOP Senate Minority Leader Mitch McConnell made multiple references to "another commission" in Congress, as though one already existed. McConnell had to have known that was a lie. There was no real reason for opposing the proposal, which had been negotiated by Republicans. McConnell was using disinformation to protect his party from being investigated for its role in spreading dangerous disinformation.

After the commission plan was killed, a House select committee was the next best option. House Minority Leader Kevin McCarthy almost immediately began sabotaging the newly created committee, which was supposed to contain an equal number of Democrats and Republicans, by appointing two of the most stalwart defenders of Trump to serve among the GOP contingent: a Freedom Caucus member, Ohio's Jim Jordan, and Indiana's Jim Banks, the Republican Study Committee (RSC) chairman.

Jordan was already on the warpath: "This is one more chance for them to go after President Trump because . . . they don't want President Trump to run in 2024," he declared, dismissing the new committee.

As for Banks, even if he was not as feisty as Jordan, he went just as hard in his fealty to Trump. I have to say, I like Banks. He was a navy man who had served in Afghanistan. I respected him for his service. But I reckon he felt he had to be completely beholden to Trump in order to advance in the Republican Party. However, both Jordan and Banks played active roles in efforts to delegitimize and reverse the election. On January 5, Banks expressed support for the masses streaming toward Washington to take up Trump's cause the following day. He used some language that was inconvenient in retrospect. "I'm writing this from Capitol Hill," Banks began, "to say I'm looking forward to welcoming the thousands—maybe millions?—of supporters of Donald Trump here in Washington over the next 24-48 hours! The crowd coming is a powerful message to politicians in DC that things can't go back to 'normal' or business as usual." Banks would later clean that post off his Facebook page.

Pelosi took McCarthy's bait. She rejected the two congressmen, thereby giving McCarthy the cover he needed to walk away from the process completely.

I understood why she did it; most people did. Letting those two men on to the committee would have been a clear case of having the foxes guard the henhouse. Still, I thought it was the wrong call. Sure, Jordan and Banks could have tried to push the committee away from pursuing questions about the involvement of Republican members of Congress in the plot against the election. And they would have been primed to hijack the public hearings at points, airing wild conspiracy theories about antifa and FBI involvement in the breach, but with many Republicans using their platforms to make those claims anyway, I've always thought it could have been healthy to take on that narrative publicly. What's more, Pelosi had the power to kick Jordan and Banks off the committee the moment she felt they were being deliberately obstructive. If she gave them a chance to act in good faith, she could have at least said that she tried to work with the GOP.

Rejecting them prematurely gave Republicans ammunition as they tried to delegitimize the committee. And to raise money! Jordan would go on to solicit donations based on the fact he was "banned" from the January 6th committee.

This was all eating up precious time.

* * *

I came into the picture on July 25, 2021, about three weeks after the committee was founded.

The members had finally been appointed. There were two Republicans: Liz Cheney and Illinois's Adam Kinzinger. Kinzinger was an air force brother, a lieutenant colonel and pilot, or "driver." As a flyboy, he tends to lean forward and go full throttle. Both struck me as people who had their eyes on higher office. But while their opposition to Trump may have fit with their ambitions by gaining them national prominence, it was also courageous. It takes real spine to walk in and out of Capitol Hill every day and face your colleagues knowing the whole conference hates your guts because you're not putting the tribe first.

On the Democratic side, the committee chairman was Bennie G. Thompson, who has represented his Mississippi district for just shy of thirty years. During my time in the House, a Democratic member once told me the way to move up in their ranks is by simply not dying. Pelosi awarded key positions based on two things—seniority and support for her. This meant that the key committee leaders generally had her back—and had done so for a long time.

Thompson fit that mold. Thanks to seniority, he was chairman of the Committee on Homeland Security. That made him the natural pick to lead a domestic terrorism investigation. It also ensured Pelosi was getting a team player who wouldn't rock the boat.

Six other Democratic members served on the committee.

Florida's Stephanie Murphy had worked as a national security specialist for the secretary of defense. I appreciated her military background and came to find her more and more impressive as our work went on. In the months we worked together, the Republicans in the Florida legislature redistricted her into oblivion and she announced late last year she would not be running for re-election. I think it's a real loss for that state.

California's Pete Aguilar was an ex-mayor. I didn't deal with him much but he asked some very perceptive questions in our meetings. Another California congressman, Adam Schiff, was one of the members who prosecuted Trump's first impeachment in 2019. I was not a big fan of Schiff from those proceedings. He began one of those hearings by reciting a conversation he suggested came from Trump. Schiff later dismissed it as parody. I was one of over fifty Republicans—including Cheney—who voted to censure him for going over the line. I don't like disinformation from anyone. Schiff always struck me as exceptionally political and his later actions on the committee didn't entirely disabuse me of that notion.

Virginia's Elaine Luria was a former navy commander. She's incredibly savvy and suffers no fools; I was glad to serve with her.

The two final members—Maryland's Jamie Raskin and California's Zoe Lofgren—were also both a part of the House Administration committee. Lofgren actually chairs that committee. I thought they were unfortunate picks since its responsibility for Capitol security meant the House Administration committee needed to be investigated along with everything else.

On the day I was interviewed about taking a position as a senior adviser, I told those I met with that it was clear to me that data would be the holy grail of this investigation. My vision was this: establish the first congressional fusion center.

These centers have become common in law enforcement and military operations. They serve as focal points for the collection and analysis of data. Earlier in my career, I had worked in intelligence centers that operated on an "eyebrow cell" model. A lead analyst works in the center with multiple desks fanning out in a semicircle around the intelligence leader. From above, it looks like an eye surrounded by its brow. It's an excellent way to share and analyze the data in broad context.

I identified three major pillars for the investigation to focus on: (1) the government's role and response; (2) the involvement of militant groups and the radicalization pipeline; and (3) foreign disinformation.

The first section would present the "day of" analysis, looking at the violence of January 6th in a detailed and technical way. We would examine the security posture at the Capitol as well as the role all links in the chain of command played. There was no question we had to understand exactly what happened in the West Wing.

The second major pillar was radicalization and coordinating functions. In other words, how people became militant and how they organized once they did. This could be accomplished by analyzing extremist networks through social media and records of communications to identify critical touchpoints. Using the fusion-center approach that helped me blend SIGINT and HUMINT in my intelligence career, we would spot the major players who linked various groups as well as highlight the major messages that changed the conversation around Trump's election fight. We would track how various far-right groups including Oath Keepers, Proud Boys, QAnon, anti-vaxxers, and neo-Nazis came together and how their rhetoric escalated from election conspiracies to calls to protest and, eventually, the plan to converge on the Capitol. A key focus would be determining who had command and control over their movements.

I recommended that the committee visually map out the connections among these groups and the escalation of their rhetoric in simple charts for the public. Once the investigation proceeded and my team had its hands on the evidence, those maps would prove more shocking than I had imagined. Our phone records analysis ultimately showed a thick web with extensive lines of communication between Trump associates and groups like the Oath Keepers and Proud Boys.

On January 6th, the militia groups were joined by people with actual military and law enforcement training. According to the George Washington University Program on Extremism, at least 101 had military experience. That amounts to about 13 percent of the over 800 people who are involved in federal cases related to January 6th. Other rioters had law enforcement experience and credentials. The data indicates that white supremacist organizations and other extremist groups have been gaining a growing foothold in our military and law enforcement communities. This is a terrifying prospect and I fear this problem will only deepen if it is not quickly and thoroughly addressed. I suggested that, along with examining the scope of this problem, the final report should recommend training programs to help prevent radicalization through all levels of service.

The final pillar would be a consideration of the "domestic and transnational disinformation linkages and coordination." In this case, we would be able to use social media analysis to determine whether foreign actors played a role in spreading the disinformation that fueled the violence on January 6th.

Lastly, after focusing on these three investigative pillars, I believed the committee should finish by looking toward the "future of social media, disinformation operations, elections, and radicalization." This grand finale would be a vision of how our world might look if we were to take no action on the domestic and foreign disinformation that is driving extremist ideology. For this section, I knew we could lean on reporting from intelligence agencies and academic experts like the NCRI. The data was already there—and horrifying.

* * *

After six days of waiting, I got the call. It was Jamie Fleet, the staff director for House Administration, who was helping build the committee.

"Can you get to Washington tomorrow?" he asked.

He wanted me to take charge of the committee's technical program. Fleet had been on Capitol Hill for over a decade. With a broad smile, he seemed like a guy you might want to grab a beer with. The affable demeanor masked the fact that Fleet was a total pro. He had seen a lot, but nothing like January 6th. When we spoke, Fleet said this committee was the most important thing he'd ever done. I felt the same way.

As I made the three-hour drive along the Shenandoah Valley and up to Washington, I thought about the enormity of the task in front of me.

There had never been an effort like this in congressional history. The January 6th select committee dwarfed the standard staff research projects where House aides created reports by relying on input from the Congressional Research Service. We were looking at hundreds of rioters, organizers who planned months of conspiracy-packed demonstrations protesting Trump's loss, and members of Congress, lawyers, state legislators, and White House aides who officially attempted to challenge the election. The committee needed to bring in the big guns.

Onboarding was an odd experience for me. I was back in the sprawling Hill complex for the first time since my farewell address. I was still devastated by losing my seat. Returning was disorienting—and also exhilarating. It was a new role, but I was back in my element, doing intelligence and operations.

As I dove in, I started calling my former military and NSA colleagues to get a sense of what we might need. I knew we would start with CDRs, call detail records, and social media data aggregation. If there was indeed a conspiracy, it was essential to identify the data, software, hardware, and subject matter experts needed to track it. For tracking social media data, I reached out to the researchers at the Network Contagion Research Institute within Rutgers University's Eagleton Institute of Politics, who had worked with me on the QAnon report. Its team was way ahead of the curve. It used computational research and collection methods to analyze the spread of disinformation and document how online rhetoric can fuel real-world events. The NCRI lab was also deep into studies on how to predict emerging threats.

That last bit was crucial since I hoped any report from the committee would include recommendations on how to stem the rising tide of radicalization and avoid future violence. Disinformation and social media had clearly been weaponized. We could fight back with algorithmic warfare—using analysis to define our battlespace and predict what might come next. It was a battle of data versus data.

When it came to call detail records, I turned to an old air force buddy, who I will just call "Spinner," and one of my intelligence colleagues, "Crazy Ivan." Both of them specialize in sensitive work. Crazy Ivan is an NSA master instructor who also worked with me at my consulting firm. He is a brilliant technical analyst as well as an operational analyst who has the rare ability to merge those two disciplines together. In other words, he knows phones and digital communications inside and out. Ivan uses that knowledge to create plans that identify data, obtain it, and turn that data into a usable investigative product. He also has a strange, dry sense of humor that leaves people wondering if he's a little bit off, hence the nickname. Crazy Ivan and Spinner helped me find a small team that would ultimately help me decode and validate Mark Meadows's text logs.

The experts I brought together are the best in the world at some of these niche technologies, analytics, and algorithmic targeting capabilities. They knew how to find the signals in the noise and spot key touch points and centers of gravity in the massive swarms of extremist online chatter and crowds that swept over the Capitol. They lent me their invaluable expertise. It was the military and intelligence community brotherhood. I called my proposed congressional fusion center the

Aggregated Communications Community Conceptualization Engine, or AC3E for short. It was going to be our ace in the hole.

The role that Republican members of Congress played in promoting and acting on Trump's "Big Lie" and the responsibility of the Democrats for security on the Hill meant this was a congressional committee that, if it was going to be the real deal, would investigate members of Congress and possibly leadership. That's an uncomfortable thing for a committee composed largely of House members and staffers. Our committee was going to need to step up to the plate and swing the bat. There was no time to sit on pitches.

As I worked on the fusion center plan for the technical team, I also began helping the committee target key evidence. We crafted records preservation requests that went out to social media and communications companies. Since digital information is perishable, these letters were an attempt to block the tech firms from deleting records that would be important for our work. Working with experts on online extremism, we cast a wide net. Along with major phone companies and sites like Facebook and Twitter, we sought records from the deepest internet fever swamps like the chan boards, 8kun, and TheDonald.win.

Edgelords weren't the only ones I had in my crosshairs. I also wanted to subpoena House members. Frankly, it was getting harder and harder to tell the difference between these two groups.

Based on what I had seen in the Freedom Caucus—and later in Mark Meadows's texts—I was certain several members of Congress were smack in the middle of the vile conspiracy theories that fueled the violence. And anyone who followed the news knew House Republicans played a major role in the official efforts to overturn the election. One issue was that in cases involving hostile witnesses, disappearing digital records aren't the only time crunch. People with means often try to get into drawn-out fights against subpoenas. The Republican members who promoted President Trump's election lies had teams of conservative attorneys behind them who would make it easy for them to wage long legal battles with the committee. More important, they also had polls showing they were likely to take over the House in 2023. If they could stall until then, there wouldn't be any committee left to investigate them. We had every reason to rush those subpoenas.

Instead, once it got started, as far as I knew, the committee didn't even bother requesting records from a single member for over five months. And even after all that wait, the records requests were just that, requests; they were brushed aside or ignored entirely. It wasn't until May 2022 that the committee sent subpoenas that would have compelled evidence. They were sent to five members.

The lack of criminal authority wasn't the only way our power was limited. My team was granted the ability to subpoena only call detail records without location data. Why was this important? Because geolocation metadata would have provided us a better sense of the physical movements of the militants and other key players in the investigation. We could have expanded our link maps and tied people who solely communicated in person, which, in spite of all sorts of new encryption technology, remains, by far, the most secure and secretive method of them all. Some of the committee staff insisted there was a court case that blocked this approach. I thought, if necessary, we should fight that battle in front of a judge. Investigating domestic terrorism isn't a time for being shy. We needed to turn up the heat.

I started to see that I had more analytical aggression than even the Democrats on the committee. I continually called for us to push the envelope and use the toughest approach possible. This ruffled some feathers on the committee. In the first week of September, as I prepared my initial presentation of the AC3E plan, I got a call from Dave Buckley, the committee's staff director. Buckley had read some of my drafts and he cautioned me that my use of phrases like "targets" and "high-value individuals" made some of the other committee staff "uncomfortable."

It was a question of public perception or, as they say in DC, "optics." I guess they wanted me to run a kinder, gentler investigation. That wasn't in my repertoire.

A threat is a threat.

In the end we settled on referring to the subjects of the investigation as POIs, or "persons of interest." While we disagreed on the terminology, Buckley and the rest of the team seemed to be on board with my overall vision.

My fusion center plan would have cost approximately $3.2 million. I didn't think this would be an issue at all since this would be the core of our technical data operation. The 9/11 commission cost $15 million—or over $23 million in today's money. Evidence from social media and phone records was clearly going to be the key aspect of this investigation. Dropping roughly 14 percent of the budget spent on the commission that probed the last major attack on the country seemed beyond reasonable for our data team.

There was one major factor behind the seven-figure price tag. The academics I wanted to work with had massive archives of the major social media sites as well as some of the more fringe digital hideouts, chan boards, and chat apps popular on the Far Right like Parler and Gab. Having access to this treasure trove of data would mean we could see deleted posts.

Paying for the internet archive was vital to understanding our battlefield. We could have constructed a complete timeline showing how lies about the election spread and morphed into calls to storm the Capitol. It would have helped us identify key drivers behind the violence.

The archive also would have helped us get around the limitation on seeking location data. Using geolocation data embedded in sites like Twitter, we would have been able to use some of the posts to see where people were at a given moment. This would have gone a long way

toward helping us tie pseudonymous social media accounts to key players in the investigation.

That's why it cost a significant amount of money. A complete record
of so many sites is a vast amount of data. Because of this, researchers
keep it in a cold storage format that cannot be searched. Integrating that
data into a live, merged interface would have required paying to transfer it to a petabyte hot storage solution that would allow for searches
and analysis. In my mind, any meaningful data we could add to our
dashboard was worth the cost since it could have exposed additional
connections between rioters, extremists, and even officials. Instead,
those links stayed hidden.

When the day came to pitch my plan, I headed up to the Capitol
complex and found myself in a large conference room. The committee
members were arrayed in front of me. Staffers sat along the walls. As I
prepared to launch into my slides it hit me. I was a former congressman
who was basically testifying before Congress. The tables had—quite
literally—turned.

I showed the committee members the types of data we could obtain.
Then, I walked them through how that evidence would be the building
block for a "triangle algorithm" where the data would be merged to
make a three-sided portrait of key persons of interest with their physical location, digital and telephonic communications, and social media
footprint. I felt like the members got it. They asked sharp questions
about how the data would be merged and I detailed the specific software and operations that would allow us to combine different types of
evidence for our complete dashboard.

It seemed like we were good to go. When I wrapped, Cheney came
up to me in the hall and congratulated me. Kinzinger, my fellow airman, offered the typically classy flyboy response.

"Bad ass," he said.

Maryland Democrat Jamie Raskin was even more effusive. He pulled me into a bear hug.

"You're going to save America," Raskin said.

That's not quite the way it worked out.

It took only a couple of days for me to realize things had gone sideways. Shortly after I briefed the committee members, I got a call from Fleet saying some of the members were worried about issuing sole source contracts. They were also concerned about keeping costs down to avoid negative public perception. There was that dreaded word again. "Optics."

I downed a dram of my wife's best whiskey to calm me down. I just couldn't believe they were fretting about keeping up appearances during an investigation into an attack on America. In government terms, $3.2 million is nothing, a rounding error. Part of me also couldn't help but wonder if the members were afraid of getting aggressive—particularly when it came to their colleagues—for fear of potential retaliation if the polls proved correct and the Republicans retook the House during the next cycle.

I knew the Trump wing of the Republican Party was going to come after the committee no matter what we did. There was no point preemptively worrying about it and it definitely didn't make sense to limit our capabilities based on expected opposition. As I told Jamie Fleet, "We are going to be attacked anyway, so we might as well give them something that actually scares them."

Amid all this, they were still freezing me out of meetings. During one of our office days in September, I needed to talk to Tim Heaphy, the chief investigator. When I went looking for him, one of the staffers told me he was in a conference room. I walked in to find the rest of the senior staff engaged in a strategic planning session. Their eyes all went big. Heaphy seemed to be grasping for words. I shut the door before anyone spoke.

This had to be fixed or I was out. I didn't want to have my name on the investigation if it wasn't going to be serious about the data. It was time to pull rank on Buckley and Heaphy. I called Cheney and gave her the rundown.

"Enough of this," she said.

Cheney pulled together a meeting with Buckley and me. She stared from across the table.

"Congressman Riggleman has access to everything," Cheney declared.

* * *

When I was hired, they thought they were getting a former congressman and whiskey distiller. That's just my cover. Since coming to Washington I have been better known for those things than my military work. In reality, I am a straight-up intelligence professional. None of my former colleagues really knew about my work at the NSA and behind the door on the fifth floor of the Pentagon.

In the end, I didn't get my fusion center funded as I wanted, but I was now firmly in charge of the technical team. Our budget was $600,000, less than 20 percent of what I had proposed. This meant we would have to be largely focused on open-source intelligence and chasing phone records. They killed the dashboard and didn't pay for the full social media archive. Not having that window into dark corners of the web meant key subjects who were linked to the violence almost certainly flew under our radar.

The intelligence officer in me couldn't help but get hung up on what we missed, but I was also damn proud of the things we did find. My call detail records and open-source intelligence teams highlighted how the groups involved in the plot to overturn the election communicated and moved on the Capitol.

We could validate what had just been guesses. Our analysis identified targets—or, excuse me, *persons of interest*—that the committee had no idea about. We identified and validated addresses for subpoenas and hidden phone numbers. We built dossiers for the investigative team with robust profiles of these individuals.

Most important, we definitively showed that the attack on the Capitol had clear command and control elements. That means mission planning, intent. It may have been decentralized, with separate leaders and distinct groups, but they worked toward a common goal: securing Trump a second term by any means necessary.

The Meadows text logs were the first hint of command and control. They showed conspiracy-addled, far-right activists and officials from all levels of the government working in concert to oppose a free and fair election. It was a written record of a democracy in peril. Our call detail records filled in the gaps from there.

The maps my team made showed robust linkages among the militant groups who were the driving force in the mob that stormed the Capitol. They were coordinating in the weeks, days, and hours ahead of the attack. The data also highlighted liaisons between the more official side of the plot and the armed extremists, including calls that seemed to go from the West Wing to rioters on January 6th.

There was a plan. There was a vision. And the lines all pointed straight up to President Trump.

CHAPTER 6

GREENSBURG, PA

Some of the biggest secrets of January 6th were uncovered on a quiet street in the Pittsburgh suburbs.

Once the competitive bidding process failed, I got a call from Dave Buckley, the select committee's staff director. Although I wasn't getting my AC3E fusion center, Dave asked me if I could build a technical plan and sole-source contract justification for what I thought was the single most important part of the investigation—a telephony analysis team that could scrutinize call detail records.

As I put together various proposals for the committee, it became even clearer to me that tracking phones would be vital to understanding what happened at the Capitol. The apparent plot was a sprawling universe, from Mark Meadows and the members of Congress who objected to the electoral certification right on down to the people who broke into the building. In my view, perhaps the central question of the committee investigation was whether these groups operated separately or in a coordinated manner. We needed to find command and control, if indeed there was any. Getting the phone records would show the major nodes and hubs. Signals—and a clearer picture of the network—could emerge from the noise.

PATCtech, the firm I chose for the telephony analysis contract in support of the select committee, ran its work for the committee out of a small space in Greensburg, Pennsylvania. Its office, which shared a squat commercial building with an AFLAC agent, an HR consultant, and a Missouri investment bank, would become crammed with computers, data processors with whirring fans, and boxes overflowing with evidence, a full-time forensics shop.

The Greensburg team started work in November 2021. It was responsible for helping the committee to obtain phone records, identify phone numbers, and turn CDRs into detailed link maps. These are the guys who cracked Mark Meadows's text logs. In a matter of months, they strung together well over eighteen million lines of data to sketch a portrait of the January 6th plot. Their work exposed an interconnected network of far-right activists that had multiple links to the former president's staff and inner circle.

As our work began, the major questions involved the militant groups who were part of the attack. The Proud Boys and Oath Keepers were all over footage of the crowds storming the building. How close were they to the political side of the push to overturn the election? Were they connected to the White House? If there weren't direct links, were there indirect ones and could we identify crucial go-betweens?

We needed to understand the whole network. Phone data was something we could get our hands on and it would help us see how the various elements of the scheme were connected. Data was the key.

Research and referrals from telephony professionals made clear that the team at PATCtech was the right one for the job. I found the company through my old air force and NSA colleagues. Glenn Bard, PATCtech's chief technology officer, was the man who had called to tell me he had finalized our analysis of the White House's call to a rioter during the attack. That was one of many jaw-dropping conversations we had as I worked with him for the committee.

Glenn had given lectures on computer forensics and telephony analysis to multiple state and federal agencies and law enforcement groups, and even created instructional courses for some of them. That's how good he was. He had a real rep. The DOJ had worked with him to set up forensics labs for American allies abroad. We needed to build a data analysis unit to assist with the massive committee investigation in a matter of weeks. They would need to build the plane while flying it. Glenn knew how to work with the wind in his hair.

Bringing in Glenn's firm also meant we were waging military warfare in the information battlespace. I liked the sound of that.

One of the most troubling aspects of the Capitol attack was that at least one hundred of the rioters who stormed into the building that day had military experience. That's per data from the George Washington University Program on Extremism. Several of the individuals who allegedly led them into battle also had backgrounds in the armed forces, including former lieutenant general Michael Flynn and Phil Waldron, a retired colonel who claims to have worked with him. Those two were supposedly instrumental in preparing a plan for Trump to declare martial law and seize voting machines.

The insurrectionists could build an army of warriors forged in the digital forum. I could put together a real military intelligence operation. If these former military men were going to forget their oaths, to hell with them. I was ready to roll and we had soldiers on our side too.

PATCtech is a four-man company, but the two guys who did the bulk of the work for my data analysis team, Glenn Bard and Mark Tomallo, were both former army pros. And they knew more about tracking phones and analyzing link maps than just about anyone I have ever come across.

Glenn, who ran the PATCtech show, was one of those eighteen-year-old kids who graduated high school in June and shipped off to basic training by that September. He did all sorts of intense training in Germany's Black Forest, fought in Desert Storm, and went on to become a Pennsylvania state trooper. Glenn would probably never forgive me if I didn't point out that Pennsylvania has what he calls "real" state troopers who do criminal law enforcement as well as traffic. He wasn't just highway patrol. Glenn's expertise in computer forensics and investigative work was unique. After over a decade as a trooper, he transitioned to the private sector and delivered technical and investigative support to the navy, Department of Justice, and district attorneys around the country, who tapped him for homicides and other criminal cases.

Mark has been with Glenn for seven years. Several years after his own army service, he started working at the local courthouse in Pennsylvania's Westmoreland County. The building is more than 110 years old, four stories, domed, and done in granite. Mark fully modernized its communications. He wired that place from bottom up. Mark wasn't just an analyst. He ran copper and terminated connections, networked complex communications suites, and programmed digital call managers. He also has practical experience running a large-scale phone system and knows everything there is to know about switchboards, Wi-Fi calls, spoofing, and cell data. That all made him a great investigator and an invaluable asset as we searched the White House phone system.

Going into the committee investigation, I was convinced call records would be the single most important part of our work. Glenn and Mark proved me right on that.

Along with putting together the committee's telephony analysis squad, I also created a technical document and contract language for creating an open-source intelligence, or OSINT, team. This was a challenge. With the fusion center off the table, we'd have to do the difficult work of building out capability piecemeal. The committee also wanted me to do it all on a budget. I felt we absolutely had to have an OSINT team. It would be vital for mining hidden corners of the internet.

Open-source intelligence means the aggregation and analysis of publicly available information. Our OSINT team would need to report on what subjects of the investigation said, what they planned, and who they linked with online. The discipline can also be called web intelligence or WEBINT.

There are three distinct layers to the internet: the open, deep, and dark web. Open web is where most people typically spend their time. It's everything you can navigate with a search engine. Deep web is defined as what doesn't show up in standard search engines. It includes some types of social media, chan forums, and chat rooms. There are specific techniques to go deep in web searches. The final and most challenging level, dark web, is actually walled off from the rest of the internet. The most famous example is the marketplace Silk Road, which was filled with all kinds of drugs and guns until the FBI shut it down in 2013.

Dark web is generally where you go if you are interested in breaking the law or are otherwise trying to stay away from prying eyes. To navigate it, you need a Tor browser or other special software. A savvy OSINT crew would know how to get there and would be able to comb through all three layers of the internet to profile the social media activity of our persons of interest.

Because many of the planners and advertisers for January 6th deleted their pages and posts, the OSINT team would need expertise in digging out those deleted materials from archives, locating hard-to-find documents, and, at times, identifying images using facial recognition. Timelines showing extremist rhetoric were another must. We wanted to track how the election conspiracies coalesced into official opposition, in the form of lawsuits and wrangling by legislators, along with calls to protest.

I turned to A1C Partners for our OSINT analysis. They're dedicated to exactly this kind of work. They regularly consult for law enforcement and intelligence agencies. Unlike my telephone data team at PATCtech, they are cagey about their methods and staffing. I won't be naming any of them individually here. Still, they know I am grateful for their contributions.

One very important thing we discovered through open-source intelligence was Trump's own apparent role in calling people down upon the Capitol on January 6th. It started well before he told the crowds on the Ellipse that day to "fight like hell" and march down Pennsylvania Avenue.

On December 19, 2020, nearly a month and a half after Joe Biden was declared the winner of the election, Trump fired off a tweet at just before two in the morning. The OSINT team would identify this message from Trump as a key turning point in paving the way for January 6th's violence.

Trump, who had just over one month left in office at the time, began the tweet by promoting a thirty-six-page report that Peter Navarro, a White House trade adviser, had compiled claiming there were "six dimensions of alleged election irregularities across six key battleground states." The whole thing wasn't worth the paper and pixels it was printed on.

In his half-baked "assessment," Navarro—who went on to face federal charges from the DOJ for refusing to testify before the select committee, and who pleaded not guilty to those charges, which are pending as of this writing—leaned hard into the fact that Trump was leading on election night in certain swing states. Navarro used this to cast doubt on the vote overall and declare it "may well have been stolen from President Donald J. Trump." But experts knew that Trump was likely to have an advantage in those first hours of the count that could disappear later on. There was even a name for the phenomenon, the "red mirage," and the explanation was simple: Democrats tend to use mail-in ballots more often than Republicans. Those take longer to count than in-person votes. And some states, such as Pennsylvania, forbid the pre-processing of mail-in ballot envelopes before Election Day, slowing down their inclusion in vote tallies even more.

The "red mirage" existed prior to 2020, but it was exacerbated because Trump, in a combination of COVID denialism and election fraud conspiracy theorizing, consistently discouraged his supporters from voting via the post office. So, as the mailed votes rolled in, Trump's election-night edge eroded.

Of course, Navarro and Trump almost certainly knew all this. Navarro's report seemed to be a wildly inaccurate attempt to spread false narratives and rile up the base. Philip Bump, a national correspondent for the *Washington Post* whose writing was actually cited in Navarro's endnotes, published an article that surmised it "might be the most embarrassing document created by a White House staffer."

Bump rightly called the Navarro report "a garbage dump." The Trump adviser exaggerated and mischaracterized information from legitimate sources, but he also heavily relied on material from the far-right ecosystem. His document was dredged up from the pro-Trump fever swamps.

The citations read like the MAGA conspiracy All-Star team. Navarro drew from Steve Bannon's podcast, YouTube videos of Rudy Giuliani, and the *Epoch Times*, a far-right, QAnon-promoting newspaper produced by China's Falun Gong religious sect. (In the *Washington Post*, an *Epoch Times* spokesperson denied any editorial support for QAnon.) It wasn't just the Christians who were drawn to the altar of 8chan. He quoted analysis from a consultant in Texas who had mistaken data from Minnesota as that from Michigan.

Navarro would later write in his 2021 memoir that he and Bannon had an elaborate plan to derail the election result. They felt members of Congress who objected to the electoral certification could generate at least twenty-four hours of heated attention during the proceedings on January 6th. Navarro believed that this would have convinced Vice President Mike Pence to delay the certification. He wasn't entirely clear what would come next in this scenario, but he claimed in his memoir it would have been nonviolent. Navarro later insisted he was bitter toward both Pence and the rioters for derailing this plan. He and Bannon had named it the "Green Bay Sweep" after a famous play from the legendary Packers football coach Vince Lombardi. It was all a bit incoherent, but the bottom line was that Navarro was quite active in the various plans to challenge the election.

The Navarro report hinted at how far-right media could often function as an echo chamber. It cited the conservative *Washington Examiner* newspaper at multiple points. When Navarro released it, the *Examiner* did an uncritical write-up hyping the report. Trump then included a link to that *Examiner* article in his December 19 tweet. One hand washing the other again and again. Just a cycling cascade of multilayered bullshit.

After blasting the Navarro document to his approximately 88.6 million followers and insisting it showed that it was "Statistically impossible to have lost the 2020 Election," Trump made a fateful pronouncement:

"Big protest in D.C. on January 6th. Be there, will be wild!"

His words lit up the OSINT team's charts. They saw a dramatic spike in anger related to the election as well as increased specific planning from militia groups.

Trump's people heard his message loud and clear. The president had issued a call to arms.

* * *

The select committee had six teams working separately. They were all code-named with different colors: Red, Gold, Green, Purple, Orange, and Blue. My operations were distinct from that structure. Part of our work involved providing technical and investigative support for the six other teams.

Red focused on the rioters and what we termed "day-of command

and control," in other words, coordination among people who engaged in violence at the Capitol on January 6th. This included the activists and conspiracists who planned the Stop the Steal and "Save America" protests that drew people to DC that day. The militant groups that took part in the attack, namely the Proud Boys, Oath Keepers, and 1st Amendment Praetorian, were also part of this portfolio. The committee was looking at the storming of the building as a military operation.

The Red Team handed my telephone team their heaviest workload. We matched names to numbers—and vice versa. We also helped them track the connections among the various violent extremist groups. We found plenty. Both my telephony and OSINT analysts prepared files on people the committee investigators were set to interview. We brainstormed to help them prepare sharp questions and catch potential lies during depositions.

Gold Team zeroed in on Trump and his inner circle. This included his family, staff, and informal advisers like Bannon, Rudy Giuliani, and General Flynn. Most folks know those names. They were some of the more hard-core voices in Trump's ear throughout his presidency. But during the election result challenge, Trump also connected with a new wave of conspiracists including the lawyer Sidney Powell and Patrick Byrne, the multimillionaire former CEO of internet retailer Overstock.com.

My OSINT team drafted deep-dive dossiers on all these major players. In particular, Byrne struck me as an underrated part of the puzzle. I came to view his role as crucial. His DeepCapture.com website published several documents related to the legal arguments people like Powell and Phil Waldron were making and hinted at their terrifying vision for how to achieve victory. We will be digging into their "war document" in later chapters of this book.

The Gold Team also benefited from the CDRs. By combing through those records, we documented every call we could that came through the White House from, approximately, the start of November 2020 through the end of the following January. Our work showed who was in contact with West Wing staff—and possibly Trump himself.

Green Team followed the money. They tracked the financing of the so-called Stop the Steal movement. This was another area where the CDRs helped prepare investigators for certain interviews. Many folks sitting for a deposition seemed to come down with severe, sudden memory issues when confronted with questions about the finances for campaigns and rallies. Knowing that we could see who they were in touch with was often a quick cure. Green Team also relied on my knowledge of the fundraising process. During my first meeting with them, I busted out a white board to chart the digital fundraising ecosystem to show how algorithms incentivized the most aggressive Stop the Steal messaging. My OSINT consultants also worked with the Green Team to tie some far-right figures to their Bitcoin wallets.

Cryptocurrencies have a reputation for total privacy, but that's not entirely accurate. Each individual transaction is generally logged in the blockchain, where it can be publicly viewed. Crypto can be tracked, it's just more difficult than going after more typical currencies.

From what I saw during the committee investigation, crypto wasn't a major part of the fundraising for the Stop the Steal movement. Fiat currency is still king on the Far Right. Still, it is all too clear that political hustlers and partisan profiteers saw opportunity in the crypto space.

In late 2021, two former Trump White House advisers, Steve Bannon and Boris Epshteyn, announced they had taken "strategic ownership positions" in a new crypto coin, FJB, short for "Fuck Joe Biden." Marketing materials touted the enterprise as "the coin that fights for America." The pair, who were both active in the efforts to challenge the election, talked up their new currency on Bannon's podcast.

Bannon described it as an "alternative currency" that was safe from "government" that's "forcing" the "continual devaluation of the dollar." His pitch was rooted in extreme conspiracy rhetoric. It cast the crypto as both a middle finger to Biden and a means to ensure survival against the sinister, global Left. Real doomsday stuff.

"We are now saying, 'Screw Joe Biden.' We've got a coin . . . the imprint is *that*. O.K.? It shows you our total and complete independence . . . our non-reliance," Bannon said. "You're going to very quickly have non-reliance on their financial systems, so no longer can they bother you. They're not going to be able to disappear you like the Chinese Communist Party, like the Bolsheviks, like the Nazis, like anybody—like any of these radicals that have ever taken control of these apparatuses."

Bannon did nothing to explain exactly how a cryptocurrency could save his listeners from summary executions by a repressive foreign regime. Behind the long-haired, wild-eyed Bannon, a sign was visible in the studio where he tapes his "War Room" broadcasts. It read, "There are NO conspiracies, but there are NO coincidences." The quote was from Bannon himself.

Crypto experts warned that Bannon and Epshteyn's FJB coin contained a locking system built into the code that could prevent users from selling it in the event the price dropped. There were multiple complaints from people who said they were prevented from cashing out. FJB also had fees that went to the currency's founders built into every transaction. And the project didn't seem to lead to Bannon's promised birth of a new financial system. Instead, according to CoinMarketCap—a crypto industry price tracker—after reaching a high price of about four and a half tenths of a penny as Bannon and Epshteyn promoted it in December 2021, one FJB plummeted to, as of this writing, three hundredths of a penny. Bannon and Epshteyn have declined to comment on whether they themselves sold off any coins as the value crashed.

Another cryptocurrency marketed to Trump supporters and created by a used car salesman, MAGACOIN, was also a one-way trip to nowhere. According to the CoinMarketCap data, one MAGACOIN went from being worth about two cents in November 2021 to, as of this writing, three hundredths of a penny. Crypto dust. That coin also took fees from each transaction. On the graph, both cryptos looked like straight lines up that immediately rocketed down. A familiar pattern, pump and dump.

These were some of the more blatant moments where it was clear how Trump's Big Lie was also the Big Grift. A lot of separate branding exercises spun off from the conspiracy theory itself. Trump's main message was essentially tested on multiple platforms and his base had already been socialized through QAnon, COVID denialism, and other online paranoia. They were easily taken in by the idea of Stop the Steal. It also had the benefit of being what they wanted to hear. Trump supporters worshiped him and they were eager to dispute his loss.

Trump backers found a million ways to make a cut from the appeal of election denialism. When the committee looked at some of the people who put themselves forward as alternate electors, several had links to online donation pages and legal funds. So many of the Stop the Steal groups were soliciting contributions. All of this was framed as a movement and likely drew sincere small-dollar donors, but the distribution of that money was all happening in the shadows. For instance, Bannon and Epshteyn's coin supposedly raised money for veterans' charities. The pair never actually said when and how those donations were made.

The select committee's Green Team showed that Trump's family and inner circle personally profited from the events of January 6th. This included Kimberly Guilfoyle, a former Fox News personality who was dating Trump's son Don Jr. Evidence uncovered by the committee showed Guilfoyle was paid $60,000 to introduce Don Jr. at that day's rally on the White House Ellipse. That's the one where Trump told the crowd to "fight like hell" and march to the Capitol. Guilfoyle urged the crowd to "hold the line."

"Look at all of us out here, God-loving, freedom-loving, liberty-loving patriots that will not let them steal this election!" she shouted.

Her remarks lasted almost exactly three minutes. That means her speech cost about $20,000 a minute. Guilfoyle also earned $180,000 from the Trump campaign in 2020, according to the *HuffPost*. That report said Lara Trump, the wife of the former president's second-oldest son, Eric, drew similar payments from the campaign. There were piles of cash associated with the MAGA movement and some of it seemed to go right to Trump's own family.

The Purple Team studied the radicalization pipeline. We didn't only want to know what people did when they charged at the Capitol on January 6th. We wanted to know how they got there and who sent them. Purple Team researched the activity of extremist groups and MAGA influencers in the months leading up to the attack. My phone records team worked with Purple extensively to help them request and identify records.

Orange Team was tasked with examining the role foreign interference played in the Capitol attack. Some of America's rivals, namely Russia and Iran, definitely contributed to fueling disinformation in the Stop the Steal space. We saw possible bot networks and coordinated actions with Twitter accounts that formed en masse on the same day. Personalities associated with English-language, Russian-state media like RT and Sputnik also pushed conspiratorial themes and hashtags. Still, the loudest and most violent stuff was coming from within our own borders. This was America's problem.

The last team, Blue, had an especially delicate challenge. They were focused on the apparent failure to adequately protect the Capitol. They were, in part, investigating House Administration, which really meant Pelosi and two of the committee's own members, Jamie Raskin and Zoe Lofgren.

Blue team was a talented group, but the sensitivity of their investigation and the multiple moving parts—House leadership, the National Guard, DC and Capitol police, and the Pentagon—created a politically explosive finger-pointing extravaganza. The end result was that the Blue Team became a bit of a backwater. Several witnesses they tried to interview remained elusive and the committee gave Blue no means to compel testimony. Later on, I would find myself smack in the middle of this mess.

Then, there were my CDR guys Glenn and Mark. Our telephone records team brought in some of the most hotly debated findings of the investigation. They proved links among Trump, members of Congress, and the violent far-right fringe. Those connections included the call from the White House to the rioter on January 6th. They found Trump's cell phone, which was operated in an extremely unusual manner. The findings never ceased to amaze us.

None of it was easy.

* * *

We called the main link map "The Monster."

The targets of our investigation were divided up into five major categories: domestic violent extremists, which included militant groups like Proud Boys, Oath Keepers, and 1st Amendment Praetorian; rally organizers; officials, which included members of Congress and local politicians; Trump associates, which included top advisers and staff; and the president's family. We also tracked a sixth group of unaffiliated individuals, who were mainly people we identified because they faced federal charges for breaking into the Capitol.

The telephony team's maps were made up of link lines. Each line represented an incoming or outgoing communication from a call detail record. If you zoomed in, you could see each line crisscrossing the white screen. The numbers were shown at the end of the line along with a small phone handset icon. Zooming out, the "Monster" looked like a lopsided hexagon with six major connected hubs representing each of our five categories and the unaffiliated rioters. It had a strong skeleton of link lines woven between each node.

They were all connected. Everyone was linked.

Loading up "The Monster" took hours, even with our military-grade computers. The map was based on a massive amount of data. It was a visual representation of a searchable database based on all of the call detail records compiled by the committee.

Putting it together required using a few different types of computer software. In some cases, they had to be repurposed to work together. The data was also in different formats. Each telecommunications company had its own version of the same product. They had slightly different fields. Some were in different time zones.

Glenn and Mark had to come up with procedures that combined all of these records across formats into a single system where they could be compared and analyzed. The software suite we used needed to be reworked so that it could look across the entire network of linked call records all at once. We had multiple technical meetings with IBM as they developed software solutions in real time. We also set up semiautomated systems for investigators to request new call detail records to add to our files. When it came in, the information needed to be entered and checked by hand—and we're talking about millions of lines of call data. The data sets for our link maps were so massive that the team would sometimes leave the computers overnight to load them up. It was an incredibly intricate, intense, and time-consuming process. Given the sensitivity of the evidence, PATCtech's lab was locked down. Everything was on site and encrypted. No data ever left the building.

Along with the issues inherent in doing in-depth analysis on such a large data set, we were dealing with some unique frustrations that came along with operating in a public, political space. Two incidents that occurred in mid-December 2021 showed how the far-right conspiracists behind Stop the Steal were ready to paint any minor mistake by the committee as proof of a grand deep state plot.

The Meadows text log, which we helped the committee acquire and decipher, was obviously a unique window into what happened inside the West Wing on January 6th. Because of that, it was heavily cited during the investigation. That was all well and good. If anything, it was validation of our hard work. However, when the texts were first unveiled, two members of the committee, Adam Schiff and Jamie Raskin, fumbled the ball a little bit.

It was December 14, 2021, and the committee was voting on whether to refer Meadows for criminal contempt charges for defying our subpoena. As they made the case that the former White House chief of staff was up to his elbows in the effort to challenge the election, both Schiff and Raskin read provocative texts from Meadows's log.

Schiff described one of the messages he highlighted as coming from an anonymous "lawmaker." He said he was declining to name them due to the ongoing investigation. I was pretty sure it was due to some sense of loyalty or propriety. You'll see what the Republicans did with that. They ate Schiff alive.

The text, as Schiff presented it, said, "On January 6, 2021, Vice President Mike Pence, as President of the Senate, should call out all electoral votes that he believes are unconstitutional as no electoral votes at all."

Jim Jordan immediately owned up to being the text's author. However, he pointed out that Schiff had truncated the message. In reality, the full text read:

> "On January 6, 2021, Vice President Mike Pence, as President of the Senate, should call out all electoral votes that he believes are unconstitutional as no electoral votes at all—in accordance with guidance from founding father Alexander Hamilton and judicial precedence. 'No legislative act,' wrote Alexander Hamilton in Federalist No. 78, 'contrary to the Constitution, can be valid.' The court in Hubbard v. Lowe reinforced this truth: 'That an unconstitutional statute is not a law at all is a proposition no longer open to discussion.' 226 F. 135,

137 (SDNY 1915), appeal dismissed, 242 U.S. 654 (1916). Following this rationale, an unconstitutionally appointed elector, like an
unconstitutionally enacted statute, is no elector at all."

That was a lot to read, right? A staffer had almost certainly tried to
summarize the message rather than going all in on the legal mumbo
jumbo.

The bottom line was that context did nothing to make the message
any better. It was a rambling supposed legal argument for throwing out
the vote. If anything, the text is far worse than Schiff made it out to be.

According to his office, Jordan forwarded Meadows a text he'd
received from a navy veteran and former Department of Defense inspector general named Joseph Schmitz. The congressman was passing on
Schmitz's brief summary of a four-page screed he'd written sketching
out a legal argument that Pence had the power to overturn the election.
Schmitz's case seemed unhinged. It cited the Navarro report directly.
Reading more of the message didn't make it more coherent. Forwarding
it also wasn't much different than writing it himself. This was the message Jordan wanted to pass along.

Despite all that, the committee had made a mistake. We should have
cited the text as an excerpt and noted it was a forward. Still, it was hard
to see how anything Schiff did justified the coverage it received in the
pro-Trump media, like a piece on the far-right site the Federalist that
called it evidence the committee was presenting "doctored" texts.

Partisans were looking for any small reason to discredit our work.
The committee needed to bring its A-game.

Raskin also had a slipup. At that same December 2021 hearing about
Meadows, Raskin read a text from the afternoon of November 4, one
day after the election. This was just as it was becoming clear the numbers were not breaking Trump's way. It outlined what the writer clumsily
called "an AGRESSIVE STRATEGY." That was the first of many typos.

"Why cant the states of GA NC PENN and other R controlled state houses declare this is BS (where conflicts and election not called that night) and just send their own electors to vote and have it go to the SCOTUS," the text said.

It was the first message in Meadows's logs that referenced some version of the alternate electors strategy, a clear call to ignore the will of the voters. Raskin was right that the text showed the kind of extreme counsel Meadows was keeping. However, he said it came from a Republican lawmaker. In fact, it had been sent by a former member of Trump's cabinet. We found multiple registrations tying it to Trump's first secretary of energy, Rick Perry. Still influential in the party and with Trump after resigning from Energy in December 2019, Perry was nearly as important as any lawmaker—but he wasn't one.

Raskin had to correct the record, which then provided conservative media a chance to pounce on his mistake. It was a painful unforced error.

The saga with Meadows's subpoena and the contempt charge shows another aggravating part of the committee investigation. We were dealing with political concerns. With Republicans likely to take over the House in 2023, we were also dealing with a political timeline. And, of course, we were dealing with the question of political violence.

There were those who continued to say they didn't want our committee's work or the Justice Department's criminal investigation to be political. That was impossible. Yet pretending to political neutrality still seemed like a paramount concern for some of my colleagues. I think those political fears stopped us from being as aggressive as we could have been. Could we have started earlier? What if we had moved harder and faster?

I worried we weren't being aggressive enough. As the senior technical advisor, I beat myself up. Had I not done enough to convey urgency to the team? Working on the investigation meant constantly feeling tortured with questions of whether we pressed enough or had missed something because we had waited too long.

At that hearing where Raskin mischaracterized Perry's text, the members voted unanimously to refer Mark Meadows for contempt charges. And yet, in early June 2022, the Justice Department prosecutors declined to prosecute Meadows for contempt. The DOJ did secure grand jury indictments against Bannon and Navarro for contempt of Congress, but it also opted not to seek an indictment of Dan Scavino, former president Trump's social media guru.

It was hard not to think the ex–White House staff was getting a pass. On one level, that made sense, since they had more plausible grounds to declare executive privilege. But there are limits to that. How exactly can the three main branches of our government serve as checks and balances to each other if one can't investigate another at all? Watching Meadows get away with defying the committee, it struck me that there seemed to be a different set of rules for the most well-connected people.

Glenn and Mark were both pretty jaded. They kept plugging away, compiling and analyzing the data, but sometimes they would question the point of the exercise. These guys have military and law enforcement backgrounds. Why were we doing an investigation if there weren't going to be any real consequences?

That's something I wonder about a lot. At the same time, I have to think it matters to share the story of what happened that day—and who was behind it. If that's the only thing any of us did, it was still worth doing.

The work of our telephony analysis team—and the committee as a whole—was important because it added to the historical record. It provided some measure of public accountability and showed us the warning signs of the new digital domestic terrorism. Glenn and Mark's work also established processes necessary for confronting the threat of political violence on a large scale. The two of them developed an evolved telephony discipline. They invented a workflow for dealing with a massive plot with militant and political components. Part of my goal in presenting our story is to help other analysts who might have to tackle something similar in the future. For all of our sakes, I hope that doesn't happen any time soon.

Many of us would like to forget January 6th. The visuals of battered law enforcement heroes, terrified lawmakers, and riotous crowds trampling our most precious symbols are painful to see. But, like it or not, this is part of our history. Smart advice can become a cliché for a reason. It's true what they say: those who do not learn from history are doomed to repeat it.

* * *

When we examined the link maps, it was easy to see the centers of gravity. They showed up as dark spots where many different link lines came together. When you searched for an individual number, all link lines associated with that number would light up in blue.

At one point, we found a cell phone that we tied to Trump himself. It appeared on the map as a kind of oval island connected to the other Trump associates by a thin bridge of a few link lines.

Over six thousand calls and messages went to that cell phone during the roughly three months between the election and the end of his term. All of it was incoming, but the phone was never turned on. Everything was forwarded to a voice-mail box, which was filled to the brim. Based on the records we had, it was unclear whether anyone ever listened to the messages or made room for new ones. That wasn't the only phone we found that seemed to belong to Trump, but I won't go into detail on the others due to the ongoing investigations.

There were people on the maps of Trump's family and their associates who seemed to regularly retire numbers. We would see lines that popped up for a few days and couldn't be tied to an individual registration. We thought they looked like burner phones or VOIP numbers generated through an app. One was active for about a week and only showed up in communication with the Trump family. It was hard to say—or to know—what that meant. Someone in the president's inner-most circle had very good OPSEC.

Another odd find came when the data team found a batch of numbers that, through the other investigators' work, we believed were associated with the White House. Those lines started with digits that didn't match any known area code or exchange.

These ghost numbers were just one of the many examples of evidence that was coming in during the spring of 2022. We kept finding new evidence for the call records team to analyze. It all added to my feeling that we should have gotten started a lot earlier. I also couldn't help but wonder how much we were going to leave on the table when the committee concluded its hearings.

Throughout our work there were four people who were extensively connected to all six clusters on "The Monster." They were in contact with militias and the highest levels of Trump's inner circle. We saw them as the key touch points: Bianca Gracia, Alex Jones, Kristin Davis, and Roger Stone.

Stone, long one of Trump's closest advisers, had a hidden phone number and a security detail comprised of extremist militia members. Glenn saw a lot of wild stuff during his time on this team, but when he found Stone on the link map, he was as excited as I ever heard him. When Glenn called to tell me about what he saw, he let me know right away that it was big.

"Denver," he said. "I found a nuclear bomb."

CHAPTER 7

DOMESTIC ENEMIES

The calls came from inside the White House.

In my mind, the evidence we found of direct communication links between militants and high-level Trump associates represented the most important findings we turned over to the committee. I was surprised when this information was not included in the first months of public hearings. This is something the American people need to see and this chapter is the story of how we found it.

The interactions between the West Wing and militant extremists went beyond the phone call to the rioter that took place during the attack. There were also texts from a leader of the Oath Keepers militia. The records the committee found are incomplete and don't tell us exactly what was said. Still, those simple lines of communication cannot be denied. They tied the executive side of the election challenge to the digital shock troops on the ground. There's no denying it. The political challenge to the election was, at least on some level, linked to a military operation.

When I enlisted in the air force, I swore to protect this country "against all enemies, foreign and domestic." That oath also included a vow to "obey the orders of the President of the United States." It's a promise that was one of the proudest moments of my life. When they are sworn in, presidents make a similar oath to "support and defend the Constitution of the United States against all enemies, foreign and domestic." Yet what I found in our CDR link maps showed that Trump, who was the commander in chief, was in league with our domestic enemies. It made me sick and, frankly, pissed me off.

That's a breakdown in the core order that underlies our national security and a deep breach of the fundamental promise Trump made to the nation. Whenever I thought too much about it, I felt my fists tighten.

And a handful of phone calls wasn't the only indication that militants had high-level connections in Trump's Washington. Other extremists—including the chairman of the Proud Boys gang—spoke with high-level Trump associates. Alex Jones, one of the most prominent and influential conspiracy propagandists, had extensive links to violent far-right groups. And Roger Stone, long known as one of Trump's closest political advisers, was directly tied to the militant network in our link maps. These two were apparently key hubs.

Stone and Jones are also a vivid example of how dark conspiracy politics was at the heart of Trump's rise. The rot went deep. That story stretches back for decades.

* * *

Roger Stone was one of over twenty high-priority targets who fought our requests for call detail records in court. Once we found him on the telephone data link maps, it was clear why he wanted to keep us out.

Going into the investigation, it was an easy guess that, if anything shady went on in the Trump White House, Stone would be right in the thick of it. Throughout a nearly fifty-year career, Stone has relished his reputation as a Republican dirty tricks man and generally slimy political operative. He cut his teeth working for Richard Nixon in the seventies. While he has always insisted he never had anything to do with the Watergate break-in that led to Nixon's resignation from the White House, he admittedly helped spy on rival campaigns, generated fake scandals, and once boasted he practiced the "black arts" for the disgraced president. After Nixon, he went on to work for Ronald Reagan. He teamed up with the infamous lawyer Roy Cohn, and with Cohn took his dirty pool to the next level. Years later, after the statute of limitations had conveniently expired, Stone claimed that Cohn introduced him to mobsters and directed him to make payoffs that could have helped Reagan win the 1980 election.

Stone next worked his dark magic on K Street, Washington's lobbying corridor. Along with Paul Manafort, another future Trump adviser, Stone founded a firm that earned a reputation for taking on the most absolutely unsavory business. The pair were early innovators when it came to circumventing rules that governed campaign contributions. They pioneered the modern influence game, helping politicians from both parties win and then lobbying them once they got in office. Their client list at times included a front group for Philippine strongman Ferdinand Marcos and Congolese dictator Mobutu Sese Seko. Stone's roster also included more conventional political figures like President George H.W. Bush, Bob Dole, and a Manhattan real estate developer, Donald Trump.

After their lobbying firm was sold, Stone focused on politics. As presidential elections increasingly came down to a few key swing states and their votes in the electoral college, Stone concentrated his efforts on disputing close races—by any means necessary.

In 2000, when the race between Democrat Al Gore and Republican George W. Bush was decided by a few hundred paper ballots in Florida, Stone was on the scene for the infamous "Brooks Brothers Riot" where Republican staffers and lawyers swarmed a government office in Miami. There, he learned that brute force could overtake an election.

That same year, Stone consulted for Trump as he considered mounting a presidential bid. For the next decade and a half, Stone advised the future president as he flirted with running for office. Conspiracies became their bread and butter. Stone and his longtime client began building a base in the far-right fever swamps.

The MAGA conspiracy movement was the culmination of Stone's years spent in an unprincipled quest for money and power above all else. Both Stone and Manafort ended up getting pardons from Trump in late December 2020, less than a month before he left office. Manafort was indicted, tried, and a jury convicted him on bank and tax fraud charges, and he pleaded guilty to other offenses, including conspiracy and witness tampering. Stone was indicted, tried, and a jury convicted him for lying to Congress about his interactions with Wikileaks as it published emails that were hacked from a top adviser to Trump's Democratic opponent Hillary Clinton and the Democratic National Committee. The charges against Stone came from the special counsel's investigation into Russian interference in the 2016 election, which included Kremlin-affiliated hackers obtaining the Democrats' emails. The special counsel also indicted Stone for, and a jury convicted him of, trying to "obstruct" that congressional investigation by, among other things, directing another witness to mimic the fictional character Frank Pentangeli's false testimony before a congressional committee in *The Godfather Part II* and threatening that witness's dog. In hindsight, it was foreshadowing for how he tried to stonewall the January 6th select committee. You don't survive a lifetime as a high-level dirty trickster without being slippery.

It was Stone who set Trump up with the far-right radio host Alex Jones, who would go on to be a key figure in the election denial movement leading up to the January 6th protests that turned violent. When Trump launched his first officially registered presidential bid in 2015, Stone arranged for an interview on *Infowars*, Jones's talk radio and online broadcast.

At the time of his December 2015 interview, Jones had spent well over a decade featuring militant far-right leaders and warning his followers about the "New World Order" of "demonic high-tech tyranny" that was responsible for all manner of evil, including harvesting babies' organs, manipulating the weather, and staging grand "false flag" attacks to manipulate the economy and keep the populace docile.

Jones's show was a breeding ground for all of the base ingredients that became the QAnon stew once Trump took office. This was not a remotely normal venue for a front-running presidential candidate. Stone was connecting Trump to the diehards.

In the conversation with Trump, Jones let loose. He went off on a rant about the "globalists that want to have a world government" and suggested there was a pro-Trump "internal war going on" in Washington.

It was an early example of the basic themes that would congeal into QAnon and cast Trump as a holy warrior in the coming "storm." Jones wanted assurances Trump wouldn't "step down . . . under death threats."

Trump spent over a half hour with Jones that day. Their conversation was only briefly interrupted by an *Infowars* ad that was an uncut blast of Jones's brand of alt-right sci-fi paranoia. In it, a narrator warned viewers that "mainstream media" was giving them "a false sense of reality."

"I mean, do you actually know what you think you know?" the narrator asked. "Break the matrix. . . . Listen to the Alex Jones show because there's a war on your mind."

Dire stakes, fear of others, blind belief in a prophet. The pitch for Jones's show used multiple parts of the cult programming playbook.

Jones wrapped up his talk with Trump by acknowledging Stone. The dirty tricks man had been a guest on *Infowars* before arranging Trump's appearance.

"Donald Trump has agreed to stay a few more minutes with us and he brought up, you know, somebody that he wanted to thank on air, that I want to thank on air," Jones said. "He came in here a month ago . . . just an incredible guy . . . a patriot fighting communism all over the world. Tell us Mr. Trump about Mr. Stone, who helped get this interview set up."

Beaming in from his corner office at Trump Tower, then-candidate Trump praised his longtime adviser.

"Well Roger's a good guy, and he is a patriot, and believes strongly in a strong nation," Trump said. "People like Roger. He's a tough cookie, I will tell you that, but people like him. . . . He's been so loyal and so wonderful and he is the one—he really wanted me to do this interview and I'm doing it."

Jones said his "respect level went up even more" for Trump knowing that Stone was his friend and counselor. Their virtual sit-down concluded with Trump plugging his new book.

"It's doing great business," Trump grinned. "I hope your audience goes out and buys it as Christmas gifts and everything else."

In March 2016, just over three months after he connected Trump with Jones, Stone was trying to help his man win the crowded Republican presidential primary. He came up with a vintage Roger Stone scheme.

Stone's political action committee launched a website that—with no proof whatsoever—claimed the primary was riddled with fraud and unspecified "irregularities." It warned that "the political establishment will stop at nothing to stop Trump." The group outlined a strategy to potentially challenge the nomination on the floor of the Republican convention.

"The Trump Ballot Security Project is committed to investigating all complaints of voter fraud. In the event a pattern can be determined, the seating of these delegations can and will be challenged," the site said.

Of course, Trump won the 2016 primary despite the supposed "fraud" against him. Stone's group kept going—and kept soliciting donations— after Trump secured the nomination. It published videos and blog posts baselessly alleging that electronic voting machines could be "rigged" and "hacked" to stop Trump. The narrative spread online.

"Why wouldn't they try to steal the election from Donald Trump? If this election is close, THEY WILL STEAL IT," the group's site read, before adding, "Plus they intend to flood the polls with illegals." Messaging that taps into fear of illegal voting is nothing new.

The project had a new name: "THE EMERGENCY COMMITTEE TO STOP THE STEAL." Its website was called simply, "Stop the Steal."

A movement was born.

* * *

Stone didn't exactly hide his associations with extremist groups.

When he appeared in Washington to speak at rallies protesting Trump's loss on January 5 and 6, 2021, Stone was accompanied by a security detail that included members of the Oath Keepers militia group. At least six of them allegedly entered the Capitol during the attack.

Stone spoke at multiple rallies around the nation's capital ahead of the electoral certification. He was billed as a speaker at the "Wild Protest," which was set to take place outside the Capitol building right as the building was stormed. On January 5, the night before the building was stormed, Stone shared the stage with Jones.

That rally was held in Freedom Plaza, blocks away from the White House. Stone and Jones stood in front of a "STOP THE STEAL" banner and spewed the full buffet of pro-Trump, election-denying nonsense.

Jones had spent Trump's presidency promoting the "Pizzagate" theory that blossomed into QAnon and fighting litigation related to his false claim the 2012 Sandy Hook Elementary School shooting that left twenty children and their teachers dead was a hoax. He was also going through a heated divorce where, in 2017, his ex-wife claimed his wild conspiracies were evidence of a dangerous instability. One of Jones's lawyers responded to that by arguing he was "playing a character" online. The jig seemed to be up, but not for Jones's true believers.

In Washington on the night of January 5, Jones was with his people. He was introduced by Owen Shroyer—his right-hand man, who is currently facing federal charges for allegedly entering restricted areas on the grounds of the Capitol on January 6th—as "the genesis in many ways of this second American revolution." After taking the stage, Jones worked his way up to his trademark hoarse shout as he railed against "Satanists"; the Rothschild banking family; Chinese "death camps" operated by the tech giant Apple; and media controlled by "globalist groups that run the genetic engineering labs," "UN martial law world government," and the COVID pandemic—or, as he described it, a "hoax" and "an engineered virus that Bill Gates owns." Jones was unloading the whole far-right conspiracy kitchen sink.

"I'll tell you who I'm excited here to see. It's you, the American people unified in resistance to the new world order! We have only begun to resist the globalists! We have only begun our fight against their tyranny! They have tried to steal this election in front of everyone," Jones yelled, finger pointing and forehead taut. "I don't know how all this is going to end, but if they want a fight, they'd better believe they've got one!"

Unlike some of the other performers who took to that small raised stage, Jones didn't have a jacket to guard against the January cold. He was plenty hot. Rolling into revival-tent mode, Jones decried Joe Biden as a "slave of Satan" and alluded to that familiar modern evangelical myth, the idea of Trump as the Lord's own imperfect vessel.

"We renounce Satan! We renounce the Democratic Party! . . . But more importantly, we embrace God, and family, and justice, and strength!" Jones bellowed. "We hold up President Trump before the creator of the universe. And we say, 'Thank you for trying to send us a deliverer though he's imperfect as we are.' . . . We pray for him, and we pray for America, and we hold him up in this hour of peril."

It was the message Jones had been delivering for years to his growing online audience. He was preaching alt-right revelations and January 6th was the day of judgment. Jones shouted "1776!," which had become a rallying cry among the self-styled #StopTheSteal "revolutionaries," and urged the audience to "commit to war against the globalists" as they chanted along with him.

"Tomorrow is a great day. We don't quietly take the election fraud," Jones said. "This will be their Waterloo. This will be their destruction. . . . We do not recognize the communist Chinese agent Joe Biden or his controllers!"

Stone, who was introduced at Freedom Plaza as the originator of the Stop the Steal movement, was hardly a natural fit for the holy roller thing. He loved tailored double-breasted suits, collar pins, custom felt hats, and suspenders. Stone's personal life was just as flashy. He was an unapologetic swinger who hung out in sex clubs and posed shirtless for magazine profiles.

Earlier in his career, Stone had explicitly distanced himself from the Christian Right. Yet by January 5, the inveterate dirty trickster and party animal had remade himself for the evangelical bent of the hard-core pro-Trump MAGA movement. Stone was a new man. He praised God for helping him cope with the special counsel's indictment and essentially declared himself born again.

"I got right with God. I confessed my sins. I pledged to walk in his way and I can tell you God will never desert you. God will never abandon his people. God will deliver you from your persecutors," said Stone. "I thank God for giving the greatest president since Abraham Lincoln the wisdom, the courage, the strength to correct this injustice."

Stone cast Trump's loss as a "heist" and "a very sophisticated psy-op" before putting it in biblical terms.

"Let's be very clear, this is not an election between Republicans and Democrats. This is not a fight between liberals and conservatives. This is nothing less than an epic struggle for the future of this country between dark and light, between the godly and the godless, between good and evil," Stone said. "We will win this fight or America will step off into a thousand years of darkness. We dare not fail! I will be with you tomorrow shoulder to shoulder."

Despite his fighting words and militia bodyguards, Stone has denied being involved in any illegality and insisted he didn't see any of the Oath Keepers engaging in anything improper. Stone maintains he stayed at his hotel, the Willard, which was used as a de facto command center by Trump allies on January 6th.

Going into the committee investigation, I knew about Stone's ties to militants. I also knew he was basically the founding father of the Stop the Steal movement. That's why I wanted to get my hands on his CDRs.

With everything that journalists and open-source investigators had compiled about Stone's long history with Trump, his extensive involvement in the election protests in DC ahead of the attack, and his Oath Keeper security detail, I had a hunch he just might be a key connection for all the various groups on our link map. It wasn't much of a reach. A quick look at the man's résumé suggested ties to both the White House and far-right militants.

Without Stone's CDRs, we were going to have to search for him in other data. At first, it was like trying to nail Jell-O to a wall. Our team couldn't find a validated number for Stone and he wasn't in the Meadows texts—or at least in the texts that Meadows delivered to the committee.

My team really started digging into Stone in January 2022. We were still working out various kinks in the process of trying to merge different types of data. Our software, although robust, had not been configured to merge separate formats of call records at the volume we ingested them—different call, text, and data identifiers are not standardized between private communications providers. The IBM partnership with the CDR team was crucial for the ingestion and linking of millions of lines of data.

Part of the problem with Stone was that he was attached to multiple companies and multiple numbers. Properly placing him on the link map would require figuring out which line he preferred and in what order he used them.

This was an issue with a few of our high-value targets. Along with using encrypted apps, a lot of the key members of Trump's inner circle operated multiple phones, including Steve Bannon and Mark Meadows. Rudy Giuliani, the former New York mayor and personal attorney for the former president, had multiple phones, and we noticed his girlfriend in text messages also. We were going to need to use military-grade intelligence.

The beauty of call detail records is that they don't just show you the link lines. They also allow for frequency analysis where you see how many times two different numbers are in contact. You can go beyond just showing two people are connected. With a detailed call history, you can also start to get a sense of the nature of their relationship.

If we had CDRs for someone who might be close to Stone, running a frequency analysis might show us his number. In January, our link map wasn't as robust as it would become, but there was one number we had that definitely could help, that of Kristin Davis, the "Manhattan Madam."

The situation with Stone was a perfect example of how much we still didn't know—and what we were up against. CDRs are the light into the tunnel. It's tough to hide from those data transfers. We also knew through other parts of the investigation that Stone loved those encrypted chat apps.

Stone, who'd already escaped criminal convictions and punishments on seven felony counts with a presidential pardon, used the full toolbox that powerful people have when it comes to avoiding a congressional investigation. Encrypted apps and Delaware shell companies can help you hide. But not completely.

While Stone's successful stonewalling exemplified some of the committee's limitations, the process of looking for his number and connections to extremists helped us home in on one of the strategies we would use throughout the investigation. As we aimed at key players, we zoomed in on their assistants and other hangers-on.

Davis and a few lesser-known characters were key to our understanding how communications routed between groups connected to Stop the Steal. Even with principals who were careful about their operations security, or OPSEC, we often found their lower-ranked aides were more lax.

Davis helped lead us to Stone. We would come to realize that, in MAGA World, looking at the B-list was crucial. Second-tier players helped us spot our top-level targets and, in the cases of Stone and Jones, to understand their ties to militants.

To hear her tell it, Davis was a former hedge fund assistant who saw while arranging dates for her bosses how much cash you could make through the world's oldest profession. Davis went on to start her own high-end escort agency staffed by ladies of the evening who charged up to several thousand dollars per hour for their services.

It all came apart in March 2008, when Davis was hit with charges of promoting prostitution and money laundering. During her case, she insisted that she had been caught up in the investigation into Eliot Spitzer, a Democrat who resigned as governor of New York earlier that month after news broke that federal investigators discovered he spent time with call girls.

Davis said Spitzer was one of her clients. Though her claim was never proven, it earned Davis tabloid infamy. Her seemingly surgically enhanced curves and dyed-blonde hair were all over the tabloids where she was given her nickname. Stone also inserted himself into the Spitzer case. He maintained that he told the FBI about Spitzer's habit of paying for dates. Stone said he found out about it from an escort that he met at a swingers club in Florida called Miami Velvet.

Stone and Davis met on a radio show while each scrounged around on their Spitzer-scandal media tours. Davis said Stone got in touch with her once they were off the air and asked what she wanted to do next in life.

For the next few years, Davis became part of the Stone show. She ran long-shot campaigns for governor and city comptroller. Her second race was interrupted by an arrest and conviction for being part of a prescription pill ring. Davis was not afraid to get her hands dirty.

By 2016 Davis was out of jail and she moved into a Manhattan apartment with Stone. She ended up testifying before a grand jury related to the special counsel's investigation in 2018. News stories from the time variously described her as Stone's "travel scheduler," "web designer," or the catchall "associate." Stone insisted their relationship was platonic.

Davis was with Stone, in Washington, at the Willard on January 5 and 6, 2021. Davis says she was present at that time and place in her capacity as Stone's longtime publicist. In a tweet sent just over five months later, she claimed that she and Stone stepped outside the Willard hotel for five minutes to evaluate whether to attend "the event" on January 6th, but that she nixed the idea. (It's not clear from her tweet precisely which event this decision relates to, but Stone was billed as a speaker at the "Wild Protest" that Ali Alexander had planned at one corner of the Capitol.)

"We had nothing to do with Jan 6th! We stepped outside the Willard hotel for 5 mins to decide if we were going to the event and I called it off! We stayed around a few hrs watching it on TV & then caught a flight to Florida," Davis wrote in her defensive tweet.

Davis was in the earlier batches of CDRs we requested. While Stone fought to keep us away from his, Davis did not. Her CDR came through right as we were looking for alternate means to find his phone number. Sometimes God smiles on the data diggers.

When we pulled Davis's record and did our frequency analysis, one number immediately jumped out. Her line was connected to this number 146 times in incoming and outgoing communications. She was on the horn with this person more than anyone in her immediate family. Mark from my call records team and the OSINT crew immediately set out to compare this certain number to the registrations we already had in hand.

Most of the numbers we looked up were tied directly to a name. Our database combined information from a variety of public records, proprietary search functions, and contact algorithms. Combining multiple data sources, including phone registrations and usage, we created a file of validated and possible numbers, emails, and physical addresses for that person. If there was some question to the validity of the information attached to a person or number, a percentage was assigned that indicated further work was needed. Even if we hit 99.9% on validating data, we sometimes dug deeper based on the importance of the person of interest (POI).

Let's have a little fun. For example, it's possible that a POI's phone number could be inactive, as determined by publicly available information and what I'll call "bespoke" sources. If we deem that POI number inactive, we can take steps to see if they migrated to another phone. We do a frequency analysis and look for numbers among those that the POI had prior relationships with. Then, we can run their closest contacts through our validating registration database to see if there's another line that they started getting in touch with after the other went inactive. In this way, we can sometimes come damn close to confirming a POI's new number—even if there's no name in the registration. We can also accomplish this type of combined analysis with a handset, which has its own unique signature, the IMEI, or International Mobile Equipment Identity number. The IMEI is just like a social security number for a phone. It can be tracked if the user switches out their SIM card. These methods even allow us to get some sense of burner phone activity. With cutting-edge telephony analysis, it's real hard to hide.

Davis's number one contact came back as belonging to a company called Drake Ventures LLC. We already knew a bit about Drake Ventures. It was based in Delaware. When we ran its corporate paperwork, Stone's wife, Nydia, was identified as the registered agent and Roger was a managing member. Stone confirmed the validity of our investigative work later in the complaint he filed to stop the committee from obtaining his CDRs. It acknowledges Roger and Nydia Stone's connections to Drake Ventures LLC and describes the subpoenaed line as "Stone's personal cell phone number."

Many, like Stone, wanted to protect their CDRs and sued to block their release. In early March 2022, I received a request from the committee to help write the technical answer to Mark Meadows's litigation from December 2021 where he had also sued to block his CDRs. I was perplexed as to why it took three months for the House of Representatives' general counsel, which represents the committee, to respond to Meadows. CDRs, in this case, could determine if Meadows released all his texts and other communications with groups involved in January 6th, including the Trump family, and to cross-reference whether he and others were truthful in their private interviews and public statements. The House's counsel has not been particularly aggressive with answering lawsuits seeking to block the release of CDR data to the committee; as of this writing, they have not entered appearances—much less motions or answers—in several cases filed against the committee months ago, including Stone's. It is possible that there are legal concerns I don't know about, or that the House counsel conducted a very thorough rebuttal to Meadows in the hope of establishing a rock-solid precedent before responding to the pleadings in other pending CDR lawsuits. In addition, House lawyers have been litigating some of the older related cases over phone records subpoenas more actively—like those involving John Eastman and Ali Alexander. (Eastman voluntarily dropped his case at the end of June 2022, citing the committee's assurance that it was only seeking his CDR data, not the content of his messages.)

Once we got Stone's line, Mark and Glenn conducted regular sweeps for his number in other CDRs as they came in. Again, we didn't have Stone's CDRs, but we could run his number as a "reference number" against the records we had in our system to see one side of a connection. We got multiple hits. Rapid fire.

On January 15, nine days after the attack, Stone had two calls with Elmer Stewart Rhodes, a former army paratrooper and Republican congressional staffer who founded the Oath Keepers militia in 2009. The group focuses on recruiting from within law enforcement and the armed forces. In their twisted logic, joining an irregular militia is a way of honoring the oaths sworn upon signing up. They buy in to various "New World Order" conspiracies that suggest our country is on the edge of full-on totalitarian martial law, where citizens will have their guns seized or even be thrown into concentration camps.

In more recent years, Rhodes has backed Trump and his militia became part of the larger MAGA movement. Rhodes and other prominent members of the group have pursued all sorts of wild election schemes, including setting up an "operation" where members monitored the polls in 2016. Many of Rhodes's comments about immigration and voting are based on seemingly white supremacist ideas that people from the "Third World" are taking over the country in concert with the "globalists."

During one of its hearings, on July 12, 2022, the committee heard testimony from Jason Van Tatenhove, a former Oath Keepers spokesman who said he broke with the group in 2018 after members began engaging in open Holocaust denial. Van Tatenhove described them as a "very dangerous organization" almost hell-bent on "armed revolution." He also alluded to their radicalization methods and the propaganda pipeline.

"I think we saw a glimpse of what the vision of the Oath Keepers is on

January 6. It doesn't necessarily include the rule of law," Van Tatenhove said. "It includes violence. It includes trying to get their way through lies, through deceit, through intimidation, and through the perpetration of violence, the swaying of people who may not know better through lies and rhetoric [. . .] I'll admit I was swept up at one point as well."

At least twenty-two Oath Keepers have been charged so far with participating in the January 6th attack. In the January 2022 seditious conspiracy indictment, one of several that have been filed against members of the militia, Rhodes and ten other Oath Keepers were accused of planning to travel en masse to DC on that day and of breaking into the Capitol, where some of them allegedly went hunting for Democratic House Speaker Nancy Pelosi. Three Oath Keepers charged with seditious conspiracy have pleaded guilty, as of this writing; the others, including Rhodes, have entered not guilty pleas. Prosecutors also said the group organized "Quick Reaction Forces," who had weapons on standby at locations in the suburbs. These guys were trying to turn the Comfort Inn Ballston into a war zone and Stone was on the phone with their leader after they did it. His phone number was also linked to a more rank-and-file member of the Oath Keepers prior to the attack. Davis spoke to an indicted Oath Keeper as well.

Stone's phone also hit—before and after January 6th—with Enrique Tarrio, chairman of the Proud Boys. Davis's phone connected with Tarrio before the attack as well. The connection between Stone and Tarrio was deep. Tarrio had previously worked as one of Stone's aides. Stone's phone was also linked to lower-level Proud Boys.

The Proud Boys are a self-described "Western chauvinist" group that was founded in 2016. They are a regular presence at protests and have earned a reputation for brawling with left-wing activists. In the weeks after the 2020 election, the Proud Boys participated in multiple protests in the nation's capital that ended in nighttime clashes on the streets. The Justice Department described the Proud Boys as "the tip of the spear" on January 6th in their arguments for keeping the group's erstwhile leader, Enrique Tarrio, in jail ahead of his trial. "The evidence shows that dozens of men in [Tarrio's] charge functioned as the tip of the spear for the mob on January 6," the prosecutors wrote, "including by conducting assaults on law enforcement, leading a charge up the stairs to the Upper West Terrace of the Capitol grounds, occupying the Capitol grounds and building, and causing lawmakers to be evacuated and the proceedings to be suspended."

According to charging papers filed in federal court, a group of about one hundred members of the Proud Boys gathered at the Washington Monument on the morning of January 6th and proceeded together to the west side of the Capitol, where the first barricade came down at 12:53 p.m. That detail is one of the reasons leaders of the Proud Boys have been charged with seditious conspiracy related to the attack. It's a rarely used charge that carries a lot of political weight. Oath Keepers are also under indictment for seditious conspiracy. It has made those two organizations appear central to the Justice Department's January 6th investigation.

A grand jury indictment filed in the US District Court in Washington, DC, earlier this year said four Proud Boys, including Ethan Nordean and Joseph Biggs, Shroyer phone contacts, were among the first people to charge through the breach and storm the building. They've pleaded not guilty. The indictment alleged that Tarrio created a new chapter for the Proud Boys, the Ministry of Self-Defense (MOSD), which he called a "national rally planning" chapter, and that he established the leadership, structure, and authoritarian ethos of the MOSD. Tarrio has pleaded not guilty too. Allegedly, Tarrio opened various encrypted chat rooms for the MOSD, dictating details of the "DC trip," forbidding the wearing of Proud Boys' colors on this trip—going "incognito" rather than wearing the group's standard black-and-yellow polo shirts—facilitating travel of MOSD members to DC, etc. He's quoted in the charging documents exchanging voice notes in one of the MOSD chats about a specific plan to, in his words, "storm the Capitol." He also was accused of directing the acquisition of handheld radios.

All of this raised my eyebrows since Stone and Davis brought together two of our key groups, the domestic violent extremists and the Trump associates. Along with the top members of the Oath Keepers and the Proud Boys, Stone's number was connected to higher-level Trump associates including Texas attorney general Ken Paxton, Bernie Kerik, a former NYPD commissioner and a close ally of Rudy Giuliani, and Arthur Schwartz, a veteran Manhattan political consultant who worked closely with Donald Trump Jr. Stone's phone certainly linked to Trump's inner circle and the militants who played a leading role in the January 6th attack.

Alex Jones also had direct links to militants and the higher-level players in the political operation. He claimed he was invited by the White House to lead a march to the Capitol on January 6th. The telephony team didn't find any records of calls between Jones and the president's team, but Katrina Pierson, a national spokesperson for the Trump campaign, would testify before the committee that the former president wanted Jones to speak at the Ellipse rally that day. In one of the texts uncovered by the committee, Pierson told rally organizer Amy Kremer about Trump's affinity for Jones and others on the far-right fringe.

"He likes the crazies," Pierson said of Trump.

While Jones didn't end up speaking at the rally amid concerns from Pierson and others, the committee investigation uncovered evidence that he helped pay for the event. Afterward, Jones was filmed leading crowds down Pennsylvania Avenue. He was outside the Capitol as it was attacked and used a megaphone to try and urge the crowds not to "fight the police."

Before that last-ditch appeal for calm, Jones did plenty to ratchet up his *Infowars* audience. He had featured members of the Proud Boys and Rhodes, the Oath Keepers founder. Jones appeared at multiple protests against the election, including at least one where he was flanked by Tarrio and other Proud Boys.

Jones was one of the highest-profile figures involved in January 6th who had direct ties to militants. We found even more on our link maps. Jones's phone number showed him connected to Tarrio's phone through calls and texts.

When I left the investigation, we still did not have CDRs for Alex Jones, and a lawsuit he'd filed but not served on the committee in December 2021 had been pending for three months. On the court's public docket, nothing has changed as of this writing, almost five months later. As far as I know, the investigators still don't have those CDRs. For me, that's frustrating. Like Stone's, Jones's initial push to block the committee from analyzing his CDRs suggests there could be data lines that he wants kept off our radar. However, Jones sat for a video deposition. I was watching and got the impression Jones was genuinely afraid.

During the deposition, he raved hysterically about being worried to speak in front of California congressman Adam Schiff, a committee member who had earned full bogeyman status on the Right for his leading role in Trump's first impeachment trial. In between the paranoid rantings, Jones's testimony was not exactly illuminating. By his own admission, he pleaded the Fifth about one hundred times. Not exactly a bold revolutionary. Jones struck me as the kind of guy who talks the loudest in the bar only to disappear into the bathroom stall once a fight is on.

As dodgy as Jones was, his fellow *Infowars* host and right-hand man, Owen Shroyer, really tied it all together. Shroyer accompanied Stone in DC that day and the day before. His phone popped on the link maps, showing us just how much Jones's network was tied in with militants. Shroyer's number connected to Tarrio, Rhodes, and two other Proud Boys who were indicted for alleged involvement in planning to bring a large group to storm the building. Assistants, or tier two, under the principals we investigated were quite helpful in providing a more complete picture of events. The B-list helped us build the bridges on our link map between militants and some of Trump's closest associates.

While prosecutors accused Tarrio, the Proud Boys' chairman, of helping to lead the group's planning for January 6th, he was not with his compatriots at the Capitol that day. Tarrio was arrested by Washington, DC, police two days earlier and charged with possession of high-capacity magazines, which is illegal in the nation's capital, and destruction of property related to the vandalization of a local church's "Black Lives Matter" banner during a December 2020 pro-Trump protest against the election.

According to the indictment, Tarrio was released from jail on January 5 and ordered to leave DC. He allegedly made one stop, the parking garage of a hotel near the Capitol where he met with Rhodes. Video taken by documentary crews who were with Tarrio show that their group also included Bianca Gracia and Kellye SoRelle, neither of whom has been charged publicly with a crime as of this writing.

Gracia and SoRelle were not really on my radar prior to learning about that meeting. But once again, examining the lower rungs of the MAGA ladder proved to be enlightening.

Gracia was president of the group Latinos for Trump, which wasn't an official part of the president's campaign. Tarrio was the group's chief of staff. The pair came with the group to Washington to speak at a protest against the election in November 2020. They flew on a private jet that cost more than twice as much money as Latinos for Trump had raised in its entire two-year existence at that point. Along with mysterious, swanky flights, the group seemed to bring the pair opportunities to rub shoulders with stars of the MAGA movement. On her Facebook page, Gracia had once posted a photo of Tarrio standing and grinning with Donald Trump Jr. and Kimberly Guilfoyle. That was back on November 4, 2019. Happier times.

Gracia's phone provided even more indication of her high-level connections. We found outgoing and incoming communications between her line and White House 881 and 456 root numbers between late November and December 2020. Four of the calls came from Gracia's phone. One was incoming—that was far more important from our perspective. I can't stress this enough: the White House switchboard was reaching out to an associate of the leader of a violent gang. She was literally dialed in. That call lasted over two minutes and, of course, there may have been more we couldn't see.

We also saw what looked like communications between Gracia and SoRelle, who was the Oath Keepers' general counsel. SoRelle was not among the members of the militia who were charged with seditious conspiracy. She also had a head-scratching attempted connection with the West Wing. We found what appeared to be a text from SoRelle's phone to a White House switchboard line on December 20, 2020. That happened to be the day after Trump's "will be wild" tweet. The text was another intriguing link—one that provoked a slew of questions. The number happened to be a landline. Why had SoRelle thought she could text it? Was she used to communicating with the White House? Had she texted with someone else there in the past? Was the fateful day of the exchange just a coincidence?

SoRelle—and the many questions surrounding her contact with the White House—have gone on to bear even more importance. In January 2022, as Rhodes was in jail on the seditious conspiracy charges, SoRelle took over as president of the Oath Keepers. The woman who was texting a White House line had made it to the top ranks of America's militant extremists.

CHAPTER 8

THE TRAITOR

I sort of knew it was coming, but the text message still hit me like a ton of bricks. It was from my mother.

> "How does it feel making touchdowns for the opposing team . . . you just keep handing over ammunition to the enemy . . . what is wrong with you," she wrote. "What happened to you . . . you want socialism . . . you want babies murdered because they are not perfect . . . I don't even know you any more."

The text came in late 2020, as I was increasingly starting to confront far-right digital disinformation. As I researched and learned more about just how much the Republican Party was being taken over by ludicrous internet conspiracy theories, I became very aggressive on Twitter. In early October, I worked with New Jersey Democratic congressman Tom Malinowski to pass a House resolution condemning QAnon. I also started going on TV to make my case.

I felt a real duty to take advantage of my final few months in office and to warn people about how extreme things were getting. It did not go over well back in Virginia.

Apart from a stray uncle or cousin, my family are solid Republican voters across the board. After a cable news appearance or two, I got a concerned call from my mother. She told me I was betraying my values just by going on CNN and MSNBC. As far as she was concerned, those were liberal networks. I had crossed over. The disappointment in her voice was thick.

We hung up after a painful hour. Since my break with the church, our relationship had had its ups and downs, but I never questioned her love for me—or mine for her. I figured we'd be offline for a while, maybe a couple months. It would not have been the first time. Then came the text, which was on another level.

It was October 14, just over a week after my QAnon resolution passed. I went on Jake Tapper's CNN show and criticized Trump for promoting a conspiracy theory that was over-the-top and sickening, even by his standards. My mother thought I was on the wrong side.

> "What will it take to wake you up son . . . I love you so, but cannot stand by and listen to your elitist attitude and being praised by elitist journalist and democrats," she wrote. "Congratulation you are now part of the swamp . . . I'm sorry you were ever elected. . . . You are officially a politician . . . I have cried over you and my heart is broken by you."

My head was swimming. I read it a second time, a third, and even a fourth. The words didn't change. As much as it hurt me, I understood her anger. Prior to Trump, if I had watched a politician claiming to be a Republican slamming a sitting president from the party, I would have dismissed them as a traitor. But didn't she see how things were different now?

I knew my mom and I were not on the same page politically, but this was something else. Any hope for a mostly normal relationship seemed dim. She was damn near disavowing me.

> "How can you do this to so many who believed in you ... loved you ... you have betrayed your values which were my values. I think you lost you," she wrote.
>
> My mom had one last angry message for me in the very long text bubble: "You are not smarter than TRUTH."

What a gut punch. I was stunned. Even though I tried to see where she was coming from, the message made me angry.

This was the woman who had worked hard and sacrificed to make sure we had good meals even when our dining table was just a cardboard box with a cloth on it. She had been there cheering at all my football games. How could she choose Trump over her own son? She was picking a pathological liar and con artist over a son who had honorably served in the military. Didn't we have some trust? Didn't she know I would never lead her down the wrong path?

As frustrated as I was with my mom, part of me was angry at myself too. Why had I started this fight? Why had I been so hell-bent on pushing into a tribal war zone?

The blowup with my mother began—like so many things did before Trump left office—with a tweet from the president. On October 13, 2020, three weeks before election day, Trump retweeted an article that was shocking even by the standards of the other crap he had been posting on social media.

At the time, Trump was trailing Biden by ten points in the polls. I suspect he was getting desperate. It was time to activate the most radical sections of the base, to ratchet up the absurdity. No holds barred.

Trump retweeted a post from someone who went by the name "Oscar The Midnight Rider 1111." Yes, that's right, in the heat of an election year and a raging pandemic, the material crossing the president's desk included an anonymous QAnon believer's tweets. The post Trump shared with his, at the time, over 87 million followers, included a link to an "EXCLUSIVE" article that claimed a "CIA Whistleblower" had proof that former president Barack Obama and his vice president, Joe Biden, had paid for the murder of the navy SEAL team that killed the Al Qaeda terrorist leader Osama bin Laden.

The "whistleblower" in question was Allen Harrow Parrot, a bearded, kimono- and turban-wearing falconer who, by his own admission, had never been employed by or worked for the CIA or any agency. Parrot had earned a bit of notoriety with a 2010 documentary, *Feathered Cocaine*, that showcased his life as a trainer and breeder of high-priced falcons for assorted VIPs in the Middle East. In the film, Parrot claimed falconry camps were the site of key meetings between Middle Eastern leaders and terrorists, including bin Laden. Parrot was cast as a would-be truth teller who couldn't get the US government to listen to his tips.

You might want to grab a snort of your favorite whiskey before trying to follow this any further. It's a category-five storm of stark raving bullshit.

A decade after his documentary appearance, Parrot's story had become much more outlandish. The article Trump retweeted contained a video where Parrot spun a wild, barely coherent tale. It began in the 1970s with the formation of an "alternate CIA" called the "Safari Club" that was working with Iran and bin Laden. As a veteran of the air force's Big Safari program, I couldn't help but chuckle at that bit. If that was what he meant, we were a declassified acquisition and technology program, not a shadowy Illuminati intelligence agency.

According to Parrot, the Iranians and some of their secret American allies spirited bin Laden out of the compound in Pakistan where he was hiding and arranged for a body double to be killed in his place. SEAL Team Six participated in the staged assassination mission and were then themselves executed by the US government due to some kind of convoluted blackmail plot that involved America giving Iran $152 billion to cover it all up.

The 2012 attack on the US diplomatic compound in Benghazi, Libya, which left four Americans dead, including two former SEALs, was also somehow roped into Parrot's global conspiracy theory. Democrats— including one who was secretly *Muslim*—were supposedly the key figures.

Parrot's tale was a long trail of blood-soaked madness, a grisly, twisted science fiction. These were ridiculous ideas dredged up from the dark side of Trumpworld. By promoting this stuff, the sitting president of the United States was scraping from the dirtiest bottom of the dankest barrel.

In the clip, Parrot claimed to have "terabytes" of data, including audio and video proof verifying his absurd story. Of course, Parrot and the right-wing activists who promoted his claims never presented any of the alleged evidence. Anyone buying in to this garbage was doing it based on nothing more than the word of an eccentric who promised he was on God's side in the holy war against the Democrats and their unseen evil empire.

"There is always an invisible hand that protects us and we're on the winning team," Parrot said in the clip.

Thanks to the internet, one man's unproven conspiracy theory was able to reach an audience of millions. Trump then increased Parrot's platform exponentially.

Parrot's deluded tale of terror, betrayal, and blood sacrifice was a vivid example of how ravings could rise up through the ranks of the far-right ecosystem before reaching the Oval Office. The original interview featuring Parrot debuted at American Priority, a conservative conference where far-right figures like Steve Bannon and Roger Stone make speeches, sell books, and push merchandise. It was presented by Nicholas Noe, a little-known right-wing activist who claimed to be a former airman and had posted videos claiming the Benghazi attack was a conspiracy, and Charles Woods, the father of one of the men killed in Libya, who had made a couple of appearances in conservative media criticizing the Obama administration's handling of the attack. Neither of these guys had a huge following.

After Noe and Woods premiered the interview, it was shared on Twitter by Anna Khait, a former contestant on CBS's long-running hit *Survivor*. Khait was increasingly building a brand and career as a pro-Trump Christian activist and influencer. However, her idea of influencing looked a lot like radicalizing. Along with sending out a steady stream of photos from professional shoots, selfies, memes, Bible verses, and inspirational quotes, Khait had posted about having alleged traitors hanged.

Khait's tweet was picked up by a website called DJHJ Media, which transcribed part of Parrot's interview. That site is operated by David J. Harris Jr., a mid-grade MAGA-world celebrity who had a book to sell along with a web page where he hawked T-shirts with conservative slogans and another site selling bottles of Enerlean vitamin supplements. Harris was a vocal election denier. He spoke at the January 5 rally in Freedom Plaza, but his daytime slot was far earlier than the headliners Alex Jones and Roger Stone. Harris's news site is still online. It is weighed down with enough ads for fad diets and autoplay videos to make your computer strain. As I write this, its top stories include one on a poll claiming "28 percent of U.S. voters think that they will have to take up arms against the government of the United States."

As the story moved from the Benghazi conspiracy fringe, to a former reality star, and then to Harris, it was climbing the escalating spiral of far-right online grift and radicalization. The story wound up with the ultimate hustler, Trump himself.

When Trump blasted out the harebrained SEAL Team Six kill mission article to his followers, some QAnon adherents said it was confirmation of Parrot's theories. Now, Parrot wouldn't need to reveal any evidence. The faithful had heard it straight from their leader.

Trump's shocking retweet made headlines. I had just passed my QAnon resolution the week before, and Tapper, the CNN anchor, invited me on his show the day after Trump's post to unpack it for people. I broke down why I thought the post was so important—and alarming.

"It's about the disintegration of, really, the trust that we have and being able to talk to each other . . . and have this dialogue that's not based on the insanity of things like QAnon," I told Tapper. "When you see what's going on with QAnon right now . . . It's exploding and the reason that I'm so worried about it is because I've worked this for so long. I worked radicalization. I worked counterterrorism for two decades."

That disintegration of trust, the communication breakdown—it was all playing out in my own family.

At the time, Trump's official, public position on QAnon was somewhere between a-wink-and-a-nod and explicit support. Less than two months earlier, Trump made his first direct, official comments about the growing conspiracy movement when a reporter asked about QAnon during a news conference in the White House briefing room. Trump, who had already spent years amplifying QAnon supporters on Twitter and seeing them at his rallies, pretended not to know about the theory, even though it had made headlines in conjunction with his campaign. Even within that implausible denial, Trump offered some praise for QAnon adherents, who he characterized as concerned about the conditions in Democrat-run cities that were seeing rising crime and violent protests during the pandemic.

"I don't know much about the movement other than, I understand they like me very much, which I appreciate. . . . But I don't know much about the movement. I have heard that it is gaining in popularity and, from what I hear these are people [. . .] that don't like seeing what's going on in places like Portland," said Trump. "I've heard these are people that love our country and they just don't like seeing it."

The reporter, Shannon Pettypiece, a White House correspondent for NBC News, seemed to be in disbelief. With an eyebrow arched in alarm, she pressed Trump on the specifics of the Q movement.

"The crux of the theory is this belief that you are secretly saving the world from this Satanic cult of pedophiles and cannibals," Pettypiece said to the president. "Does that sound like something you are behind?"

There it was. Trump was standing behind the White House podium. He had the perfect opportunity to use the full force of his presidential platform to denounce the most unhinged and angry aspects of QAnon. The chance to have a positive impact on the segment of his base that was going off the rails was all teed up for him. Trump didn't take it. Nope. Rather than doing what any remotely decent person would have done, he actually doubled down and almost endorsed QAnon's dark, apocalyptic vision of world affairs.

"I haven't heard that but is that supposed to be a bad thing or a good thing?" Trump asked, adding, "If I can help save the world from problems, I'm willing to do it. I'm willing to put myself out there—and we are actually—we're saving the world from a radical-left philosophy that will destroy this country. And when this country is gone, the rest of the world would follow."

The end-time death-cult conspiracies were now coming from behind the White House podium.

QAnon rejoiced. According to the Associated Press, which monitored the internet response in real time, the Q believers who pored over Trump's appearances for coded messages saw his comments as "validation."

"On Twitter, one user claimed Trump's choice of a pink tie . . . was another signal of support," the AP's report said. "Within minutes, dozens of Instagram users began celebrating Trump's acknowledgement of the conspiracy theory."

One user quoted by the news wire said they had been "waiting for this moment for a while." Another simply exclaimed, "Holy Smokin Q."

On Tapper after the SEAL team tweet, I tried to explain why all of this was so disturbing. When Trump flirted with QAnon and offered them bits of validation and praise, he wasn't just dragging the discourse into the gutter and far outside the realm of objective reality. He was tiptoeing right up to the brink of advocating for violence. Trump's retweets gave him one degree of separation from the Anna Khaits of the world, who were openly calling for the public executions of political rivals. He was greasing the social media wheels and helping radicals build their own followings.

"It's a dangerous tweet and that's the kind of things that we cannot do," I told Tapper. "That is the language of radicalization and people go down these rabbit holes [. . .] Let's use the technical term for what's going on here. It's batshit crazy."

Tapper noted that, as we were speaking in October 2020, Marjorie Taylor Greene, a Georgia Republican who had openly aired QAnon beliefs, had just won a primary and was on her way to Congress. I, on the other hand, was on my way out. I gave Tapper and his audience a description of the dramatic changes underway on Capitol Hill.

"It's almost this federated conspiracy theory and we have to stop the spread of it," I said. "I grew up during the Reagan years. I grew up when it was, 'Morning in America.' . . . Right now with the members of Congress we have coming in, I think it's almost 'QAnon After Dark.' It's just a ridiculous thing and it has to be stomped out."

That's why I was going on CNN. As I put it in that interview, I wanted to "fight speech with speech." Tapper had a question for me.

"Are you at home in the Republican Party anymore?" he asked. "I mean, they are embracing this insanity that you condemned."

I acknowledged that my experience in Congress had been "pretty awful for me" and said it was getting "harder and harder to find a home in the GOP."

"My loyalty isn't to a party," I said. "My loyalty is to the people who elected me and my family."

Little did I know, certain members of my family might not remain loyal to me. With my QAnon resolution and TV appearances, I had inadvertently strained my relationship with my mother. We had disagreed before, but something about the Tapper interview struck her last nerve. She fired off that text calling me "lost" and accusing me of betraying our values.

I texted back that I was sorry she was disappointed in me and thanked her for the input. My response was bitterly curt. What else could I say? I wasn't going to debate her about whether Osama bin Laden had been replaced by a body double before Obama ordered the secret summary execution of a SEAL team. She was fully submerged in a fantastical, fanatical belief system. Our relationship seemed to be broken.

My personal experience with my mother was a major reason that I focused on "the damage being done to family relationships and friendships based on a multi-pronged digital radicalization" in the report on QAnon that I wrote with the NCRI in December 2020. That effort and those early public experiences calling out the conspiracy theory threat were a big part of what eventually led me to the select committee.

I knew both sets of my parents had some far-right conspiracy-tinged leanings. Both my mother and stepfather had expressed fear about airplanes spouting dangerous "chemtrails," a thoroughly debunked conspiracy theory that's been flying around since the nineties. My biological father slapped a "Trump Is My President" sticker on his car after Biden won. They were not fond of liberals and, as Trump railed against the deep state, they got on board with the idea the Left was in league with global elites in an attack on our traditional American way of life.

My own mother was buying in to the idea that there was some kind of dark force in Washington and I was a part of it. Her anger was intense. I had betrayed Republicans. I had betrayed Trump. I had betrayed God. I was putting us all in danger.

She was worried for my soul and—no matter what—I love her for that. I also love her enough that I can't stand by while she falls in thrall to sick conspiracies.

*　*　*

My relationship with my mom made it through my break with her Mormon Church. I wasn't sure if it could survive the Church of Trump.

After I abandoned my Mormon mission, my mother didn't let me live under her roof. But she never cut me off.

From that point forward, we always had some degree of distance between us, but we stayed in touch. My time in the military helped. I was moving around so there was no pressure to be in constant contact. That time apart provided an opportunity for some healing. My service was also a point of pride for my mother. As I built my family with Christine, we made sure the kids had visits with my mom. I called as often as I could.

With time, Mom also seemed to drift away from the church. She still prayed, believed, and, like me, she hadn't removed herself from the LDS rolls, but her attendance dropped off almost completely. I never asked why. It was one of the many things that remained unspoken between us.

My biological dad had never been part of the Mormon Church, but we had our own bridges to build over the years. After he left my mother, my father existed on the edges of my everyday life. We weren't particularly close. As I grew, we connected more and more. We laughed, worked, and had beers together. My stepdad shared my mom's devotion to LDS. Although he and I have had our strained periods, I appreciated him for stepping up and sticking by us from the moment he came into our lives.

My relationships with all my parents improved when I ran for office. They were very supportive when I ran for governor in 2016. It was all so quick, but I invited them to a few events, and they seemed to get a real kick out of it. We all thought I was done after that, so they were quite pleased when I threw my hat in the ring for the House seat in 2018. That was a weird race, a whirlwind, so before they knew it, we were all together for my swearing in at the Library of Congress. My folks were all beaming and backslapping. Dad, as usual, had his own way of expressing joy.

"I can't believe you're a fucking congressman!" he exclaimed.

My mom wasn't as surprised. She'd always said God had blessed me with special talents. She believed in the idea that God's hand placed us in the time and place of his choosing. There was a great purpose behind it all. I had won with almost no experience in 2018, an election year that was really challenging for the GOP. She was so proud. It was God's will. I was ordained.

Of course, a big part of the excitement for my family was that I was on the right team. But as I served and came into more and more conflict with my party, I heard rumblings from back home that they worried I wasn't sticking to Republican values. Still, even amid the uproar over the gay wedding, there was nothing so serious that it caused a rift between us—until I took on QAnon.

I told my biological dad a bit about the struggles I was having as I pushed back against disinformation and did what I thought was right. He was always a fighter. Dad didn't necessarily agree with all of my positions, but he was proud that I was being, as he put it, a real motherfucker who wasn't backing down. Hearing that people were calling me a "tool of the Antichrist" got him hot. He wanted to fight. Whatever side I was on, Dad would be at least a bit proud as long as I was standing my ground.

My mother was different. While she'd always been a Republican, she had never been too enamored with any individual politician apart from Reagan. All that changed with Trump. I could only surmise that Mom was spending a lot of time on Facebook. She was falling hard for Trump and becoming angrier and angrier at all of his perceived enemies.

Once I came out against QAnon and gave that Tapper interview, I made it onto her list of people who were turning on the president. I was slowly becoming lost to her. We might never have spoken again if it wasn't for my little sister.

Shelly was just shy of two years younger than me. I had seven brothers and sisters, but she was my only full sibling. We were alone together for her first five years, and we always protected each other. That kept up when she started sneaking out of the house. I would cover for her when she turned up missing. We took a few whuppings together for these schemes. Shelly's defiance started real young for that sort of thing. She had been through a lot and was acting out, a wild child.

Eventually, slipping out windows, seeing boys, and getting drunk turned to darker, harder stuff. The quick-witted kid who shared my love of bad, off-color jokes and eighties music gave way to an addict who barely kept in touch.

As we got older, Shelly became something of a nomad. She moved up and down the East Coast before ending up in West Virginia. Like so many people in our corner of Appalachia, she got caught up in opiates and other drugs. Shelly endured terrible abuse in her life. She also suffered from lupus. Shelly was always sick. I know that fed into her struggles. However, I also see a link between the recent surge in overdoses and addiction and the disinformation wave.

Both drugs and digital disinformation provide an outlet for those who might feel like they're stuck or falling behind. You can turn to pills or a needle for a quick hit, or you can get your dopamine boost from clicking or commenting on an article that reinforces your biases.

People are looking for escapes and answers. Some of the solutions we're getting hooked on are self-destructive. And these addictions—whether to opiates or extreme ideologies—can tear families apart.

Once drugs became part of her life, Shelly was a hard person to stay close with. We would sometimes go months or even years without speaking. Yet even when we weren't in touch, she was on my mind and in my heart.

During my time in Congress, one of my proudest achievements was being part of the Freshmen Working Group on Addiction. It was a bipartisan collaboration of new House members. The second I heard about it, I knew I wanted to be on board. I did it for Shelly. Among other things, we passed legislation that provided $5 billion in grants for opioid response in the states. There's still a lot more to be done.

In November 2021, as I was digging into my work on the select committee, I heard from my mother. Shelly was sick. Again.

Due to her lupus, Shelly had been in and out of hospitals for decades. The substance abuse didn't help matters. She was having another rough stretch, and Mom was worried Shelly couldn't take it anymore.

I was facing my own health issues at the time. For much of my life, I have dealt with something called supraventricular tachycardia. That's a medical way of saying superfast heartbeats caused by coronary electrical issues. My system had been on the fritz since I was a teenager.

Throughout 2020 and 2021, my SVT episodes were getting more frequent. It might have been the constant stress I felt in Congress the prior two years pulsing through me retroactively. This was also as I was struggling through those difficult early days on the committee, when simply putting my team together felt like a dogfight. Maybe it was the campaign fights, death threats, taking on QAnon, or fighting with my own family because of my stances. It was probably a combination of all these things. Either that or I was just getting old.

Every other day I was having fluttering and tightness in my chest. My breath became labored. I was terrified, but I was also very afraid of going to the doctor and hearing bad news. One afternoon in November, Christine caught me straining for air and grabbing my chest. I had been to the emergency room a couple times over the preceding months. Christine wasn't having any more of it. She got me an appointment with a specialist.

Over the years, doctors had failed to find a concrete cause for my SVTs. The specialist at UVA had bad news, but it came with a silver lining. I hadn't been properly diagnosed. There was a congenital defect no one had noticed—a pulmonary arteriovenous malformation, as they say in the medical books. To put it in plain English, I had veins and arteries between my lungs and heart that weren't connecting properly. That was the bad news. The good news was they could fix it with a surgery. They scheduled me for the next month, December 2021.

A little over a week after that appointment with the specialist, my mom called me about Shelly. She was being transferred from a hospital in West Virginia to one in the DC suburbs. Shelly was on life support. It didn't look good.

I drove to the hospital. My mom met me on the ground floor. She delivered a dire prognosis for Shelly. It had been over a year since the text message blowout. This was our first verbal conversation since then. We didn't address the rift as we rode the elevator up to the intensive care unit.

Shelly was all hooked up to tubes. Unrecognizable. I stared at the machines pumping fluids into my sister. Her heartbeat was steadily rising along with her temperature.

Almost a year of silence had passed between my mother and me. Now, my arm was draped around her four-feet-eleven-inch frame as our other family members went home and left us alone with Shelly.

My mother quietly prayed. Despite our issues—and my ambivalence toward religion—it was comforting. I'd always wanted to have faith, and I needed it more than ever now. This was how it was supposed to feel. Not the cultish black-and-white, us-versus-them world of judgment and division. Just prayer. And love.

It all hit me in that hospital room. I had almost lost my mom and stepdad. If it wasn't for Shelly's condition, we would have remained in a silent ideological cold war. I was doing all I could to try to help our country out of its mess, but I just didn't know if the committee would do enough to make a real difference. It was all so far gone. Now, I was losing my little sister and facing my own trip to the hospital in a matter of weeks. I was overwhelmed.

It wasn't clear that Shelly would make it through the night. A nurse slowly approached my mom with a piece of paper. My mom glanced at me with wide eyes and a trembling lip as she accepted it.

"What's that?" I asked.

"It's a DNR, honey," Mom said. "Shelly wanted this."

I stared at the document. My mom set it down, let out a breath that was a mixture of a deep sigh and a pained whimper, and then signed on the dotted line. No parent should have to do that for their child. I told her we should take a break. Time to leave the harshly lit hospital for a quick shower and change of clothes.

I patted my mother's shoulder and gently guided her out of the ICU. She leaned on me as we walked down the breezeway that connected the hospital to the parking garage. My vision started to get blurry. I was trying to be the strong son. I turned us left, but I meant to go right. Disoriented.

Suddenly, my chest thumped. I took a knee. My heart was flying. I gasped for air. A passing doctor ran up to us.

"Sir, are you all right?" the doctor asked with a look of clear concern.

I could barely talk. The words came out in ragged gulps.

"I've got . . . an SVT," I wheezed. "It's a doozy."

The doctor cried out, "Someone get me a wheelchair!"

Everything whizzed along with my shaking heartbeat. I was whirled into the ER and lifted onto a bed. My mother stood alongside me holding my hand.

"I'm so sorry," I mumbled to her.

I couldn't imagine what she must have been feeling. My sister upstairs in the ICU and me downstairs in the ER.

"You're going to be okay," she said. "God won't take you. Not now."

This time I was glad my mother thought she knew what the Lord intended. I needed that confidence.

"Go be with Shelly," I said. "I'm in good hands."

I would make it out of the hospital. My sister wouldn't be so lucky.

That night—and the next couple of weeks as I waited for my surgery—I was forced to think about how little time I might have left. Was taking a stand against QAnon and disinformation worth fighting with my family and stressing myself nearly to death?

I made it out of that operation on December 8, 2021. That's a hell of a gift. I can't think of a better way to make the most of it than trying to do some good. Nearly losing my family and myself made me appreciate everyone in my life—despite our disagreements.

It took a death—plus a very close call—to bring my mom and me back together. Some of the relationships being torn apart by conspiracy culture are not going to be repaired. That's unbearably tragic. The loss and pain I experienced in my first few months with the committee only hardened my resolve to fight. I decided it was worth the potential costs.

I never told my mother I was investigating January 6th. I'm not sure if she ever saw it on TV or in the papers. She's almost certainly going to hear about this book. I really hope she reads it—and keeps an open mind. She might see that I am not betraying our values. I am living up to them and trying to take on the groups that have co-opted Christian and American ideals.

People like my mom are being taken advantage of. If they read this book, they might start to see how.

Based on my research and training, I believe a facts-based approach can have a real impact on those who are losing their way. Addressing disinformation head-on by identifying and exposing the networks that distribute it is necessary to stem the QAnon epidemic. We're in an information war, and it's house-to-house fighting.

If I can help even one person turn away from this fringe conspiracy culture or recognize Trump for the un-American grifter that he is, it would make everything worth it. I'd be especially happy if that one person was my mom.

CHAPTER 9

FOG OF WAR

Just before Christmas 2021, I found myself in the back of a restaurant waiting for a House staffer to deliver a box of files. A classic document drop.

The cloak-and-dagger episode started a few days earlier when I got a call from Illinois Republican congressman Rodney Davis. We had been pretty close during my time in Congress. Davis always struck me as a reasonable, moderate guy who hadn't fully gotten on board the Trump train. He also always appreciated a good beer.

Davis was the ranking minority member on the House Administration committee, which shares responsibility for day-to-day operations and security at the Capitol. It was obvious to anyone with a television or cell phone that there were major security failures at the building on January 6th. Which is putting it mildly. The place was stormed easily. Total system collapse.

Davis was trying to dig into what went wrong, but he told me that the House Administration's Democratic leadership wasn't cooperating with his requests for documents and information. He felt he was being stonewalled.

I don't know why Davis didn't go to Cheney or Kinzinger, our other fellow Republicans, but I understood why he was coming to me. We had a good relationship.

Still, speaking to me was a real risk. Trump diehards would roast him if they knew he was talking with anyone working on the January 6th investigation, even me. Plus, two of the members leading the select committee were part of House Administration: Zoe Lofgren, who was its chairwoman, and Jamie Raskin. If I shared what Davis told me with the Democrats, it could give them a chance to clean things up. It would also conceivably provide a preview of the playbook Republicans would use to launch a counteroffensive against the January 6th committee when they had a House majority, which everyone expected would happen in the coming election cycle. Politically, it was fraught.

But Davis seemed to genuinely want answers.

When I spoke with him, his voice was tight. He didn't want anyone to know we were talking.

"I don't know what you'd have me do," I told him. "I work for the committee. They're the ones who are paying me."

This was a tricky spot for me. I couldn't go behind the committee's back. And our work was for the people, all of them. Not one party or the other.

But what happened to security that day was part of what the Blue Team was looking into and, well, hell, Davis might have some solid leads.

Davis said he had documents outlining key questions about the law enforcement and intelligence breakdown that allowed for the Capitol breach. He claimed to have evidence showing mistakes that were made. And he said that his requests for information and records were being blocked by Lofgren. Basically, Davis thought there was a cover-up. And he wanted the two of us to run our own secret investigation.

"Denver, I want to deliver you all our documents, all of our questions, and all the requests that have been denied and ignored by House Administration," Davis told me.

Very sensitive stuff.

"And I'd like to keep this quiet," he said.

That kind of off-the-books work seemed to me to break every protocol. But at the same time I too wanted answers. How did we get the Capitol's security posture so wrong that day? This was a crucial part of ensuring that nothing like this happened again. I also wanted to know where the Administration committee was resisting inquiry. At heart, I'm an old intelligence officer. I want all the facts I can get. Part of me didn't care what Davis or anyone on the select committee or Administration committee thought about the situation. I just wanted to get my hands on the documents to make my own assessment. Trust is not my default mechanism.

I had a decision to make. Should I do what Davis wanted or immediately notify the committee? Forgive the mixed metaphors: I tried to split the baby and, frankly, cover my ass. I told Davis I would have to loop in Liz Cheney and Jamie Fleet, the staff director. However, before turning the evidence over, I promised Davis I would go through all of it by myself.

"I can do my own investigation, but I can't keep it a secret from the senior members of the committee," I said. Davis agreed.

After our conversation, I called Cheney and told her that Davis had reached out to me and that he wanted to deliver documents. I told her I would make sure they got to the proper people on the investigative team.

"Fantastic," Cheney said. "Please do the work."

Fleet was also on board.

"We have nothing to hide," he said. "And you do need to look at these materials."

Davis and I needed to arrange the handoff. He wanted secrecy, somewhere quiet and discreet where there was no chance we'd run into someone from the Hill. Steakhouses were out. Really, the whole District of Columbia was a no-go zone.

I knew just where to go.

Mama Mia Pizza in Manassas is in a strip mall down the road from Coverstone Apartments, where I lived as a kid. Underneath the complex, a maze of big rounded groundwater tunnels links drains on every access road, parking lot, and the highway, about a mile away. My friends and I used to run those tunnels all day, every day and sometimes at night. We called it sewer diving. You could sneak through those stormwater drains without seeing daylight for miles and pop out at 7-Eleven—or right by Mama Mia.

Manassas is about thirty miles from Capitol Hill along Route 66, which is always backed up with traffic. The drive takes at least an hour most weekdays. That distance—and annoyance—meant the town wasn't full of staffers or members. And Mama Mia does mostly takeout during the day, so the dining room is pretty empty then.

Mama Mia opened in 1976 and the inside doesn't look much different than it did back then. The place is lined with brown booths, plastic tabletops, faux Old World paintings of Italian landscapes, and chintzy lamps with flowers etched into the glass.

On the day we set up, I made sure to get there early and grab a seat facing the door. Davis sent a staffer. When they showed, we were basically alone. I waved them over and got our sandwich order going (Italian ham and tomato; it's knee-buckling good). The staffer, whose name I am leaving out of this because, as I said before, Republicans are likely to vilify anyone who was involved in working with the committee, explained to me what Davis and his team believed had happened. Their take was tinged with conspiracy. They weren't suffering full-blown fever dreams, but their suspicions were rooted in political bias.

Davis was concerned that the Democratic House leadership had ignored warnings about January 6th, that they had avoided hardening the Capitol in the face of an obvious and imminent threat in order to have something to criticize Republicans for. Essentially, Davis felt the Democrats wanted a dash of chaos in order to tarnish Trump.

I didn't buy that, but I wanted to see the documents. I told the staffer that I would keep an open mind.

After polishing off our subs, we headed to the parking lot. I pulled my car up next to the staffer's and we transferred the documents. For a brief moment it felt exciting, like old times in military intelligence. And then it was time to return to the more sober intricacies of jurisdiction and law enforcement in the nation's capital.

* * *

In order to understand how everything went to hell on January 6th, you have to understand that the District of Columbia has its own rules. The city was established as a federal district in 1790. In the years since then, Washington has gained a greater degree of autonomy and home rule, but it doesn't operate like a normal state or city. A congressional committee reviews laws passed in the city and retains authority over its budget, and of course there's still the thorny issue of taxation without representation in Congress. Local DC Metropolitan police officers often have to take a backseat to specialized federal police forces in the city's many national parks and federal buildings, including the Capitol. There, the primary law enforcement agency is the US Capitol Police. According to a Metropolitan Police Department (MPD) directive issued in 2003, the department's policy is to "extend assistance" to the Capitol police if it is required. However, that general order guiding the department's relationship with USCP also specifies that "no member of MPD shall, except with the consent, or upon the request of the Capitol Police Board, enter [the Capitol] Buildings or Grounds to make an arrest in response to a complaint, serve a warrant, or patrol."

Translation: stay off our turf unless we let you in.

Like all of the fifty states, DC also has National Guard units. However, unlike the states where the National Guard is generally overseen by the governor, the only commander in chief of the district's National Guard is, well, the commander in chief.

The Capitol police department has a unique command structure. It's overseen by a board that includes the sergeants at arms of the House and the Senate and the architect of the Capitol—two offices rooted in the traditions of medieval parliaments and one that echoes the founders' Masonic proclivities. The department's chief is an ex officio member. In addition to the board, the USCP is overseen by the United States Senate Committee on Rules and Administration and by the Committee on House Administration, which is currently headed by Zoe Lofgren. A bureaucratic smorgasbord.

It's a lot to keep track of. This complex command structure was a major reason why the response to the January 6th attack was such a mess, and why investigating the security failures was a political minefield.

But that's exactly what Davis wanted me to do. I dug into his cache of documents.

Davis's primary question was whether Pelosi should shoulder blame, and how much, for the time it took National Guard troops to show up in support of the besieged Capitol police. It took roughly four hours after the first barricades were breached on January 6th for the DC National Guard to deploy troops. Why so long? During that time, police officers were brawling with the militants and rioters on the Capitol steps. Was that Pelosi's fault?

There was plenty of blame to go around. In a letter Davis and three other Republican ranking members on various House committees sent to Pelosi on February 15, 2021, he focused on another letter that former Capitol police chief Steven Sund had sent to the Speaker two weeks earlier. Sund claimed that on January 4, 2021, he went to Paul Irving, the

House sergeant at arms, and asked about the possibility of getting National Guard support for his officers on January 6th. According to Sund, Irving told him he didn't think available intelligence indicated a need for the National Guard—and that he was concerned about the "optics."

There was that damn word again. Keeping up appearances in a time of crisis.

Irving allegedly sent Sund to Michael Stenger, the Senate sergeant at arms, who similarly told him it would be preferable to request support as needed rather than proactively.

According to a Senate investigation report, Irving and Stenger both disputed Sund's testimony; neither of the two sergeants at arms recognized their conversations with Sund as a formal request to the Capitol Police Board.

Sund, Irving, and Stenger all resigned in the aftermath of the attack. In congressional testimony about six weeks after January 6th, Sund said he regretted resigning and that he had only done so under the pressure of Pelosi's public call for him to step down.

Even if the sergeants at arms were more worried about optics than the slow-rolling boulder of an angry, militant election-denialism movement bearing down on their city, they weren't the only ones.

Major General William Walker, the commander of the DC National Guard, testified before the US Senate Committee on Homeland Security and Governmental Affairs in March 2021. "Good optics," he said, were what the Pentagon brass were concerned about on January 6th. Sending in the National Guard, according to Walker, would not be good optics, and could further "incite the crowd."

There was another person involved in the response who clearly discouraged a more preventative National Guard presence before January 6th. Washington, DC, mayor Muriel Bowser, a Democrat, wrote a letter that Davis also included in his files. That letter, which Bowser made public herself after sending it, was addressed to Trump's acting secretary of defense, the secretary of the army, and the acting attorney general Jeffrey Rosen. In it, she told them that local police were "prepared" for the protests of the electoral certification and asked them not to send in any reinforcements without coordinating with her.

"To be clear, the District of Columbia is not requesting other federal law enforcement personnel and discourages any additional deployment without immediate notification to, and consultation with, MPD if such plans are underway," Bowser wrote.

As strange as that letter might seem, you must recall the context in which it was sent. DC spent much of the second half of 2020 being absolutely rocked by the civil rights protests that erupted following the death of George Floyd. For weeks protesters took to the downtown streets, vandalized buildings, and engaged in nightly clashes with law enforcement. Trump's administration had no qualms about squashing those protests. Trump sent in an alphabet soup of federal agencies, including DEA agents, Secret Service, and National Park police. He mobilized soldiers to nearby bases; he even put guards from the Bureau of Prisons on the streets to get the crowds in line. Military helicopters flew low over the city's residential neighborhoods, and then there was the incident in which peacefully protesting crowds were driven from Lafayette Park with tear gas and men on horseback so Trump could walk across from the White House for a photo op.

In short, the response was heavy-handed. The city was on edge. There was not a lot of trust to go around.

Bowser may have had her reasons, but there were clearly worthwhile questions about her role in the insufficient presence at the Capitol. The DC police, which of course had to get approval from the USCP to respond at the complex, didn't show up on scene for nearly twenty minutes after permission came through. Once there, the commander on the scene reportedly had to make at least seventeen calls—in less than an hour and twenty minutes—for backup.

Christopher Miller, the acting secretary of defense, has said part of his reluctance to send in troops was a concern that Trump "would invoke the Insurrection Act to politicize the military in an anti-democratic manner." I think that was a legitimate fear. With a president actively working to overturn an election and seize power, you don't necessarily want to see troops at the Capitol.

So there were a lot of cooks in the kitchen when it came to security at the Capitol. There were also a lot of political concerns and complex command structures involving high-level elected officials rather than law enforcement professionals. People in political positions making operational decisions is usually a nightmare. January 6th was no exception. If it were up to me, the whole operational plan for emergencies in the District of Columbia would be totally revamped. January 6th was a comedy of bureaucratic errors that had built up for years with major consequences.

The bottom line: there was more than enough blame to go around. Speaker Pelosi was not blameless—and she had a lot of company in that regard.

That was not as exciting as Davis's theory that the Democrats turned a blind eye toward the attack in order to have ammo to use against Trump. But it was the truth. The security failure wasn't the result of a nefarious plot. It was more of a standard, not-so-everyday cascading effect of governmental fuckups.

Before I go any further in laying out the intelligence failures that contributed to the chaos, and the one area where Davis seemed to have a point about Pelosi and the Democrats, there's something I need to stress. When I am critiquing the operational response to the Capitol attack and the security failures that day, I am talking about leadership and commanders. When I refer to the response as a failure I am talking about the command and control breakdown that took place between multiple agencies. Make no mistake, the police officers who spent hours battling at the Capitol in hand-to-hand combat were nothing short of heroic.

Failures of leadership usually result in those on the ground taking the brunt of the punishment. The Capitol police and, later, MPD officers who put their bodies on the line kept the members of our Congress safe as the building was overrun, and they kept our government running. They showed astounding leadership and courage. One of the most disgusting aspects of the efforts to deny and diminish what happened on January 6th has been the attempt to debate the deaths of the five police officers that have been linked to the attack, and the lasting trauma to so many others.

When it came to leadership failures, the worst clearly belonged to Trump himself. In a hearing on July 21, 2022, the committee would document in painstaking detail how the former president stood by for 187 minutes as the riot unfolded without making a single call to military leaders or the heads of any law enforcement or national security agency. During that time, despite the protestations of aides, many of whom testified before the committee, Trump also made no attempt to tell his supporters to go home. To my military mind, it was the ultimate dereliction of duty.

* * *

While I didn't buy in to Davis's theory that Pelosi and the Democrats had primary responsibility for the mess, there was one thing his box of files did appear to show: the Republicans were getting stonewalled. Some of Davis's requests were being ignored. He had sent many, many letters to various entities requesting documents and answers. He didn't receive them. It seemed as if the Democrats on the committee were none too pleased about receiving information requests from the likes of Davis, Jim Jordan, and Jim Banks.

At the same time, it was clear the Republicans weren't acting in good faith, either. They were accusing Democrats of not holding hearings on the security issue at all, which simply wasn't true.

Ideally, this issue would be fully chewed over with congressional leadership, including Pelosi, Lofgren, and Mitch McConnell, sitting down with investigators. But I doubt any congressional committee—for now—will ever deeply dig into that. Despite all of its divisiveness, Congress is a club; it is inclined to cover up its own messes.

As for me, I wanted to see Pelosi and Lofgren talk to investigators, but I was also way more intent on subpoenas to those who showed up in Mark Meadows's phone. Democrats may have dodged the hot seat, but far more Republicans got lucky on that front.

* * *

At the end of January 2022, I wrapped up my review of Davis's documents. I sent a memo summarizing my findings to Davis and to Cheney. There were questions that needed to be answered about why the Capitol Police Board reportedly went to congressional leadership before authorizing the request for support from the National Guard. I also concluded Sund, Irving, and Stenger should have been interviewed as part of a security review before stepping down from duty. Lastly, I noted other agencies had provided actionable intelligence to USCP indicating the potential for violence. USCP officials should have done more to act on that information. Mistakes were made. More than a few people had dropped the ball.

In my analysis, I may not have gone where Davis might have wished, but he was pleased. I had kept my word. And now, he had written documentation that the committee had considered his concerns.

But in addition to whatever legitimate criticism they had of the security response, Davis and the other Republican ranking members were also attempting to use the issue to muddy the waters over the violence that occurred that day. In their letter, they criticized the Democratic

Speaker for a "hyperbolic focus on fabricated internal security concerns" that they said had "taken critical resources away from the real threat, which is from outside the U.S. Capitol."

This was a pretty laughable assertion from a group of Republicans that, along with Davis, included Ohio congressman Jim Jordan and California's Devin Nunes, two of the most prominent participants in the drive to overturn election results.

Davis's own trajectory was a bit more interesting. He had been inclined to hold Trump accountable, and he didn't vote to overturn the election. He supported the effort to have an independent commission investigate January 6th, until the Republicans shot it down. Of course, with Trump's iron-fisted sway over the GOP, that alone constituted a major break: Davis was an apostate.

Thanks to redistricting, in 2022 Davis found himself in a primary fighting for the Republican nomination against Congresswoman Mary Miller, a Freedom Caucus member from Illinois. Miller—who had echoed conspiracies about "voter fraud" in the 2020 election and voted to overturn the results—secured Trump's "Complete and Total Endorsement" as a reward for her hard-line loyalty.

Davis was in political trouble. As he faced the realities of that race, Davis went further down the rabbit hole of conspiracy and January 6th revisionism. I assumed it was a desperate, last-ditch attempt to appease the far-right base. He was probably getting the same craven advice I heard from consultants in my last race: sometimes you have to be a little crazy to beat the crazy.

And Davis sure seemed willing to throw meat to the more rabid elements of the base. In June 2022, he teamed up with Jordan shortly after a crew from Stephen Colbert's *Late Show* were arrested for being inside the Capitol without authorization. They were there to film a segment with the famous puppet "Triumph the Insult Comic Dog" and had been let in by House staffers. It was a breach, to be sure, but Jordan and Davis tried to propose a full-fledged investigation and preposterously compared that security lapse to what happened on January 6th.

Of course, no one with half a brain would compare a television crew ditching their required escort to the events surrounding January 6th. We're talking about a couple of comedians, cameras, and a cigar-chomping rubber rottweiler, not a massive assault.

Jordan and Davis's letter could be easily dismissed. Davis—a man I'd had a good deal of respect for—was fully debasing himself for Trump. He was paying what increasingly seemed to be the price of admission in Trump's Republican Party.

It wasn't enough. On June 28, eight days after Davis sent the ridiculous Colbert letter, Miller beat him in the primary. She cast the win as a victory for the "forgotten men and women of Illinois" over the "D.C. elites."

Davis's fall, like my own, was a good example of how, as bad as things already are in Congress, it's getting a lot more extreme. His replacement, Miller, is a straight-up lunatic. That's not something I say lightly. Three days before her win, Miller appeared at a rally alongside her big backer, Trump. As she praised the former president, Miller thanked him for the Supreme Court's overturning of *Roe v. Wade*. She called it a "historic victory for white life." Aides quickly said Miller had "a mix-up of words," but it wasn't the first time she flirted with openly racist language. In early 2021, shortly after she was sworn in to Congress, Miller appeared at one of the pro-Trump demonstrations. As she boasted of her commitment to "Christ" and "conservative values," Miller went full Nazi.

"If we win a few elections, we're still going to be losing unless we win the hearts and minds of our children. This is the battle," Miller said. "Hitler was right on one thing. He said, 'Whoever has the youth has the future.'" Miller would later apologize for that remark.

In the upcoming midterm elections, Republicans are projected to make major gains and to retake the House majority. If they do, Lofgren will lose her position as chair of House Administration. Thanks to Davis's departure, her place is set to be taken by Georgia representative Barry Loudermilk. The day before the siege of January 6th, Loudermilk was filmed leading a byways and backways tour of the Capitol. One of the group would be filmed the following day marching back toward the Capitol with the mob and threatening Democratic lawmakers. Before the committee presented its full findings, the Capitol police issued a statement that the tour group was not suspicious, and Loudermilk would use that determination to claim the committee's continued scrutiny of this tour was a smear campaign against him.

It's going to get a lot crazier.

* * *

Although Pelosi didn't sit for interviews with the select committee's Blue Team during my time on the committee, she did set up a task force to review what went wrong at the Capitol on January 6th. It was led by retired Lieutenant General Russel Honore, the swaggering Louisianan who earned a national reputation from heading the relief efforts after Hurricane Katrina.

Davis and the Republicans criticized the task force because Pelosi gave them no input. Still, I think Honore put together a strong report. He interviewed members of Congress and didn't exactly go easy on them.

Honore's task force faulted the Capitol Police Board for its "deliberate decision-making process [that] proved too slow and cumbersome to respond to the crisis in January." It recommended giving the Capitol police chief the capability to request National Guard or other support without approval from the board in the event of an emergency.

Overall, the task force also suggested—for purposes of both intelligence and operations—the establishment of an "overarching integrated security plan" for the national capital region, which includes Washington, DC, and six counties across Maryland and Virginia.

"Some law enforcement elements, like the U.S. Park Police and USCP, have geographic jurisdictions. Others, such as the U.S. Secret Service, are functional. Reporting chains are even more complex, with various entities reporting to different governors, the D.C. mayor, or federal agencies," the report said.

The goal of the integrated security plan would be streamlining the chaotic command structure in Washington so law enforcement could be more responsive to emergency situations.

Along with creating greater operational coordination in DC, Honoré's task force recommended upgrades to the physical security and fencing of the building and to the US Capitol Police force. The report described the USCP as undermanned and underfunded, particularly when it came to intelligence. According to the task force, "only a handful of people in the USCP have significant intelligence training." The task force called for a larger intelligence team as well as more coordination with other agencies.

Both of which were badly needed. My experiences in the air force and at the NSA taught me the value of quality intelligence. Airmen and soldiers are much safer in the field if they know what they're up against. Police officers are no different. Intelligence is the preventative medicine of the military and law enforcement world. There's no replacement for it.

Reviewing Davis's documents and our own work for the committee also made it clear to me how badly the data was ignored before the Capitol attack. Our OSINT team saw massive spikes in violent rhetoric at two key points: on December 1, 2020, when Trump's attorney general Bill Barr definitively declared there was no election fraud found by federal authorities; and on December 19 when Trump tweeted, "Big protest in D.C. on January 6th. Be there, will be wild!"

We didn't just dig up that data in hindsight. In the months between the election and the attack, countless journalists, open-source intelligence analysts, and other experts on extremism were banging the drum about the increasing militant insanity of the election conspiracy movement. There were warning signs extremist groups were converging on DC—including the prior clashes with the Proud Boys in the streets. The intelligence was there ahead of January 6th. It evidently just didn't make it to the right people who needed to make the right calls for that day.

Honore's task force largely identified two factors behind the intelligence breakdown: insufficient coordination between the USCP and other agencies and a lack of resources. The report began by noting its recommendations "may require Members to overcome institutional reluctance to appropriate tax dollars to fund necessary security improvements in support of the legislative branch." It concluded with a stark warning:

"As you consider the recommendations of this Task Force, we must not forget it was the riotous actions of an angry mob that laid bare the vulnerabilities of the Capitol Complex. We must not long endure any discourse that prevents or delays efforts necessary to strengthen the security of the U.S. Capitol Complex and enhance the safety of those who serve the American people in Congress."

In other words, we need to stop the bad-faith, partisan posturing. We need to invest in intelligence to understand the new domestic terror threat rather than denying it. We need to invest in democracy and difficult conversations rather than worrying about politics and fucking optics. It's time to get serious.

CHAPTER 10

THE BYRNE IDENTITY

Make no mistake, the hard-line Trump loyalists and dead enders had a plan.

If everything had gone their way on January 6th, we likely would have seen a chain of events beginning with federal agents seizing the voting machines in key swing states. In Congress, the results would have been disputed, delayed, or overridden entirely. Troops would have taken to the streets in major cities. The two-hundred-and-forty-plus-year-old American democratic experiment as we know it would have come to an end.

On January 6th we were on the edge. The Trump legal team was, on one level, fundamentally a joke. Their supposed evidence, half-baked arguments, and simple mistakes were all laughable. Yet they had a horrifying vision that was deadly serious. Some of the president's advisers were eagerly working to plunge the country into civil unrest and toward autocracy. The scariest part of all was the fact that, if Trump's most extreme allies were just a little bit smarter, their plans might have worked.

You're probably thinking that all this talk of occupied cities and seized ballots sounds a lot like something from the internet-addled conspiracists I've been criticizing. I assure you, this is different. When I say that there was an organized, militarized plan running through Trump's push to overturn the election, I am not making it up based on some hunch or my own personal biases. I'm not out here sniffing for coded messages in Trump's tweets or tie color.

I know they had a plan to implement an authoritarian America because I saw it in the data. There were war documents.

* * *

This was one of the most shocking aspects of the January 6th plot. But it wasn't hidden behind closed doors. We didn't need a subpoena to get at it. It was all available through open-source intelligence. And there was no one who provided us with more OSINT than Patrick Byrne. He was a relatively new and little-known addition to Trumpworld, but he would make it into the Oval Office. Most important, Byrne wrote about what he discussed there. According to Byrne, Trump was nearly on board with the plan to send federal agents into the swing states and grind the peaceful transfer of presidential power to a halt. If Mark Meadows was the House select committee's MVP, then Byrne was our rookie of the year. The man was a gold mine.

By January 2022, I had my teams set up and humming along for the committee. After my operation, my blood was also properly oxygenated for the first time in my life. I had the time and energy to start digging into evidence like Rodney Davis's documents, the CDR maps, and OSINT my analysts were producing. Outside experts who knew me from my work on QAnon were also reaching out. Many of them had the same question: Had I seen Deep Capture?

The site was written by Byrne. It seemed to be a detailed digital record of one man's intense persecution complex. Byrne's writings also described his dealings with some of Trump's most aggressive and unhinged legal advisers in the months after the election.

Byrne is the polar opposite of a reliable source. His web page was filled with fantastical, self-aggrandizing conspiracy theories. That said, some aspects of Byrne's story can be checked against and backed up by other sources—and it's one of the most important episodes of the entire election fight.

We need to confront the grave realities of the events Byrne described without fully trusting his account. So while anything from Byrne should be taken with a jumbo-sized grain of salt, I am including some of his claims here where there is corroboration. Byrne did work with Trump's legal team and, together, they cooked up the war document plot to send federal agents into states to seize their voting machines. And Trump nearly adopted their plan. We have data showing all of it. Plenty of it. These people left a long trail.

Byrne was a CEO who—well before his involvement in MAGA election denialism—was dubbed a "Mad King" of the business world by *Forbes*. He is the son of an insurance magnate who built the family's fortune while working closely with legendary investor Warren Buffett, whom Byrne is fond of referencing as his "Omaha Rabbi." As a young man, Byrne, who has a shaggy shock of blond hair and piercing blue eyes, battled testicular cancer. He tried to distract himself during his health troubles by throwing himself into his studies. Byrne's education included stints at Dartmouth, Cambridge, and Stanford, where he earned a doctorate in philosophy. Thanks to that degree, he would go on to identify himself as "Dr. Patrick M. Byrne" when promoting wild allegations about the 2020 election.

With loans from his father, Byrne began to build a business empire in the late eighties. His investment holding company ended up launching Overstock.com in 1999. The company exploded during the initial dot-com boom and went public in 2002. Three years later, the stock took a dip.

Byrne was convinced Overstock's 2005 price drop was the result of unethical short selling practices on Wall Street. He launched a crusade that included a lawsuit against a hedge fund and a conference call with analysts and investors where he claimed to be on the wrong end of a massive conspiracy.

According to Byrne, his company was being targeted by a cabal that included the business press and other executives. He said it was spear-headed by "a master criminal from the nineteen-eighties" whom he referred to only as the "Sith Lord." Byrne also feared he was under sur-veillance—a real hard-core paranoia and persecution complex.

Not everyone at Overstock shared Byrne's suspicions. In 2006, his father, then chairman of the company's board of directors, resigned after expressing misgivings over his son's "jihad."

Byrne was undaunted. His feud with the financial industry seem-ingly became an obsession. He created a website called Deep Capture, complete with a forty-five-minute presentation narrated by Byrne on video, focused on exposing what he described as a "massive circle of corruption." The name came from Byrne's view that America had been "captured" by powerful financiers. Byrne played fast and loose with the facts as he cast himself as a heroic figure dodging hit men and fat cats. His questionable claims led him to lose at least one libel suit and nearly a million American dollars in a Canadian court in 2016.

In 2014, Overstock made a splash when it became the first major online retailer to accept payments in Bitcoin. Crypto seemed to be Byrne's new-est obsession. He planned to launch Overstock's own coin and talked up the technology as a solution to global poverty. Overstock's various block-chain ventures ended in at least one SEC investigation, which resulted in an Overstock subsidiary paying an $800,000 fine (but not admitting wrongdoing), and over $60 million in losses. Byrne spent months on the speaking circuit trying to win crypto converts. It put him on a collision course with a Russian spy.

Maria Valeryevna Butina was a twenty-six-year-old graduate student when she met Byrne in 2015. They were attending FreedomFest, a libertarian and conservative conference that was held at the Planet Hollywood casino in Las Vegas. Byrne was there to deliver a speech about his newfound passion. The title of his talk was "Turtles All the Way Down: How the Crypto-Revolution Solves Intractable Problems on Wall Street." According to the FBI, Butina was there to make contact with influential Americans and report back to a Russian official. In late 2018, Butina pleaded guilty to acting as an unregistered agent of the Russian government. She was sentenced to eighteen months in prison. Before her arrest, she and Byrne had an on-again-off-again romance.

The relationship with Butina plunged Byrne deeper down the rabbit hole. It also led him to Trump.

Byrne went public about his connection to Butina in the summer of 2019, roughly a year after she was arrested. He gave a pair of interviews to Fox News contributor Sara Carter in which he confirmed his involvement with the Russian spy and suggested that, in carrying on the relationship, he was cooperating with FBI investigations into both Butina and Hillary Clinton, Trump's 2016 rival. Then things got really strange.

After Carter published her second story, Byrne had Overstock send out a press release that has got to be one of the most bizarre moments in the history of corporate communications. The release, issued on company letterhead, was titled, "Overstock.com CEO Comments on Deep State, Withholds Further Comment."

Byrne described his statement as confirmation of Carter's articles. Of course, this was another one of those echo chamber cycles. Carter's stories were recaps of comments by Byrne. She specifically noted that she had not reviewed the documents he claimed to have provided the government and that the FBI declined to comment on his involvement.

Byrne had made a series of intense allegations, so he tried to confirm them by simply saying them again in a new space. But none of the articles or his subsequent writing included any definitive evidence of a supposed deep state plot. As much as he probably wished it were otherwise, his word was not proof.

This is something I see a lot in the conspiracy space. In traditional media, the phrase "confirmed" is used by journalists when they have hard evidence or independent sources verifying something. Grifters tend to throw that word around a lot. "Confirmed." One person just saying something is not "confirmation." That's especially true when what they're saying is as completely improbable as Byrne's story.

Without proof, Byrne's statement suggested that deep state members of the government, or as he put it the "Men in Black," were engaged in "political espionage" against Trump, Clinton, and two Republican senators who ran for president in 2016, Ted Cruz and Marco Rubio. Byrne also roped Buffett into the statement.

"In July 2018 I put the pieces together. I immediately (last July) came forward to a Congressman and a senior military officer, to the Department of Justice this April, and (upon my Omaha Rabbi reminding me of my duty as a citizen late this June) to a small set of journalists this summer. Ms. Carter was among them. Her two stories are accurate," Byrne wrote in the statement. "Having confirmed Ms. Carter's two articles, I have fulfilled those citizenship obligations of which my Rabbi reminded me. I will speak no more on the subject."

Byrne never explained why, if he figured it all out in 2018, he had waited a year to escalate the matter beyond that initial congressman and military contact. Overstock sent out that press release where Byrne described himself as embroiled in some kind of battle against the deep state. Overstock shares went into a tailspin after the press release was issued. They plummeted 36 percent over three days. A lot of people lost a lot of money.

Ten days after his shocking pronouncement, Byrne resigned as the company's CEO. After Byrne's departure, the stock price climbed back up more than 8 percent in a single day.

Having exited Overstock, Byrne was unleashed. Despite declaring that the statement would be his final word on the matter, Byrne went on Fox Business, the financially focused sister channel of the conservative cable outlet Fox News, to discuss his exit with a panel of hosts.

Wearing a "Make America Grateful Again" hat and a black T-shirt, Byrne began by painting his departure from Overstock as an effort to spare the company from the blowback that would come from his courageous fight against the nefarious forces in our government. To hear Byrne tell it, he was a patriot facing grave danger for speaking out, a hero willing to sacrifice himself.

"This is me ejecting and I have to," said Byrne. "I've been warned that, if I come forward to America, that the apparatus of Washington is going to grind me into a dust, and that's going to happen, and I have to get that away from the company."

Byrne claimed he had "assisted" the "Men in Black" up until the point he realized they were engaged in "political espionage." In the end, Byrne said he was able to put the "jigsaw" together to discover who was behind the sinister scheme that targeted members of both parties.

"I took some orders that seemed a little fishy," said Byrne, unblinking. "Last summer, watching television I figured out the name of who sent me the orders . . . the name of the man who sent me the orders was a guy named Peter Strzok. . . . Got it? Capisce?"

By invoking Strzok, a former FBI agent, Byrne was tying his personal issues to one of the Right's favorite bogeymen. Strzok, a more-than-twenty-plus-year veteran of the bureau, had helped lead an investigation into Hillary Clinton's private email server and was also part of special counsel Robert Mueller's Russia investigation.

In 2018, an inspector general's report showed that Strzok had sent text messages criticizing then-candidate Trump and saying he wanted to "stop" him to Lisa Page, an FBI lawyer with whom he was having an affair. The report concluded that Strzok's personal opinions didn't affect investigatory work. Strzok had people layered above and below him. Still, the texts were unprofessional and cast doubt on the investigation's impartiality. Strzok was removed from the Mueller investigation and eventually fired.

Trump and the conservative media latched on to the Strzok episode as proof that the whole Russia probe was a "witch hunt." Fox News ran a story that built on the implication in a Republican senate report that an out-of-context text from Page to Strzok showed how former president Barack Obama personally interfered in the email server investigation to help Clinton. Even though there was never anything to connect that text to the Clinton email matter, the claim then rocketed around the MAGA sphere with rolling coverage on Fox and headlines on the Drudge Report, *Infowars*, and Breitbart, among others.

Now, almost two years later, Byrne had the Strzok story back on Fox. It was yet another example of one of the far-right bullshit spirals. A questionable allegation was promoted on Fox, another even more wild tale sprung out of that story, and now the double-strength conspiracy was back on the air. The echo chamber had the capability to endlessly amplify itself. I liked to call it the self-licking ice-cream cone. Strzok, for his part, told the *New Yorker* in November 2020 that he had never met Byrne and had "no awareness" of the businessman until reading about him in the news in the summer of 2019—one year after Strzok was fired.

I had never seen any of this until my OSINT colleagues turned me on to Byrne. Once I watched the clip, I couldn't believe it hadn't been bigger news. The leader of a major American company was embroiled in a spying scandal and had seemingly unraveled on live cable television.

David Asman, the Fox Business host of Byrne's segment, ate it all up. He uncritically accepted Byrne's claim that Strzok was heading some type of spy operation inside the FBI.

"That's huge news," Asman said. "That hasn't been revealed so far as I know as of yet."

Byrne, who was coming in via satellite from his home state of Utah, said there were "other whistleblowers" and suggested he was coming forward because of the fear he might "disappear" due to the sheer enormity of "the big cover-up" he had discovered.

"There was political espionage conducted," Byrne said. "This isn't a theory of mine. This isn't some political position. I was in the room when it happened. I was part of it. I thought I was doing law enforcement. Sorry."

Then it looked like Byrne got emotional. He seemed to be on the verge of weeping as he explained that sitting on this knowledge was eating him up inside. Byrne alluded to America's epidemic of mass shootings, which—somehow—tied in to his personal situation.

"This country's gone nuts," he said, choking up. "I feel a bit responsible."

Byrne declared that everything would be exposed in another "massive federal investigation."

"I believe I was offered a billion-dollar bribe to be quiet," Byrne added.

The interview was one of those split-screen segments. Byrne was on with five other panelists. They all sat there wide-eyed and open-mouthed, except Fox's Asman, who nodded along and empathized with Byrne as he broke down.

"It's understandable when you think of all you've been through," Asman said.

Then author and investor Zachary Karabell cut in to note how little sense Byrne was making. He was incredulous.

"You're the CEO of a company. . . . You have a board. You have shareholders. You've got employees," Karabell said. "I've just got to ask you, why are you involved in any of this—whatever any of this is and I don't really know how to make heads or tails of it . . . but why?"

Byrne, eyes reddened, declared he was simply "a citizen," and "as a citizen, we have duties too," said Byrne, his voice faltering.

Another one of the panelists, hedge-funder Jonathan Hoenig, stepped in and brought the discussion back to the actual topic at hand, Byrne's resignation.

"How does it feel to see the stock rally when you stepped down?" Hoenig asked.

Byrne initially answered with a plug for his company. It was a little bit of profiteering mixed in with all the conspiracy. Another great moment of grift from this self-styled anti–deep state warrior.

"I'm a shareholder now. . . . I didn't choose this fight. I'm doing it. If you want to help me, go buy your daughter a rug at Overstock dot com," Byrne said, before starting to stammer. "If you want to help me out because the entirety of Washington, DC—even though I've left the company—is going to be coming after who the heck knows . . ."

Byrne trailed off. He was careening completely off the rails.

"What's your question? It seems silly to me," Byrne said. "I thought I was doing—helping—with legitimate law enforcement. I helped them. It turns out I was a tool in a game of political espionage. I didn't know that. I only figured it out last summer. I thought I was doing something legitimate."

Asman, the host, began to speak, but Byrne cut him off. He was turning back to Hoenig's question about the stock price. Byrne shook back and forth in his chair and pointed his finger at the camera. He was irate.

"Who the hell was that? Who was asking that question? What's the name of that fool? You're a fool!" he said, jabbing his finger at the camera and rocking in his chair.

Rage, the last resort of hucksters who find themselves cornered and true believers who run out of real excuses. It was hard to tell which of these boxes Byrne fit into, but his anger was incandescent.

After Byrne capped off his nearly fifteen minutes of unhinged, unproven ramblings with an insult toward one of his fellow panelists, he received no pushback from Asman. Instead, the Fox host praised Byrne as "an incredible man in the history of business in the United States."

"We have to have you back, Patrick," Asman said, as though he'd just finished a cordial conversation. "Please come back and see us again."

"I'm laying low," Byrne replied.

But Byrne didn't exactly go into hiding. The day after breaking down on air, baselessly alleging a conspiracy, and berating another guest, he moved from Fox Business to the main Fox News channel, where he was given another chance to accuse Strzok of giving him a "fishy" order as part of some unspecified scheme. During that conversation, Byrne claimed he had turned over evidence to John Durham, a federal pros-ecutor who was reviewing the origins of the Russia investigation for Trump's Justice Department. No near-tears from this TV spot, at least.

Along with airing his allegations on cable television, Byrne wrote a long, four-part series on his website describing his encounters with Butina. In it, he provided more details about the alleged plot by Strzok and the Obama administration.

Byrne suggested that, when he met her in 2015, Butina told him she was working with people in Russia who wanted to take out the coun-try's strongman leader Vladimir Putin. Butina said they were grooming her to become the country's next president. Things only got more far-fetched from there.

In his rambling recap of his romance with Butina, Byrne claimed he instantly found her suspect and sent the "proper notification" to the authorities, or, as he again put it, the "Men in Black."

In Byrne's telling, he already had extensive contacts with law enforcement and intelligence agencies. On his site, Byrne claimed that he was working with the authorities when he took on the short sellers. This led him to become an informant for the Senate Judiciary Committee and being given a letter ensuring he should be "afforded extraordinary latitude under the laws of the United States of America to pursue his activities investigating and disrupting corruption within the federal government." The thing is, this letter was locked away in a secret safe somewhere in Washington, so he couldn't provide a corroborating copy.

Byrne insisted it was actually his CIA and FBI handlers who ordered him to continue the relationship with Butina. According to Byrne, the two agencies were collaborating and had him working a top-secret assignment "undertaken at the personal request of President Obama."

Got all that? He was like a quadruple agent working under deep cover for two of America's key intelligence agencies, the president, and some kind of shadowy spy division of the US Senate. All of them were demanding that he sleep with Butina for the good of the country.

It's situations like these where I try to remember Occam's razor: start with the simplest theory. To me, the idea that Byrne was one of several men taken with a twentysomething Moscow Mata Hari was a heck of a lot simpler than Byrne's triple-agency double-spy scenario.

As convoluted as Byrne's story already was, it spun out even further. He claimed that, in 2016, as he was communicating with the feds about Butina, they asked him to be the point man in an effort to catch Democratic presidential candidate Hillary Clinton, who was running against Trump, in a bribery scandal. Byrne said that plan was aborted shortly after he realized it was "a soft-coup by Barack Obama against Hillary Clinton." He also came to believe that the deep state was letting Butina cozy up to Republicans to hurt them.

That would mean the Obama administration was mounting conspiracies against its fellow Democrats *and* the GOP, tapping the CEO of an online discount retailer to be an instrumental piece of both schemes.

Byrne claimed he refused to be used as a pawn any longer. He cooked up his own plan where he falsely made the agents think he had raped Butina. This would somehow be used against them to expose the whole thing. The sordid plan is in Deep Capture's four-part story. Byrne wasn't really clear about how faux rape was supposed to redound to his benefit, enabling him to best his would-be manipulators. However, through it all, Byrne stressed he was a total gentleman who was doing the best he could for his country.

The story was an all-you-can-eat conspiracy theory buffet. And it was well stocked: Obama, Clinton, sex, foreign spies, the global financial industry, and multiple "deep state" intelligence agencies. Byrne was like a one-man QAnon band. He seemed to have developed his own personal conspiracy mythology that neatly dovetailed with popular far-right themes.

While Byrne kept hinting that Durham, the Trump administration's investigator, was going to blow the lid off it all, nearly three years later those promised revelations have yet to materialize. In that time, Byrne has also provided no concrete evidence to back up his claims. Somehow, after a billion-dollar bribe offer, multiple high-level assignments, associations with several government agencies, and a sincere desire to come forward, Byrne hadn't ended up with a shred of paper or real data to back up his story.

That's the thing about so many conspiracies: they don't need much oxygen to breathe on. It's not impossible to prove a negative, but it's not easy. An unproven, unspecific, and rambling yarn like Byrne's would be hard to directly debunk. At the same time, its contentions are clearly outrageous and it's hard to believe such a massive plot would leave no kind of trace, digital or otherwise.

Byrne's soft-coup, deep state spy story didn't really go anywhere. And yet, as Trump was trying to undermine the 2020 election, Byrne's conspiracy fantasies swept him straight into the Oval Office.

* * *

After "ejecting" from his job and plunging into deep state paranoia, Byrne—months before any vote—began predicting the election would be "stolen." He was pre-committed to the narrative. So in the days after Trump's election loss was projected, Byrne's Deep Capture site began to question the vote. He warned of "goon vote counters" in Michigan and a media "cone of silence" that was suppressing the truth.

On November 17, ten days after media outlets declared Joe Biden the winner, Byrne was back on TV, only this time he wasn't in the big leagues. Instead of Fox, Byrne was on Newsmax, an ascendant far-right channel run by a friend of Trump's, Christopher Ruddy. Sporting at least a day's worth of stubble, Byrne identified himself as a "small *l* libertarian" who had "never voted Republican or Democrat."

"This election was hacked. The outcome was rigged and should be completely ignored," Byrne said.

The anchor, Emma Rechenberg, pressed Byrne for evidence of this blockbuster claim.

"I have the data, the electronics, everything," Byrne replied.

Byrne revealed that he had been "funding" a team of what he described as "ethical hackers and cybersecurity people" who were reviewing election systems. According to Byrne, who kept rattling off his various credentials and degrees, his team had determined "an eighth grader could hack this nonsense."

"I'm putting it all on the line," Byrne said. "This entire election was hacked. It's far easier to hack this than a Paypal or your Venmo account."

Newsmax was bush league compared to the major cable outlets. Byrne wasn't taping in a studio. The angle of his laptop screen and the ornate embroidered silver curtains behind him made it pretty clear he was in a suite at Trump's DC hotel. Still, Rechenberg pushed Byrne to prove himself more directly than any of her colleagues who interviewed him about his previous fantastical conspiracy had.

"Would that be provable in court?" she asked.

Byrne answered by alluding to the "red mirage," the phenomenon where Republican candidates run hotter in the early vote counts because Democrats are more likely to vote by mail and have their ballots counted in later waves. It had been observed before this presidential election, and was a known feature of the process, but the politicization of COVID protocols ensured the mirage shone brighter than ever in 2020.

"Doesn't it seem a little odd that Mr. Biden was behind?" Byrne asked, leaning forward into the camera.

Nope. It wasn't even a little bit odd. There was an easy, obvious answer. If Rechenberg knew it, she didn't say. Instead, the anchor amplified Byrne's election skepticism.

"That is what a lot of people are asking," she said.

Once again, thanks to the far-right media ecosystem, Byrne was getting a large television platform to broadcast his wild claims without meaningful scrutiny in the moment.

Rechenberg may not have pushed back on Byrne, but she did make a sharp observation. As Byrne baselessly questioned the integrity of the vote, the anchor said, "You sound like Trump's legal team."

He sure did—and that wasn't a coincidence. The man who had fallen for a Russian agent, arguably tanked his own company's stock, melted down on live television, and published screeds about an improbable "soft-coup" was actually advising the president of the United States.

CHAPTER 11

EXECUTIVE DISORDER

Less than a week after the election, Patrick Byrne claims he was in an office outside of Washington, DC, meeting with two leading figures of Trump's legal team, Rudy Giuliani and Sidney Powell. With all of his byzantine deep state conspiracy theories, Byrne was a hard man to follow—and even harder to believe. However, I dug into his long and winding accounts of alleged Washington intrigue because they provided a unique window into the frenzied personalities who became Trump's counselors as he battled to remain in office and the rabid plans they had to help him do it.

Byrne was bankrolling a group of what he called "cyber guys," who were trying to find evidence of election fraud and irregularities. He would later tell the *Washington Post* that he'd been introduced to Powell by Russell Ramsland, a failed Republican congressional candidate and self-styled security consultant who was part of Byrne's ragtag election research operation. Powell then connected Byrne with Giuliani. We know about their initial meeting because Byrne published a five-part series (not counting the lengthy introduction) about his work with the lawyers challenging the election for Trump on his site, Deep Capture.

As I huddled with my OSINT researchers and pored through the committee's records, I came to believe the trigger for this draconian plan was an executive order that Trump signed in 2018. It was the baseline for a bunch of the screwball legal scenarios that were dreamed up by the various legal minds of MAGA world.

Executive Order 13848 came during special counsel Robert Mueller's investigation into Russian election interference in the 2016 presidential election. Then, in March 2017, FBI Director James Comey revealed in a congressional hearing that the FBI was "investigating the nature of any links between individuals associated with the Trump campaign and the Russian government, and whether there was any coordination between the campaign and Russia's efforts." Trump consistently dismissed the allegations of links and coordination with the Kremlin as a "hoax." But there were many indications his campaign had been eager to receive help from Russia and that Russia had actually pitched in. With all of the controversy, Trump was facing mounting pressure.

Executive Order 13848 was an attempt to address this. Trump signed it on September 12, 2018.

The EO declared a national emergency to deal with the threat of "unauthorized accessing of election and campaign infrastructure or the covert distribution of propaganda and disinformation" by a foreign power. The order called for the director of national intelligence to begin assessing any indication of interference from another government within forty-five days after the conclusion of each US election.

The DNI released a declassified version of the first such report in March 2021. The national intelligence council's conclusion was in line with the findings of the select committee's Orange Team. There were foreign attempts to influence the 2020 presidential election, however, they were largely influence operations and nothing that tampered with the final result.

The report concluded "a range of" foreign actors, including Russia, Iran, "Lebanese Hizballah," Cuba, and Venezuela conducted "influence efforts" or propaganda operations during the race. It also said "cybercriminals disrupted some election preparations." Iranian hackers obtained voter registration information. According to the DNI, Iran's "overt and covert messaging and cyber operations" were probably authorized by the country's Supreme Leader Ali Khamenei. This is heavy stuff, but the spooks were also clear it didn't go beyond influence and propaganda efforts to more direct interference with the machinery of voting and tabulation.

The report specified that there were "no indications that any foreign actor attempted to alter any technical aspect of the voting process." The official assessment of the US intelligence community was that it would be "difficult" for any foreign actor to alter the voting "at scale" without detection due to cybersecurity and postelection audits. Still, that same report also claimed "Some foreign actors, such as Iran and Russia, spread false or inflated claims about alleged compromises of voting systems to undermine public confidence in election processes and results." This meant that the various Stop the Steal conspiracists panicking over foreign interference that didn't actually occur were unwittingly playing into the hands of the real foreign influence operations. Our domestic disinformation was helping our rivals around the globe.

Along with commissioning the intelligence report on foreign interference, EO 13848 outlined steps to take in the event such meddling was suspected. But the order was incredibly broad—especially since foreign influence operations and cyberattacks have been a known feature of the election landscape for some time now. It said the treasury secretary could "impose all appropriate sanctions" in light of the intelligence community assessment in consultation with the secretary of state, the attorney general, and the secretary of homeland security. It also said the treasury secretary and the secretary of state could jointly recommend further sanctions against foreign persons to the president in consultation with "the heads of other appropriate agencies." Nothing in the order specified or limited exactly what that key phrase "all appropriate sanctions" meant. For some of Trump's more extreme allies, that was the beauty of it.

After Trump's loss was projected on November 7, 2020, some MAGA hard-liners turned to EO 13848. They had their own expansive interpretation of what the order allowed. These Trump allies thought it could be a trigger to push members of Congress and Vice President Mike Pence to refuse to certify Biden electors on January 6th or perhaps that the order could even be used to invoke martial law or the Insurrection Act. We know all of this because it played out in full public view. Trump advisers openly talked about using the order to reverse his defeat or to get the military involved for that same purpose. They were musing and writing memos about Civil War.

* * *

Presidential campaigns are major operations. They have high-powered lawyers who are ready to fight in court if a race is close. The Trump campaign's attorneys made a few standard efforts to challenge procedures and COVID protocols in key states. Normal election stuff. Legal battling in the margins. It didn't work. Trump was too far down. That's when he called in Rudy.

Giuliani was the most famous member of the legal team that assembled in the days after the election to help Trump challenge the vote. Internationally known as "America's Mayor" for his stint leading New York City through September 11, he'd been a mob prosecutor and a presidential candidate. In more recent years, though, Giuliani had gone through a pair of messy divorces, made a pile of money working for foreign governments, and became one of Trump's most reliable hatchet men. He'd gotten up to his ears in the 2019 scheme to pressure the government of Ukraine to dig up dirt on Joe Biden's son that resulted in Trump's first impeachment.

Powell, the other leading figure on the legal team, was much less well known. A former federal prosecutor in Texas, Powell had made it onto the Trumpworld map by representing the president's former national security adviser, retired army lieutenant general Michael Flynn, in the long-running court fight over false statements he made to the FBI during the investigation into Russian interference in the 2016 election. Flynn, who lost his West Wing gig in that mess, had pleaded guilty in December 2017. However, in June 2019, Flynn hired Powell and tried to reverse that plea.

On November 13, 2020, right around the time Byrne said he met with her, Powell appeared on Fox Business Network and said Trump won in a "landslide." Powell claimed to have proof that "hundreds of thousands of votes" were manipulated—and she vowed to air it all.

"I'm going to release the Kraken," Powell declared.

The online Far Right was ecstatic. Powell's appearance garnered over 1.3 million views. Her declaration of war trended on Twitter.

Behind the bluster, according to Byrne, the Trump legal team was not firing on all cylinders. In his story about their initial meeting less than a week after the election, he recounted seeing mostly empty rooms at the Trump campaign offices. Based on tensions in the air, Byrne was convinced Powell and Giuliani had a "blow-up" shortly before he arrived. And sitting in Giuliani's office, Byrne said he got a serious whiff of "medicine" or "booze." In subsequent days, Byrne said, he heard the ex-mayor had a taste for "triple scotches on ice."

Byrne described Powell as convinced that a huge "hack" or algorithm had stolen the election from Trump while Giuliani was fixated on the idea votes had been cast on behalf of dead people. Of course, both of these theories were equally off. It was just like the "algorithm" paranoia I had seen in the Freedom Caucus, when my former colleagues were worried some master code was censoring conservatives online. The idea that an algorithm rigged the presidential race was technologically impossible for the same reason. States run elections and they each do so differently. You'd need to have a program or hacking protocol that could simultaneously work across multiple operating systems. Plus, the machine systems in key states had paper backups. The results were double-checked without serious discrepancies.

There was simply no basis for Giuliani's claims about dead and illegal voters. He actually had his law license suspended in New York over those allegations.

In spite of how messy Powell and Giuliani's relationship was, Byrne said he left with a clear mission. Byrne and his "cyber-buddies" would work with the Trump lawyers as they hunted for evidence the election had been fixed for Biden. According to Byrne, he then consulted with Flynn, who encouraged him to headquarter his team somewhere far from Washington. Byrne was part of Powell's Kraken.

Who formed that cyber team? Prior to linking up with Byrne, Ramsland gave speeches at events and posted videos on YouTube, dabbling in all the paranoia hits of the conservative fringe in both. Also, Byrne exaggerated the credentials of several other people whose work he would feature. A "military intelligence expert" who the *Washington Post* reported in 2020 was actually just one of Ramsland's associates, had failed to complete various army programs—including the entry-level training course for a military intelligence unit—and had never actually worked in military intelligence. Byrne talked up Ed Solomon as a "mathematician," but he was really an ex-con who worked construction and installed children's swing sets, according to the allegations against

Byrne in a defamation lawsuit filed by Dominion, which cited his court cases and his social media.

Byrne and his supposedly crack squad came up with a whole lot of nothing. He published much of the research on Deep Capture.

Solomon's analysis, which focused on key swing states, didn't draw from actual election results. His algorithm premise couldn't have worked at all in at least one of the states he cited—Georgia. A key system there wasn't connected to the internet at all. Moreover, as part of its postelection review of the vote count, Georgia recounted all paper ballots by hand—an analog method that would have fully busted any discrepancy introduced digitally. That hand tally reduced Biden's lead, but only by 0.02 percent, not nearly enough to change the outcome. The small change was attributed by county officials to ballots mistakenly not being put through the scanners, not to any fault in the machines.

Ramsland mixed up numbers from different states in his main report, which was focused on Antrim County, a Michigan jurisdiction that Trump actually won. Ramsland falsely claimed modems were used in Antrim's voting machines, used "red mirage" logic, and fixated on unofficial numbers that were released while counts were ongoing.

A report released by the Michigan Senate's Republican-led oversight committee in June 2021 devoted substantial space to debunking Byrne and Ramsland's claims about Antrim County.

"Ideas and speculation that the Antrim County election workers or outside entities manipulated the vote by hand or electronically are indefensible," the report said. "Further, the Committee is appalled at what can only be deduced as a willful ignorance or avoidance of this proof perpetuated by some leading such speculation."

The committee urged Michigan's attorney general to "consider investigating those who have been utilizing misleading and false information about Antrim County to raise money or publicity for their own ends." That's how bad this stuff was.

Bottom line: the work product from Byrne wasn't real research; it was a dressed-up version of the internet comments section.

Even though they could be so easily picked apart, the claims from Byrne's crew were featured on major media outlets like Fox News and One America News, one of the cable giant's more extreme little siblings. These television stations would all eventually have to air dramatic corrections based on glaring errors with the central theory of the election fraud case. But before that reckoning with reality, Fox and OAN blasted dubious claims out to millions of viewers.

One doubtful theory was a crazy fantasy that Ramsland had been promoting for months. Its gist was that leftist Venezuelan strongman Hugo Chávez, who died in 2013, had developed software for the express purpose of stealing elections and it was still embedded in the US's systems. Various versions of the story also connected China and Spain. The theory zeroed in on an election software company, Smartmatic, which had Venezuelan founders and obtained their first contract in that country. Smartmatic was not a Venezuelan government operation and the company had only supplied voting equipment to one American county—Los Angeles—in 2020. It could not have played a part in the kind of campaign-defining mass conspiracy that Byrne and his "cyber guys" had cooked up.

As they attempted to use the ghost of Chávez to cast doubt on the election, Ramsland and others tried to tie Smartmatic to another company, Dominion, which actually is the second-largest seller in the American voting machine market, supplying voting systems to twenty-eight of the fifty states. The only problem was that Dominion and Smartmatic had no relationship whatsoever. They are competitors, walled off from coordination by antitrust law.

Dominion and Smartmatic each pushed back aggressively against the disinformation campaign. I loved the companies' mettle. They scored major wins that showed the real value of taking this stuff head on.

Threats from the legal teams for Dominion and Smartmatic got the far-right cable channels to correct the record and stop allowing conspiracy theorists to slime the companies on their air—or to stop them midstream when they tried. That matters. Hyperpartisan audiences will only listen to voices from their tribal leaders. The companies forced the people who were promoting this garbage to come clean with their flock directly. Independent of one another, they also filed billion-dollar defamation suits against the cable channels, Powell, Byrne, Giuliani, and others. The two companies' cases are similar, and they're still ongoing.

It was easy to see Ramsland's angle. As he pushed election nonsense, it seemed to me that Ramsland was promoting his company, Allied Security Operations Group, or ASOG. Even before the first votes were cast in 2020, the *Washington Post* reported, he tried to raise hundreds of thousands of dollars from Republican donors to fund legal challenges that he said would ensure election integrity. Whether or not he had inhaled enough of his own fumes to buy what he was selling, Ramsland was clearly in a position to profit.

Byrne's motivation was another story. Even with his dramatic exit from Overstock, he had earned a fortune with the company. He didn't need small donations. It seemed like he had his own money to spend on the effort to overturn the election. But did he want more?

In its August 2021 defamation suit against him, Dominion alleged Byrne's efforts were all about crypto. The lawsuit pointed out that, under Byrne, Overstock had invested in two companies with blockchain voting programs. As a shareholder, he was literally invested in alternative voting systems and had a material interest in questioning the current infrastructure.

Regardless of its intent, the consequence of Byrne's fake research was very real rage. Showing the dangerous turn lies can take, Dominion's lawyers quoted threats to company employees supposedly received during the conspiracy blitz. One caller allegedly left a bone-chilling phone message on Dominion's main line:

"You're all fucking dead. We're bringing back the firing squad and you fuckers are all dead, everybody involved up against the wall, you motherfuckers. We're gonna have a fucking lottery to fucking give people a chance to shoot you motherfuckers, you fucking wait, you cocksuckers, you commie pieces of shit. We're going to fucking kill you, all you motherfuckers," they said.

Another message had an explosive threat.

"Yeah, good afternoon. Fuck you, fucking scumbags. We're gonna blow your fucking building up. Piece of fucking shit," said the caller.

Byrne's research wasn't just key to providing content for right-wing media and rationales for violent threats. It also formed the core of Powell's legal argument. She released the Kraken of Dominion conspiracy theories on November 19, 2020, when she and Giuliani held a press conference to make their case. The setting for their arguments, which the Associated Press dubbed a "batch of false vote claims" and the *Washington Post* called "truly bonkers," was the Republican National Committee headquarters on Capitol Hill. The party had been fully taken over by the conspiracy crazies. They were on the main stage. At least in person. Their press conference was only carried live by far-right outlets, as major broadcast and cable channels declined to give the Trump legal team a platform for their uncut conspiracy theories.

While Giuliani was still pushing the false idea of "illegal ballots," he also joined Powell and Byrne on the Dominion crazy train.

"We use largely a Venezuelan voting machine, in essence, to count our vote," Giuliani said, falsely. He added an ominous, unhinged prediction, "We let this happen, we're going to become Venezuela."

Giuliani also made another completely false assertion.

"Our ballots get calculated—many of them—outside the United

States and are completely open to hacking," Giuliani declared. "And it's being done by a company that specializes in voter fraud."

Not a single American vote is counted outside the country. In fact, many of the machines Powell and Byrne's researchers implied were pinging with foreign servers were not even connected to the internet. Giuliani was papering lies one over the other. Then, Powell stepped behind the podium. She outlined a plot involving a global leftist network headed by the dead Venezuelan dictator.

"What we are really dealing with here and uncovering more by the day is the massive influence of communist money through Venezuela, Cuba, and likely China in the interference with our elections here in the United States," Powell said. "The Dominion Voting Systems, the Smartmatic technology software, and the software that goes in other computerized voting systems here as well, not just Dominion, were created in Venezuela at the direction of Hugo Chávez."

Byrne's Deep Capture fever dreams were now being broadcast live from the headquarters of the Republican Party.

Powell and Giuliani stayed on that stage for over an hour. Giuliani was hunched over, with sweat and hair dye rolling down his face. Trump campaign staffers could be overheard on a hot mic laughing at the former mayor. It was an absurd, sad spectacle.

Powell and Giuliani were joined at the press conference by a new addition to their team, Jenna Ellis, a regular on the conservative cable circuit.

While Ellis promoted herself as a seasoned constitutional lawyer, when the *New York Times* looked into her résumé they found that her branding was mostly based on a self-published book she wrote on the Christian interpretation of a "moral Constitution." When the paper asked about Ellis's credentials, the Trump campaign only provided evidence that she participated in one single federal case. The *Times* reported that Ellis wasn't who she played on TV.

When it was her turn to speak, Ellis described their press conference as "basically an opening statement," a public preview of the legal arguments they were set to make.

"This is an elite strike force team that is working on behalf of the president and the campaign," she said.

Already hobbled, that force was headed for a brutal courtroom massacre.

* * *

Behind the scenes, White House chief of staff Mark Meadows's text messages revealed that not everyone in Trump's inner circle was on board with Powell and Giuliani's carnival road show.

Meadows's tepid response to Utah senator Mike Lee's texted attempts to put Powell in touch with the president hinted that Meadows was also lukewarm on the dynamic election denial duo's contentions.

As Lee warned Meadows that Powell was complaining the Trump campaign lawyers were "obstructing progress," it's likely those attorneys shared Meadows's reservations. Nonetheless, Powell texted Meadows directly on November 10. She only sent an image. We don't know what the file contained. It's one of those messages in the log that remain a mystery. Still, the pair clearly had an open line of communication.

On November 20, Powell sent Meadows a text that seemed to indicate she had shown him Ramsland's Antrim County affidavit.

"This portion of Russ' aff is accurate for Michigan and reflects enough fraudulent votes to flip the state," Powell wrote.

Looks like even Powell was admitting only a "portion" of Ramsland's work was up to snuff.

Eleven minutes after Powell texted Meadows about her work, the White House chief received another message from a donor with whom he appeared to be on friendly terms, who asked if Meadows was buying into Powell's claims about the voting machines.

> "How confident are you Mark on this Dominion Fraud?" the friendly donor asked.

About half an hour later, Powell texted Meadows again. She claimed federal prosecutors in New York were "harassing" her "key whistleblower." Did she want the White House chief of staff to interfere in a federal investigation? According to the logs, Meadows did not respond. About an hour later, Powell followed up by changing the subject; she sent a series of messages that claimed without evidence that a "shredder truck just left Dominion in Denver" and instructed Meadows to "Save" a "Hugely important thread" by a random Twitter account unspooling another Dominion conspiracy.

Meadows's response to Powell's series of texts was a terse "Thanks." Then he answered the friendly donor's question about the Dominion claims Powell and others were advancing.

> "Dominion, not that confident. Other fraud. Very confident," Meadows wrote.

Meadows, who bought into other election conspiracies, was clearly not impressed with Powell's ideas. Nor was Jason Miller, the Trump campaign spokesman. On November 21, Powell went on Newsmax, the far-right cable channel, and accused Georgia's Republican governor, Brian Kemp, of taking bribes from Dominion. At the time, Kemp, who had been a Trump ally, was resisting a push from the former president to use his gubernatorial "emergency powers" to overturn Biden's win in Georgia. The day after Powell's appearance, at around noon, Miller wrote to Meadows and shared his thoughts on the Newsmax interview.

> "Chief-I can't stand Gov. Kemp just like everybody else, but Sidney
> Powell is getting into dangerous territory here," Miller wrote.
>
> "I will see what I can do," replied Meadows.

A little over five hours later, the Trump campaign put out a clipped statement from Giuliani and Ellis.

"Sidney Powell is practicing law on her own. She is not a member of the Trump Legal Team. She is also not a lawyer for the President in his personal capacity," the statement said.

The ax.

On November 23, Charles Archerd, another associate who was once a Republican primary candidate for North Carolina's Eleventh, wrote Meadows to ask about the turbulence around Powell.

> "What is going on with my neighbor, Sidney P? She is either a nut case
> or is on to something so big it will rock the world," Archerd wrote.
>
> "Not optimistic it will rock the world," Meadows replied.

The next day, Miller sent Meadows another message.

> "Excellent job this week with Sidney Powell [. . .] in case nobody
> had said thank you yet!!!" Miller wrote.
>
> "That means a lot. Thank you," answered Meadows.

Despite being cut from Trump's official legal team, Powell kept up her courtroom offensive. On November 25, 2020, the same day Trump pardoned Flynn—his former adviser, who was allegedly working with Byrne—Powell, who had been Flynn's lawyer, filed suits in Michigan and Georgia. The cases leaned on the Dominion and Chávez conspiracy.

Powell's filings also featured the research that Byrne had bankrolled and published on his site. The Deep Capture work wasn't the only shoddy part of Powell's swing-state legal challenges. One of her team's filings in Georgia somehow managed to misspell the word "district" three different ways. Overall, Powell lost at least four straight cases. She is currently facing sanctions and possible disbarment for her handling of some of the election cases and has been forced to backtrack and publicly admit some of her claims were exaggerated. The mythical "kraken" went out with a whimper.

Between the Dominion defamation suit and the potential loss of her license, Powell might seem to be an example of the system working and making sure a potentially dangerous liar faces appropriate consequences for their actions. However, in the last month of 2020 and the first seven months of 2021, as she fought to overturn the vote, a nonprofit headed by Powell raked in over $14 million. She was getting quite a lot of support for her troubles.

Also, the backlash and the courtroom losing streak didn't keep Powell away from Trump. On December 18, 2020, she met with the president for hours. Byrne and Flynn were with them. They were there to deliver Trump the war document.

The night before the meeting, Flynn went on Newsmax, where he discussed his preferred strategy for the president. Sitting in front of the same silvery Trump Hotel luxury suite curtains that featured in Byrne's past Newsmax broadcast, Flynn said Trump "needs to appoint a special counsel immediately" and "needs to seize all of these Dominion and these other voting machines that we have across the country." Flynn suggested Trump wasn't aware of all the tools at his disposal.

"He's got a couple of options that he can take and he needs to take them. He needs to take them right now," said Flynn. "He could immediately on his order seize every single one of these machines around the country on his order. . . . He could order the—within the swing states—if he wanted to he could take military capabilities and he could place them in those states and basically rerun an election in each of those states."

After calling for Trump to seize the machines and send troops into swing states, Flynn, preposterously, said the situation would not be "unprecedented." In his telling, this was all just business as usual.

"I mean these people out there talking about martial law like it's something that we've never done . . . martial law has been instituted . . . 64 times," said Flynn.

Flynn neglected to mention the fact that presidential or federal declarations of martial law are exceedingly rare. Under current law, it's not even clear whether the president has the power to call for martial law. Flynn and his crew were offering a decidedly aggressive interpretation of executive power—and they were about to mainline it directly to Trump.

Byrne wrote about the meeting on Deep Capture. He claimed the group essentially barged into the Oval Office uninvited.

Meadows and other White House staffers were trying to keep Powell at arm's length from the president, but she had friends on the inside. Byrne said a "fine young [National Security Council] staffer" he knew got the group through security. (That aide, later identified as Garrett Ziegler, said Meadows revoked his guest-admitting privileges in the White House complex after the incident.) From there, Flynn used a contact to get them deeper into the West Wing. Suddenly, they were with Trump in the Oval Office. Byrne described the start of that meeting.

"Sidney and Mike began walking the President through things from our perspective. In brief: there was a quick way to resolve this national crisis because he had power to act in ways he was not understanding," Byrne wrote.

According to Byrne, they believed that power came from Executive Order 13848, the document Trump signed in 2018 that granted the president power to "impose all appropriate sanctions" if they suspected foreign interference in an election, and from an unspecified executive order former President Obama had signed in 2015. Byrne laid out the basics.

"He could 'find' that there was adequate evidence of foreign interference with the election, and while doing so would give him authority to do a number of *big* things, all he had to do was one *small* thing: direct a federal force . . . to go to the six counties in question (the Problematic 6), and re-count (on livestream TV) the paper ballots."

According to Byrne, his group recommended Trump send in the US Marshals Service or National Guard. You know, just that one small thing.

Byrne said some administration staffers—including White House counsel Pat Cipollone—came into the Oval Office and pushed back on the extreme plan. According to Byrne, some of the lawyers started "being bitches" and suggested calling the National Guard into American cities would be "terrible optics." Flynn, Byrne, and Powell suggested using the Department of Homeland Security as a compromise. Cipollone was allegedly apoplectic. The exchange that follows is all according to Byrne's account.

"Never in American history has there been this kind of a challenge to an election!" Cipollone said.

This was one area where he and Flynn agreed—though for very different reasons.

"Never in American history has there been a situation like this, with counting being shut down for hours, foreigners connecting to our equipment," Flynn replied.

Byrne said Cipollone "thundered" and said Trump "does not have the authority to do this!" Powell countered with EO 13848 and the Obama-era order.

"Of course he does," she said. "Without question he has the authority."

Byrne recalled the president being intrigued.

"You know, Pat, at least they want to fight for me," Trump said to Cipollone. "You don't even fight for me. You just tell me everything I can't do."

The meeting went on for hours. According to Byrne, it stretched until after midnight and then Trump brought the group back to his personal residence as they continued talking through the plan.

Along with pushing Trump to use EO 13848 to send federal agents or troops into swing states, Byrne, Powell, and Flynn encouraged the president to name Powell his "special counsel." Before the meeting had adjourned upstairs, in Byrne's account, Trump had reached a decision that showed he wanted to proceed with the plan. Brushing aside his lawyers' objections, he had verbally appointed Powell to a White House special counsel position and granted her a top-level security clearance. By the time they wrapped up, Byrne said Trump was still "decisively" on board with the strategy, including Powell's appointment.

The plan was in motion.

Days later, the Powell aspect of the plan was "called off."

In his write-up of the meeting, Byrne stressed that "at no point in the evening or in any segment of the discussion was there mention of martial law, or Insurrection Act, or anything of the sort." That seemed like a distinction without a difference. While he didn't want it described as "martial law," Byrne was fine with the National Guard in the streets rerunning an election.

In my mind, Byrne is obviously not the most reliable witness, but other, far more credible sources have also described the meeting. On December 19, the day after the meeting, the *New York Times* published a report that Powell and Flynn met with Trump. That article said Powell faced withering pushback on her ideas from "every other Trump adviser present" as they discussed using an executive order to seize voting machines and making her a special counsel. According to the *Times*, the meeting got "raucous," with Cipollone and Meadows "repeatedly and aggressively" rejecting the group's proposals. Following the contentious sit-down, the *Times* said it was "unclear" whether Trump would move forward with the plan to tap Powell for a special post. The news site Axios's story about the meeting was published in early February 2021 and confirmed more details, including that Byrne was at the meeting, that it moved to the residence, and that Trump had a copy of the executive order printed out to review. Byrne's characterization of this meeting also aligns with that by the select committee during its seventh hearing.

Evidence we found as part of the committee investigation showed even more about how much traction the war doc plan got in Trump's White House. On December 23, 2020, five days after the White House meeting, Zenger News—an obscure "digitally native wire service" run by David Martosko, the former US political editor of the *Daily Mail*— posted online a compilation of documents stretching to several hundred pages that it said it had received from Sidney Powell's legal team, along with an interview with Powell herself. Powell touted the binder on her own websites, but as Zenger News itself would conclude several days later, it contained only previously published materials—a mixture of government documents printed from the web and repackaged versions of Powell's familiar, debunked claims like the fatally flawed Antrim County report and the affidavit from the supposed military intelligence expert who never worked in military intelligence. Some of the government documents printed from the web were announcements made in October 2020 by the FBI and the Cybersecurity and Infrastructure Security Agency, which warned Iranian actors were trying to obtain publicly accessible voter registration data. Subsequently, on her own website, Powell published a two-page set of talking points that claimed those announcements had triggered EO 13848.

"Under that National Emergency he has all the authority needed to: Secure and analyze the voting machines in all the contested States, appoint an Election Fraud Task Force, immediately Appoint a Special

Counsel or Principle Deputy Attorney General to lead this effort, [and] Utilize National Emergency Funds," the talking points said.

Powell described the situation as "a crucible moment in United States history."

Looking through these materials and Byrne's Deep Capture site I became convinced that the order was central to the various crackpot legal strategies being cooked up by Trump allies. In January 2022, as I dove deep into the documents, I flagged them for the committee's Gold Team, which was focused on Trump's associates and advisers. They were as intrigued as I was. Due to how compartmentalized the investigators were, it's hard to say if my warning was what drove them to take a closer look at Byrne or if that avenue came from someone else. Either way, I was gratified when, roughly six months later, they called him in for a deposition. Byrne reportedly testified for about eight hours. I had left the committee by that point, but that's one interview I truly wish I could have watched.

In my air force days, I was a mission planner. That requires mission planning documents: you need to know the things you have to prove to authorize the use of force and, once you're in the air, which targets you have to hit. In my view, EO 13848 laid all these out for anyone looking for an excuse to implement an aggressive undemocratic version of presidential power. Powell and her associates didn't seem to be the only ones operating from the document.

It was right out of the Trump textbook. In his real estate days, Trump was known for setting up competing power centers in his company. He felt having underlings jockey with each other was the best way to get them to push for results. Trump carried that approach to Washington, where his White House was known for having rival factions engaged in near constant backstabbing and plotting. I suspect he ran his last-ditch power grab the same way with several different groups pushing to develop a plan of action based on EO 13848.

The committee obtained memos and emails showing that, even as members of the White House team may have rejected Powell and Flynn personally, they were nonetheless considering plans based on the executive order—and some of these strategies came from a onetime close Flynn associate, who was now working closely with Rudy Giuliani and John Eastman. In one email dated December 22, 2020, four days after Flynn, Powell, and Byrne's midnight meeting, Phil Waldron, who's said he worked under Flynn at the US Defense Intelligence Agency—where he specialized in psychological operations, or PSYOPS—sent Meadows a note referencing a "conversation" he supposedly had in the chief of staff's office the previous day. Waldron also circulated a PowerPoint presentation that detailed different strategies for overturning the election. His name was all over various documents and questionable pieces of evidence that were flying around the different Trump legal teams. Many of Waldron's schemes seemed to draw cues from the executive order and, according to comments Waldron made to the *Washington Post*, he spoke with Meadows as many as ten times in the weeks after the election, often alongside Giuliani.

In his email to Meadows following up on their conversation, which was obtained by the committee, Waldron said he was sending in a "National Asset Tasking request to support EO 13848." I knew just what that language meant. Tasking can happen under the auspices of other intelligence agencies, but foreign interference in the cyber realm falls under certain authority given to the National Security Agency. This seemed to be the start of an effort to claim foreign interference and launch the executive order.

Another document meant for Trump also caught my eye. The *Washington Post* reported in February 2022 that there was a memo of uncertain origin dated December 18, 2020, entitled "Counter-Election Fraud NSPM-13 Request." The committee found out about the document from the newspaper. The memo encouraged Trump to bring in three men to form a "core advisory team" on foreign interference in the election: Frank Colon, a Department of Defense lawyer and retired navy man; Richard Higgins, a former National Security Council staffer; and Michael Del Rosso, a former consultant to US Special Operations Command.

That memo suggested the trio would "run targeted inquiries of NSA raw signals that may not have been processed yet to pursue suspected foreign interference of the 2020 election vote count manipulation." Those people pushing this strategy—seemingly including Waldron—wanted this trio to get access to raw intelligence from the NSA so that they could search for indications of foreign meddling in the vote.

The NSPM-13 memo specified that the trio should accomplish their analysis as private contractors. Requesting raw NSA data is highly irregular. Controls on the data are rigid. Were these three men even eligible for such access? Had they been through extensive background checks? Did they receive any training?

The memo strongly implied that this access would help them find evidence that would be sufficient to allow military "remedies." It framed this as something that could happen in secret and "in parallel" with legal challenges to the election.

"Those targeted inquiries will likely identify hard evidence of foreign involvement in DOD data which will support all other efforts to reverse the fraud," the memo read. It went on, "If evidence of foreign interference is found, the team would generate a classified DOD legal finding to support next steps to defend the Constitution in a manner superior to current civilian-only judicial remedies."

These were nightmare scenarios. High-level players around the president were encouraging the use of military power to overturn an election result. Many of the people linked to this operation—like Colon and Higgins—had actual military and intelligence experience. They wanted that firepower again and were asking to get full access to NSA data as part of the push.

It all smelled like military intelligence: clandestine operations, parallel courses of action, messaging plans, information operations and, most of all, arguments based on the war document. Military planners use operational documents to dictate their next moves. These guiding plans often include establishing priority intelligence requirements— that is, the information that needs to be obtained about an enemy to trigger action. The proponents of EO 13848 worked in this manner. The executive order was their central planning document. It identified the intelligence they'd need and set the rules of engagement.

The evidence showed military planners were involved in the efforts to overturn the election. Waldron gave lawmakers a PowerPoint presentation on "Options for 6 JAN" that focused on using alleged "foreign interference" as a pretext for reversing Trump's loss. Waldron's presentation contained a bulleted list detailing a frightening order of operations that culminated with overriding the election.

"Brief Senators and Congressmen on foreign interference . . . Declare National Security Emergency . . . Foreign influence and control of electronic voting systems . . . Declare electronic voting in all states invalid," the presentation said.

Another ex-soldier who worked under Flynn at the DIA, former Green Beret Ivan Raiklin, posted a memo dubbed "the Pence Card" that argued the vice president could block the electoral certification on January 6th. Seth Keshel, a former army captain who worked in intelligence and supposedly connected with Flynn on LinkedIn, was a prominent promoter of false election fraud claims. Meadows's texts indicated he was communicating with Waldron about Keshel's data.

These were intelligence officers working in parallel and in concert. So far, this book has shown that January 6th had both political and military components. The saga of EO 13848 demonstrates that the military component was formal and Flynn was one of the central figures.

As an intelligence veteran, I find Flynn sickening. He's a pretender to the uniform, a pardoned shell of what a military man should be. I watched as Flynn was interviewed by the select committee investigators. It was an embarrassing retreat. Flynn pleaded the Fifth Amendment at every turn, including to questions he was asked about his own tweets, his communications with the Trump campaign, and his interactions with members of the Oath Keepers, Proud Boys, and 1st Amendment Praetorian. There was one exchange that I found to be particularly ridiculous.

"What were you relying on when you said that President Trump could seize all voting machines during that December 17th, 2020 interview with Newsmax?" the investigator asked.

Flynn tersely said, "The Fifth."

I think Flynn is a shameful and spineless disgrace. I also recognize him as a clear and present danger.

High-ranking military officers are serious adversaries. Their training is incredibly effective and they know how to get other soldiers to follow them into battle. Chain of command is a powerful belief for many military members, even after retirement or separation from service.

I lose a lot of sleep thinking about how many members of the armed forces and how many veterans are joining the ranks of the authoritarian Far Right. I also get a twist in the pit of my stomach when I think about EO 13848. Trump was sure as hell interested. What if Cipollone and other White House staff hadn't pushed back?

We're probably all lucky Powell was one of the major backers of the plan. She had a mixed reputation in Trumpworld and was coming off a string of losses. What if Powell hadn't filed all of those suits? What if she just made her crazy claims in public while pressing Trump to work with executive orders rather than in court? Could she have been able to persuade him to pull the trigger? Who knows. Looking back, it seems like there were a lot of close calls and we had a lot of good luck.

On January 6th, Trump had the military option on the table. America was right on the edge.

CHAPTER 12

AGENT PROVOCATEUR

Ray Epps was an easy target.

Tall, wide, and loud, Epps stood out in video footage of the Capitol attack and the protests that led up to it. On the evening of January 5, he was filmed near the White House wearing a red "TRUMP" hat in the crowds of supporters that swarmed the city streets the night before their big rally for the former president. He solidly represented the mob of foot soldiers on the ground who thought they were following orders from on high.

"I'm going to put it out there," Epps bellowed. "I'm probably going to go to jail for it, okay? Tomorrow we need to go into the Capitol! Into the Capitol!"

Epps's comments made some fellow rally-goers uncomfortable. Tensions were high. Multiple livestreams were running. They were worried Epps was a plant trying to get Trump supporters in trouble. Some shouted incredulously and yelled at him.

"What?!"

"No!"

The crowd started a chant accusing Epps of being a government agent.

"Fed! Fed! Fed! Fed! Fed!" they yelled.

Epps tried to calm them and clarify that he only wanted to go into the building "peacefully!"

Raising his voice a little higher each time, Epps insisted, "Peacefully! Peacefully! Peacefully!"

It was too late. The damage was done. So Epps leaned in.

The next day, January 6th, as people surged away from Trump's speech on the Ellipse toward the Capitol dome, Epps was there, easy to see and hear in videos of the crowd, still wearing his red "TRUMP" hat, as well as tan and camouflage tactical gear. He had a military-style backpack. Epps cupped both hands around his mouth and shouted at the other demonstrators.

"As soon as our president is done speaking we are going to the Capitol where our problems are," Epps said, waving his hand down Pennsylvania Avenue. "It's that direction. Please spread the word."

Once again Epps seemed to be encouraging the people around him to storm the building. He was dressed for a fight.

And there he was in the footage again a few minutes later, at the exact moment the Capitol barricade was breached. Epps walked up to a Pennsylvania man named Ryan Samsel and put a hand on his shoulder. Epps seemed to whisper in Samsel's ear. Moments later, Samsel was part of a group that pushed the barricade over a cluster of Capitol police officers, at least one of whom was injured and knocked unconscious.

Epps's presence at the breaching of the Capitol caught the FBI's eye. A photo of Epps standing with Samsel was included on posters the bureau's DC field office put out on social media on January 8 seeking information on people who may have participated in the Capitol attack. In the photo array, it was labeled photograph number sixteen.

It wasn't just law enforcement who had Epps on their radar. He also attracted the attention of some on the Far Right. They made him a central figure in a new conspiracy theory designed to deflect blame for the attack away from Trump's supporters. Republican politicians—including Trump—also homed in on Epps. He became their agent provocateur.

* * *

False flag theories are the refuge of the most weak-minded and uncreative conspiracy theorists. They're the lowest-hanging fruit. False flags, unlike so much else of what's in the fever swamps, actually have some basis in reality.

Historically, the term "false flag" refers to a ship or armed force misrepresenting themselves by flying the flag of their enemy. This subterfuge can have political purposes, such as drumming up support for a cause or creating a pretext for a more justifiable military strike. False flag attacks are illegal under the commonly adopted conventions of international law. They're also fairly rare. I could point to a few international examples of such operations since World War II, but the fact is, the handful of authentic false flags are far outnumbered by the countless double-agent scenarios that conspiracy theorists incessantly dream up.

False flags are one of the most common tropes of the misinformation and disinformation space. They're easy and politically expedient. Does something look bad for your side, an event that went sideways into violence or illegality? It must have been the work of the enemy; surely things must be the exact opposite of what they seem. Even if your false flag claim gets debunked, you can still hold your ground because of the shadow of doubt you've cast. Deflect. Delay. Deny.

That's why I think this type of theory is the weakest sauce in the conspiracy cookbook. It's lazy and unimaginative. Unfortunately, it's also quite effective. Proving that something didn't happen has always verged on the impossible.

The strongest conspiracy belief systems spring from a grain of truth. Plausible stories with real players and historical precedents are much harder to stamp out than something that's ridiculous on its face—like the falconer's SEAL team body double kill mission or Patrick Byrne's deep state soft coup. False flags are like the drug-resistant bacteria of the conspiracy world. On January 6th, Ray Epps was patient zero.

Mark Meadows's texts showed Trump supporters—including members of Congress and the chief of staff himself—immediately trying to blame the violence on "antifa." At just 3:45 p.m. on the 6th, Jason Miller texted Meadows:

"Call me crazy, but ideas for two tweets from POTUS: 1) Bad apples, likely ANTIFA or other crazed leftists, infiltrated today's peaceful protest over the fraudulent vote count[. . .]."

Marjorie Taylor Greene chimed in seven minutes after Miller: "Mark we don't think these attackers are our people. We think they are Antifa. Dressed like Trump supporters."

Louie Gohmert weighed in five minutes after Greene: "Cap Police told me last night they'd been warned that today there'd be a lot of Antifa dressed in red Trump shirts & hats & would likely get violent. Good that Trump denounces violence but could add & well demand justice for those who became violent & well get to the bottom of what group they're with."

The evidence-free push to blame the attack on someone else began before the Capitol had even been cleared of rioters.

Theories that leftists or secret deep state agents orchestrated the violence in order to discredit and damage the MAGA movement kept bleeding out in the days after January 6th. Antifa was central to many of these right-wing conspiracies; Marjorie Taylor Greene was just one Trump apologist who invoked it in texts to Meadows:

"Antifa was mixed in the crowd and instigated it, and sadly people followed."

Antifa is not an organized group. It is an ideology and a set of tactics, namely, violently confronting the right wing. Antifa is short for "anti-fascist." The name is borrowed from World War II–era German anti-Nazi activism. Here in America, the antifa movement became an increasingly large feature of the political scene after Trump's election. Alt-right groups like the Proud Boys also saw a surge in membership during this time. The two factions brawled in the streets at protests. They fed off each other. Trump and other Republicans spent the second half of 2020 criticizing violence and vandalism from antifa and Black Lives Matter activists during the civil rights demonstrations that erupted around the country after the police killing of George Floyd. Then January 6th took place.

It's no surprise that Trump supporters raised the specter of an antifa false flag; such conspiracies are the bread and butter of the online Right. The only problem for conspiracy theorists is that there is no credible evidence of a large leftist presence at the Capitol on January 6th.

While left-wing violence has risen recently—particularly in 2020— the Far Right has gotten much more militant much faster. Multiple Department of Homeland Security reports in the past few years have identified white supremacists of all stripes as the country's top domestic terror threats.

I don't want to minimize or ignore far-left violence, but the fact of the matter is, the Far Right has gone way beyond them when it comes to violence based on fantastical beliefs or ideologies. It's more organized and has higher-level support on the Right. You don't see the kind of coordination between the institutional Democrats and the extreme militant Left that our link maps exposed among the Republican Party and right-wing extremists. Also, I can't help but think the Left is lacking some of that religious and nationalist fervor that has made the QAnon movement so crazed.

When I was studying the former Yugoslavia back in my air force

ROTC days at the University of Virginia, I had a professor who knew Serbia very well and still had close family in the region. During a conversation after class one day, he shared a fear that's stuck with me all these years: if America ever encountered a force with serious numbers that was as dedicated as the Serbs under Slobodan Milošević, we would be in for a real challenge. Of the Serbs, he said, "What they lacked in numbers, they made up in ferocity." They were shaped by hundreds of years of history, violence, and belief. Religious ethnonationalism is an aggressive driver.

As they tried to pin the Capitol attack on antifa, some far-right posters pointed to a self-styled "video journalist" named John Sullivan, or "JaydenX," who was on the scene that day. While Sullivan had organized ostensibly left-wing protests in Utah, at least one of those protests reportedly featured the Proud Boys, and he was viewed by the left-wing activist community as an exploitative interloper. The *Washington Post* reported he had also organized a pro-gun-rights rally in Utah. It's possible his politics skewed all over the map, or maybe he was just out to make a buck. (He sold the rights to part of the video he took inside the Capitol to the *Washington Post*, and later got arrested for what he was seen and heard doing in it.) In any case, this one man's attendance was the closest false flag adherents could come to "proving" a leftist presence at the Capitol.

That didn't stop them from trying for more "evidence." The attack had been livestreamed, Instagrammed, and taped by tons of surveillance, news cameras, and cell phones. The MAGA sphere instantly started digging through the footage to find anything that looked like it was proof of antifa or federal involvement. They cobbled together heavily edited clips. In the overheated rush to explain away the attack, a man who appeared to look up and pause before opening a door he had previously struggled with became proof that someone on the inside was coordinating with the horde that rushed into the building. Video of crowds passing police became evidence the mob was allowed in rather than an indication law enforcement was overrun. Black-clad rioters surely weren't MAGA. They must have been leftist anarchists. Confirmation bias cut with the fog of war and a shot of deliberate misdirection is a hell of a drug.

It's exactly what you shouldn't do in an investigation. They went looking to confirm a specific political point instead of letting the data do the talking. The digital brigades had an answer in search of a question— and they found Ray Epps.

Epps is a man in his early sixties, and before all this, he was settled in Arizona. A retired marine sergeant, he came from a farming family and worked for years as a contractor before meeting his wife. In 2010, they bought a farm of their own in Queen Creek, just outside of Phoenix. The couple stocked it with cattle, horses, chickens, emus, and a pair of dwarf Nigerian goats that were a favorite with kids. Their dream was to turn the place into a venue for weddings and family gatherings. It came true in 2019 when they opened up a barn on the property to host parties and children's field trips.

Behind all of the baby goats and sweet dreams, though, Epps's story had a darker side. In 2011, Epps was listed as the Arizona chapter president of the Oath Keepers. In the decade leading up to January 6th, he gave interviews, conducted vigilante investigations, and appeared at events with the militia group's founder, Stewart Rhodes, who would go on to be charged with seditious conspiracy related to the Capitol attack.

Counterintuitively, that association is part of why the Far Right turned on Epps. He was a militant who showed up at the Capitol and apparently seemed eager to incite the crowd to charge into the building. Epps was on the FBI's posters, and the bureau was rounding up hundreds of people from that list. Why wasn't Epps in jail? And then, suddenly, Epps's photo disappeared from the FBI's posters. Their list of suspect photographs now skipped from number fifteen straight to seventeen. Epps, pictured in suspect photo sixteen, had vanished.

The internet exploded. On June 17, 2021, just as the debate was rolling on Capitol Hill over how to investigate the attack, a Twitter user with the handle @BrebDaily set their sights on Epps. They posted a typo-filled recap of the footage showing Epps in Washington. The Twitter account was affiliated with the Breb Room, a group chat on the encrypted social media app Telegram where users trade theories about January 6th and accuse various pro-Trump figures who promoted the protests that day of being secret deep state plants. Breb Room posts have taken aim at Michael Flynn, Roger Stone, Oath Keepers leader Kellye SoRelle, Proud Boys chairman Enrique Tarrio, and some members of the Trump legal team. They suspected all of these people in the false flag plot.

Despite its silly name, Breb Room was hard-core internet extremism—and thousands of people were participating. Now the @BrebDaily account had aimed its internet conspiracy cannon at Epps.

> "On Jan 5th, the night before the infamous Jan 6th Capital Event, this Fed was caught on camera encouraging the crowd to raid the capital on the next day," they wrote. "Who is Ray Epps?"

Epps had already been a topic of conversation on far-right forums. The Breb thread, which mocked Epps as the "Boomer Fed," was filled with screenshots from chan board posts where users shared clips of Epps and posted his personal information. It was another example of the Far Right's online echo chamber. Telegram group chats were drawing from other message boards and compiling the content for tweets. The outlandish thread was part of a tangled web that drove Epps's infamy skyward. He was rocketing through all the levels of the MAGA mis- and disinformation chain, on his way to the very top.

* * *

As the Far Right fixated on Epps, echo-chamber influencers collected supposed evidence that he worked as an undercover federal agent. They presented the supposedly incriminating footage of Epps in the DC streets and at the Capitol barricade, when he seemed eager to storm the Capitol himself and was urging others to do so too. More important for the conspiracy grifters was the fact that Epps had been dropped from the FBI's posters. This one seemed like a smoking gun to the MAGA analysts. What had happened to suspect photo number sixteen? Where was Ray Epps?

Not all of this was as exciting as it seemed at first glance. There were alternative explanations that were less far-fetched than the idea Epps was a government plant. A local paper in Arizona identified Epps in the footage and interviewed him about it for an article that was published on January 11, 2021, five days after the attack. Epps told the reporter that he "didn't do anything wrong." Just like when the Trump supporters in the street became angry at him on January 5, Epps insisted he was only encouraging people to "peacefully" go into the Capitol.

"The only thing that meant is we would go in the doors like everyone else," said Epps, adding, "It was totally, totally wrong the way they went in."

Epps stuck to his story. The idea that he was trying to encourage violence at the Capitol relied on a selective viewing of the videos showing him turning up the volume at the protests. There were also clips where Epps seemed to be attempting to de-escalate.

In one video that appeared to be taken just before the barricades were breached, Epps walked up to a man who was shouting at the Capitol police with a megaphone. The man had been seen with a can of bear spray, an irritant designed for use on grizzlies. Epps urged the man not to carry it past the barricade.

"When we go in, leave this here," Epps said. "You don't need to get shot."

As the backlash over his presence at the Capitol attack mounted, Epps hired a lawyer, John Blischak, who denied his client had ever worked with the FBI—as an agent or informant.

Blischak said he believed the video of Epps whispering to Samsel at the barricades was probably an attempt to calm things down. That seems a lot more plausible once you look at the footage of him pulling the man with a megaphone aside a few moments before. Of course, there's also the footage of Epps specifying that he wanted to protest "peacefully" in one of the videos that went viral. But there's more seemingly exculpatory evidence. Another clip from after the fencing went down showed Epps on the Capitol steps. Once again, his voice was loud. This time, though, he stood between a group of angry men on the Capitol steps and a line of police officers in riot gear, encouraging the crowd to stand back and not engage in any violence.

"We're holding ground—we're not trying to get people hurt," said Epps. "You don't want to get hurt. Let's back up."

Granted, video clips did show Epps seemingly riling people up and himself eager to enter the Capitol. However, a significant amount of footage appeared to show Epps doing the opposite, and trying to keep the peace. Far-right posters who suggested Epps was on a mission to fire up the crowd were ignoring half of the video evidence.

I can't say for sure what Epps did that day or what his exact intentions were. He sometimes looked angry, and some of his actions seemed reckless. Epps came to the Capitol in defense of Trump's lie. He's not what I would consider one of the good guys that day, but I stick to the data. If Epps really was an agent provocateur, he sure seemed to do certain things that would have undermined his own goal.

But what about those FBI "wanted" posters? Again, what had happened to suspect photo number sixteen?

The videos showed Epps behind the barricades and on the Capitol grounds. These areas were technically restricted; however, as of this writing, the Justice Department's criminal investigation has focused on people who were part of coordinated extremist groups, rioters who injured police officers, and individuals who went inside the building.

The crowds that charged over the broken barricades but didn't hit the cops and stayed outdoors have largely received a pass. So far, no clips have emerged of Epps going inside the Capitol or engaging in acts of violence.

According to his attorney, Epps reached out to the FBI within days of the attack. If Epps cooperated with the bureau, participated in an interview, and presented evidence that he had not entered the building, he would have most likely been removed from the suspect list. Online, the FBI's January 6th flyers were often incorrectly referred to as "Wanted" posters. The suspects in the photos were not actually labeled "Wanted." Those posters were headlined "Seeking Information." The photos showed the people agents were looking for and those who had been arrested. A handful of others were removed. A quick glance at the photo array of suspects reveals sixteen is not the only number that is now being skipped over.

The Epps false flag theory was, at the very least, questionable. None of that stopped the far-right MAGA media ecosystem from barreling full steam ahead with the conspiracy though. Republican politicians added fuel to the fire.

On October 21, 2021, just over four months after Epps went viral on Twitter, Republican Kentucky congressman Thomas Massie pulled out his iPad while he was questioning Joe Biden's attorney general, Merrick Garland, at a Justice Department oversight hearing. Massie was sitting across from Garland on a dais with the other members of the House Judiciary Committee. Show-trial time.

"There's a concern that there were agents of the government or assets of the government present on January 5 and January 6 during the protests," Massie said. "And I've got some pictures that I want to show you."

Massie began to play clips of Epps on the iPad as he cast an accusatory glance at Garland. The tinny sound coming from Massie's tablet was barely audible in the cavernous hearing room. A staffer handed

Garland pictures of Epps so he could see what Massie was talking about.

"You have those images there and they're captioned," Massie said, adding, "As far as we can find this individual has not been charged with anything. You said this is one of the most sweeping investigations in history. Have you seen that video?"

Massie was channeling the deep web in a congressional hearing. The attorney general was being forced to answer questions that had bubbled up from chan boards. Garland brushed it off.

"So, as I said at the outset, one of the norms of the Justice Department is to not comment on pending investigations and, particularly, not to comment about particular scenes or particular individuals," Garland said.

Of course, Massie knew all that. Law enforcement officials are always tight-lipped during an ongoing case. Asking Garland a leading, provocative question, knowing he wasn't free to answer, was one of the oldest items in the bag of disingenuous congressional tricks. This setup guaranteed a nonanswer, but that was the point. It seemed to me that Massie wasn't looking for real data. He was hunting for Twitter likes and backslaps from the base. Massie rubbed his official stink on the now-exploding internet belief in a nefarious FBI cover-up around Secret Agent Epps.

"I was hoping today to give you an opportunity to put to rest the concerns that people have that there were federal agents or assets of the federal government present on January 5 and January 6," Massie said. "Can you tell us without talking about particular incidents or particular videos how many agents or assets of the federal government were present on January 6, whether they agitated to go into the Capitol, and if any of them did?"

Garland, as Massie almost certainly knew he would, declined to answer.

"So, I'm not going to violate this norm of the rule of law," Garland said, his hands folded in front of him. "I'm not going to comment on an investigation that's ongoing."

Massie shared the exchange, which he overhyped as a "refusal" by Garland, on his Twitter. It was picked up by a slew of right-wing sites and had a starring role in multiple segments on Fox News.

* * *

Four days after Massie questioned Garland, the far-right website Revolver News published the first of two long stories on the Epps theory. The initial piece began with Massie. Revolver was created by former Trump administration speechwriter Darren Beattie after he'd been fired in 2018, when CNN published a report revealing he had been a speaker at a white nationalist conference two years earlier. The site had received major help with establishing itself in the MAGA media ecosystem from tweets by Trump himself. Now, Beattie was going all in on Epps.

The October 2021 Revolver article and its sequel that December were about 21,000 words long when added together. For reference, that's a quarter of a typical book. The articles ran alongside ads soliciting donations and subscriptions to Revolver, as well as for a store selling the site's merchandise. If the first long-form piece hadn't worked, there wouldn't have been a second. There had to have been money being made here.

Beattie drew two conclusions. Of course, he had no real proof for either of them.

"Ray Epps appears to be among the primary orchestrators of the very first breach of the Capitol's police barricades at 12:50pm on January 6," Beattie wrote. "Epps appears to have led the 'breach team' that committed the very first illegal acts on that fateful day."

Epps was definitely on hand for the initial breach. However, the only sign he supposedly orchestrated it was his quick whisper to Ryan Samsel. And that cut against other activity that seemed aimed at calming the crowd. According to his interview with the FBI, obtained by the

New York Times, Samsel says Epps "came up to me and he said, 'Dude'— his entire words were, 'Relax, the cops are doing their job.'"

Beattie's second takeaway was even more jaw-dropping—and he had even less to back it up.

"It increasingly appears that we now know how rogue elements of federal agencies pulled off the January 6 Fedsurrection," he wrote. "If the Ray Epps Breach Team hypothesis is correct, a group of government-sponsored provocateurs were all instructed separately by handlers to arrive at the Peace Monument before 12:45 p.m., where they front-ran the arrival of the Proud Boys, who would serve as the scapegoat for the breach."

The word "if" is doing a lot of work there. Beattie had yet to prove his first theory and was already basing another one off it. In his articles, Beattie largely focused on describing footage of Epps and other organizers to argue their movements were suspicious and indicated coordination.

Of course, there certainly was a degree of coordination between some of the extremists who stormed into the Capitol. My team and I spent months mapping it. But it's a bizarre logical leap to go from noting that people seemed to be working together to assuming those groups were working for the feds.

Other than obsessively analyzing the video clips, Beattie's case for the "Fedsurrection" mostly hinged on two points that proved to be completely boneheaded.

His headline described Epps as a "Fed-Protected Provocateur," a characterization that was rooted in Epps's association with Stewart Rhodes and the Oath Keepers. Beattie suggested that the fact Rhodes had not been charged while other Oath Keepers were facing legal consequences for their involvement in the attack was proof the group's founder was under "inexplicable and puzzlesome FBI protection." He then took another logical leap to suggest this showed Epps must have a similar arrangement.

Now, even if Rhodes had some kind of deal, it wouldn't prove anything about Epps. But it doesn't seem like the Oath Keepers leader had any sort of cover at all. Rhodes's arrest on seditious conspiracy charges came in January 2022, less than a month after Beattie published his second story on Epps. As of this writing, Rhodes is still in jail. Some protection. Beattie had built a lot of supposition on top of the premise that Rhodes would not face serious charges for his role in January 6th, and that premise had absolutely crumbled. From my perspective as an intelligence professional, it was a major analytical misjudgment.

Beattie's other main "point"—and I am being charitable in using that word—was that Epps's picture was suspiciously removed from the FBI's photo arrays. Throughout the Revolver articles, Beattie repeatedly incorrectly referred to the photos as the bureau's "Most Wanted" list. The FBI's "Most Wanted" list is the well-known list of the country's top ten criminals. Epps was never on that. In fact, the FBI had never declared him "wanted" at all. As we've seen, the flyers featuring Epps did not contain the word "wanted" and instead specified that the FBI was "seeking information" from and about the pictured individuals. That's a pretty huge difference.

Beattie's reports were arguably filled with small factual errors. At one point, he claimed a January 5 incident where two men were arrested after DC police allegedly found a weapons cache on a bus full of Trump supporters went "completely unreported by DC media." In Beattie's own article, that stunning accusation appeared exactly one paragraph of screenshotted tweets away from an editor at a local CBS affiliate who had covered the incident live. So much for the media blackout.

Beattie's stories were amateur hour. I thought he was no more than a grifting propagandist with a partisan agenda.

As shoddy as Beattie's work was, the far-right media lapped it up. On October 25, the day Revolver's first Epps post went live, Massie was invited onto Laura Ingraham's prime-time Fox News show. Ingraham began the broadcast by simply repeating some of Beattie's flawed logic and errors.

"According to a new investigation from Revolver, Epps may have led the breach team that first entered the Capitol on January 6. Moreover, Revolver also reports that the FBI stealthily removed Ray Epps from its Capitol violence most wanted list," Ingraham said. "Why would they do that?"

It's simple. They would not do that. They had not done that. Ingraham was sitting on a prime-time cable news perch before an audience of over two million people simply parroting easily disproved, inflammatory allegations dredged from the digital swamps. Ingraham was inserting quarters into the rinse-and-repeat bullshit cycle. A theory that originated in the deep-web basement had now made its way into Congress and on the air. The Epps story migrated from Massie's iPad to Revolver to Fox, the biggest stage in cable news. And it was only just beginning.

After introducing the Revolver report, Ingraham paused for a moment. She shook her head and gave a big eye roll before expressing disbelief about the FBI's work on January 6th.

"This Epps thing . . . they were getting grandma, you know, hauling grandma in for questioning, but this guy doesn't get—he just kind of disappears. Very odd," said Ingraham. The implication was that, in rounding up the people who stormed the Capitol, the bureau was arresting harmless and sweet senior citizens.

Ingraham's gross downplaying of the brutal attack was a pitch-perfect example of the deluded strain of January 6th denialism that was taking hold on the Right. Epps was just a part of it. In the months after the attack, right-wing media figures and Republicans began an active effort to minimize and mischaracterize what happened that day. The false flag narrative was merely one piece of a larger disinformation offensive.

A Republican member of Congress called the mob a "normal tourist visit." Others—including Arizona's Paul Gosar and Georgia's Marjorie Taylor Greene, who had both played an active part in the push to overturn the election—seemed to openly sympathize with the rioters.

Gosar called them "political prisoners who are now being persecuted and bearing the pain of unjust suffering," and Greene joined him—as well as Gaetz and Gohmert, who'd also texted Meadows claiming that antifa had been to blame for the Capitol's storming—in protesting the conditions in the DC jail where many of those arrested in conjunction with the case were being held.

Along with these other denials, Republican leaders kept poking around on the Epps theory. On January 11, 2022, Texas senator Ted Cruz used the Massie maneuver—asking an FBI executive about the Capitol case and acting shocked when they declined to respond—during a hearing. Four days later, Trump, flirting with another White House bid, also brought up the issue during his first campaign rally of the year.

"Exactly how many of those present at the Capitol complex on January 6 were FBI confidential informants, agents, or otherwise working directly or indirectly with an agency of the United States government?" Trump asked. "People want to hear this."

Trump then pivoted to Epps. He had the same question as Ingraham.

"How about the one guy? 'Go in, go in, get in there everybody.' Epps . . . nothing happens to him. What happened with him? Nothing happens," said Trump. "Did any of these individuals play any role whatsoever in proving or facilitating the events at the Capitol? That's what we want to know."

The unproven and unlikely stories about Epps were now a campaign talking point for the country's top Republican.

Fox News was in lockstep with the party when it came to January 6th denial. They refused to carry some of the House select committee hearings live. Tucker Carlson, the network's top-rated host, put together a documentary special called *Patriot Purge* that promoted the idea that January 6th was a false flag designed to crack down on dissident speech. It featured extended interviews with Beattie and jump cuts to black helicopters, a common motif of anti-government conspiracies in the nineties. Carlson suggested the government was at war with its own people.

"The helicopters have left Afghanistan," Carlson said. "And now they've landed here at home. They've begun to fight a new enemy in a new war on terror."

Fox was fanning the flames while assuring the world nothing was on fire. It was maddening—especially since our data showed some of the network's hosts knew what had really gone down. One of them, Sean Hannity, was deeply, personally involved with Trump's efforts to overturn the election and informed enough to express grave concerns about Trump's plans for January 6th starting a week beforehand.

Ingraham, Carlson, and Hannity all showed up in Mark Meadows's texts—that last host much more than the other two. One set of messages from mid-November 2020 indicated Meadows and Carlson tried to get in touch as the host was writing a broadcast. On November 29, Hannity texted Meadows an article from a website, the Federalist, and suggested he was convinced the election result was wrong. Hannity was eager for any shred of evidence he could use to question the vote.

> "I've had my team digging into the numbers. There is no way Biden got these numbers. Just mathematically impossible. It's so sad for this country they can pull this off in 2020. We need a major break-through, a video, something," Hannity wrote.
>
> "You're exactly right. Working on breakthrough," Meadows replied.

This came as Mike Flynn, his supposed associate Phil Waldron, lawyer Sidney Powell, and Patrick Byrne were all mounting their effort to invalidate the vote.

On December 6, Meadows texted Hannity to criticize another Fox News host, Chris Wallace, for correcting a guest from the Trump administration when they refused to refer to Biden as the president-elect.

"Doing this to try and get ratings will not work in the long run," Meadows wrote after sharing an article about the incident.

Hannity had been pressing colleagues to toe the delusional Trump election line.

"I've been at war with them all week. We will talk wen I see u," he replied.

Hannity went on to indicate that, if Trump was unable to hold on to power, he had big plans for Meadows. He wanted them to team up against Biden and to get into business together—and possibly with Rudy Giuliani.

"If this doesn't end the way we want, you me and Jay are doing 3 things together. 1- Directing legal strategies vs Biden 2- NC Real estate 3- Other business I talked to Rudy. Thx for helping him," Hannity wrote.

The text logs didn't contain a response from Meadows. Five days later, on December 11, Hannity texted the White House chief to vent. Biden's victory had been projected for over a month. He seemed to finally be coming to grips with it.

"3 years we expose the deep state, what happens? Nothing," Hannity wrote. "The Media protects Joe and Hunter. They steal an election. What am I missing Mark? We r so F'd as a country."

Meadows concurred.

"I am afraid you are not missing anything. The evil prevails for a time and they are rejoicing. But we must continue to fight," Meadows wrote.

As December rolled on, Hannity sent Meadows strategic advice about how Trump should handle Senate races in Georgia. Meadows was grateful for the support.

> "You are a true patriot and I am so very proud of you! Your friend-ship means a great deal to me," wrote Meadows.

Hannity appreciated the kind words, but he was distraught over Trump's loss.

> "Feeling is mutual," Hannity replied. "I am not particularly optimis-tic for the future. Biden is a semi conscious corpse, and he will be controlled by a very radical left wing element. [. . .] The country has foundational corruption that likely can never be fixed. The ramifica-tions of this are incalculable."

On the last day of 2020, Hannity texted Meadows a warning. The Fox News host was worried Trump was taking it too far. He wanted the lame-duck president to acquiesce to Biden taking office and start thinking about staging his comeback from Mar-a-Lago, his private club in Florida, after Biden took office.

> "I do NOT see January 6 happening the way he is being told. After the 6 th. He should announce will lead the nationwide effort to reform voting integrity," Hannity said of Trump. "Go to Fl and watch Joe mess up daily. Stay engaged. When he speaks people will listen."

Again, the logs did not include a response from Meadows. While Han-nity was encouraging Trump to step aside, Lynda McLaughlin, a producer at Hannity's radio show, was working on the election challenge.

> "Hey it's Lynda from Hannity," she wrote to Meadows on January 5. "I am down here presenting this information [. . .] Rallying the troops."

McLaughlin had texted Meadows a PDF document entitled "DIG Press Release" about an hour before. During this period, McLaughlin had spread lies about the election, including in testimony before Georgia legislators and in videos for the *Epoch Times*, in her capacity as communications director for a mysterious outfit, the Data Integrity Group, composed of purported data scientists and intelligence operatives.

> "Wonderful," said Meadows. "Thanks."

McLaughlin asked Meadows if he would agree to listen to her group to present its "data" to him or if he would arrange for some Republican members of Congress to hear them out. Meadows connected her to Ohio congressman Jim Jordan.

> "Jim jordon will gladly coordinate with the house team," Meadows wrote, before sharing the lawmaker's number.

McLaughlin also tried to score a direct meeting with Trump for her group.

> "Mark-are we able to present our data to POTUS? It seems there are many ppl presenting arguments that are based only on speculative information," she wrote. "We have hard data which shows proof of the fraud and is irrefutable."

The logs did not show a response from Meadows.

It's unclear how much Hannity knew about his radio producer's seeming final-hour election-fraud push, but he mentioned some of her activities with her group on the air. On the night of January 5, Hannity sent Meadows another text of his own. He was concerned that Pat Cipollone, the White House counsel, and Vice President Mike Pence were not on board with the various plans to keep Trump in office.

> "Im very worried about the next 48 hours," Hannity wrote. "Pence pressure. WH counsel will leave."

The next day, January 6th, at 2:32 p.m., as the crowds stormed the Capitol, Ingraham string-texted Meadows:

> "Hey Mark, The president needs to tell people in the Capitol to go home."
> "This is hurting all of us."
> "He is destroying his legacy and playing into every stereotype . . . we lose all credibility against the BLM/Antifa crowd if things go South."
> "You can tell him I said this."

Hannity wrote in just about an hour later. He also wanted Trump to calm the crowds.

> "Can he make a statement. I saw the tweet. Ask people to peacefully leave the capital," Hannity wrote.
> Meadows responded five minutes later, "On it."

Hannity's and Ingraham's messages showed they knew the violence was real, that it could have been stopped by Trump, and that it was unacceptable. Despite all of this, that very day they aired segments on their shows downplaying the role of Trump supporters in that violence and legitimizing and defending the anger of the crowds gathered outside the Capitol. It seemed clear to me that they were actively, willfully spinning and misleading their huge audience.

Four days after the attack, Hannity texted Meadows and Jordan. The Fox News host indicated he was trying—and failing—to soothe Trump.

> "Guys, we have a clear path to land the plane in 9 days. He can't mention the election again. Ever. I did not have a good call with him today. And worse, I'm not sure what is left to do or say, and I don't like not knowing if it's truly understood. Ideas?" Hannity asked.

The text logs did not include a reply from Meadows or Jordan.

The select committee aired some of the Fox News hosts' texts, but it mostly focused on the messages from January 6th decrying the violence. It was an effective strategy to highlight Trump's inactivity during the riot and to publicly expose how—despite what they were broadcasting to millions—even the partisans at Fox knew what happened that day was wrong. Still, I personally would have liked to see more emphasis on the messages that showed how solidly in bed Fox, largely through Hannity, and the Trump administration were.

The Fox News stars weren't just bystanders alarmed by January 6th's violence. The channel promoted the lies that led to it and spearheaded the effort to deny it. Behind the scenes, they floated business deals with administration officials, coordinated on strategy, and—even if Hannity's radio producer was acting alone—actively furthered the push to overturn the vote. Fox was part of it. They were there every step of the way.

* * *

The Ray Epps saga was a perfect demonstration of the power of the far-right media cycle—and its lack of principles. It also showed how the MAGA movement was willing to eat its own.

Epps seemed to be a true believer. He showed up in DC to—depending on which clip you saw or how you interpreted it—raise hell or lodge a peaceful complaint. Either way, he was a dedicated Trump supporter and the movement made him a fall guy.

In January 2022, as the theory about Epps bounced around the far-right digital sphere, I had a talk with one of the members of the select committee, Illinois Republican congressman Adam Kinzinger. We both thought the committee needed to directly refute the false flag conspiracies about supposed FBI involvement. Not doing so might undermine the investigation. It would also leave Epps and other individuals the Far Right was locked in on vulnerable to harassment.

Adam and I scheduled a private Zoom meeting limited to the committee's sitting members. Both of us discussed how conspiracies could damage the credibility of our investigation. Skeptics could paint our work as the political sequel to the inside job the FBI had supposedly started. We were in danger of losing the information battlespace.

After the meeting, the committee posted a pair of tweets that described the theories as "unsupported" and noted Epps denied any relationship with law enforcement. It was an effort to try to stem the tide of garbage swirling around online. Then I dug into Epps's phone records.

I promised the committee that I would thoroughly run the data. My team had Epps's CDRs. We could conduct frequency analysis to see his most-called numbers and call chain analysis to get a sense of his network. After a review of every number that had been in touch with Epps's phone, we could not find contacts between him and the FBI besides his call to them after his picture appeared on the flyers. Just to be certain, the CDR team conducted a deep dive on all the numbers in his logs to see if he was connected to any law enforcement agency or extremist group. There were no hits. Based on the data, Epps's time in the militia movement really did seem to be behind him.

I watched when Epps spoke to the committee in January 2022. I was curious to see this man who had ended up in the eye of the storm and wondered which rumors were closest to the truth.

My bullshit meter is well tuned. I wanted to see how he answered questions. Epps struck me as forthcoming and honest. He had no apparent awareness of encrypted apps that could have masked his communications.

Possibilities and probabilities are what drive intelligence analysis. It is possible that Ray Epps had communications we missed. He could have used encrypted chats, burner phones, or alternate means of communication. All of that was "possible." But, with the mountain of data we processed, including the call analysis and Epps's testimony, it was not probable that he secretly worked for the FBI. His initial inclusion on the flyers was actually another data point that indicated he was not affiliated with the bureau.

Investigators deal with probabilities and ambiguities. Total certainty is a rare thing. However, it was certain that Tucker Carlson, Darren Beattie, Thomas Massie, Laura Ingraham, Donald Trump, and so many others were culpable in spreading a conspiracy theory that had little basis. To me, it was undeniable that they had perpetuated the radicalization of MAGA supporters and put Epps's life in danger.

When I watched Epps as he video-conferenced with the committee, my main impression was of his deep regret. He hated what had happened to his family.

Epps and his wife had experienced death threats. She moved out for safety. They had to sell their beloved farm. The full force of the conspiracy theory media complex had come down on Epps. It crushed him.

CHAPTER 13

THE BETTER HALF

Virginia Thomas had been brainwashed.

As the wife of Supreme Court justice Clarence Thomas, Virginia, who goes by Ginni, is a major player in conservative activist circles and a powerful figure in Washington. However, when she first came to the capital, Thomas almost lost her way.

It was the mid 1980s and Thomas had moved from Omaha, Nebraska, where her parents were wealthy Republican Party insiders. Thomas had always loved politics and, after finishing law school, she got a job as a congressional staffer. She also became a "Lifespringer."

Lifespring was a company that offered group seminars on personal growth. The courses cost hundreds of dollars and involved emotionally charged and confrontational activities. Students stripped down to bikinis and berated each other about their bodies. The program was designed to humiliate them.

The mastermind of the project was a real hustler named John Hanley. He had been convicted of mail fraud for a scam involving toilet-cleaning services. Although Hanley has denied it, there were reports that he was inspired to start Lifespring after attending a leadership training program where he was locked in a coffin and people were made to, literally, eat shit.

Lifespring was intense. Some attendees described significant pressure to enroll friends and social circles that would cut you out if you left the program. Others claimed they left with psychotic breaks. The group was hit with a slew of lawsuits and linked to multiple deaths and mental hospitalizations. Critics called it a cult.

Thomas was totally sucked in. In later speeches, Thomas said she felt brainwashed and that the experience had hurt her personally and professionally. She broke out only with the help of a cult deprogrammer. Afterward, Thomas had to move out of her house to avoid what she said was harassment from Lifespringers who were pressuring her to come back into the fold. The experience drove her to become an anti-cult activist.

When Thomas's texts with Mark Meadows leaked to the press in March 2022, the world was shocked. The messages showed Thomas, the wife of a Supreme Court justice, ranting about Democrats being dragged off to detention camps and ballots labeled with hidden quantum blockchain watermarks. No one was more surprised than the people who knew Thomas from her time fighting Lifespring. Some of her former associates talked to the press and expressed amazement over the fact she'd gone from warning people away from cults to seemingly losing her grip to one.

As Thomas's texts made headlines, a cult expert named Steven Hassan tweeted an old video that gave a glimpse into her mind. Hassan had hosted an event for former Lifespringers in Kansas in 1986. Thomas was there. She spoke about how she got out of what she called a cult—and hinted at what had gotten her in.

"When you come away from a cult you have to find a balance in your life as far as getting involved with fighting the cult or exposing it," Thomas said. "The other angle is getting a sense of yourself, I mean, what was it that made you get into that group and what are the questions in there that still need to be answered?"

Thomas recognized herself as someone who was susceptible to cults and mental manipulation. She even worried that she might go too far in her anti-cult activism.

"I also don't want to go overboard in that regard so that I can reconnect with my own needs in a spiritual way, which I still haven't done, and I still have so many questions," said Thomas. "All those things that got me to Lifespring are still there and, I guess, I struggle with not going overboard in fighting the cult."

With her need to seek out answers and tendency to go all in, Thomas feared she could get drawn into another extreme ideology. Which is exactly what happened.

* * *

I found Thomas in Mark Meadows's text messages after a hot tip and a case of mistaken identity.

Before my CDR team got set up and started working, committee staffers had tried to decode the Meadows text logs. They did fairly well in matching names to numbers, but the databases and services used were mostly basic online phone directories. My team had experience with tricky searches. I also procured for the committee a subscription to a high-grade database that is used by law enforcement to dig for records. What happened with the messages that turned out to be from Thomas gave me cause to worry that other original identifications might have been off. All of the earlier staff work needed to be double-checked.

Thomas's messages highlighted the challenges in having untrained, although intelligent, individuals conducting name and number lookups with inferior tools. Before my team came in, Thomas's text messages were originally attributed to a University of Virginia professor, but the name Ginni appeared to be in a sign-off position in one of the texts—

were we just dealing with a UVA professor whose first name happened to be Virginia? Another text referenced Connie Hair, who is the chief of staff to Republican Texas congressman Louie Gohmert and Thomas's good friend. In the intelligence world, we'd call that an indicator. These indicators were more like giant red flags. Why would a UVA professor with a different name include the word "Ginni" in a message? It seemed very odd.

The messages that supposedly came from the professor were deeply crazy stuff. They were militant, messianic, and loaded with fringe web conspiracies. If "Ginni" was Ginni Thomas, it would be further proof the QAnon conspiracies had penetrated, and influenced, the upper echelon of the Republican Party.

At the time, I was running a bit of a human intelligence operation. Many Republicans who were disgusted by what they saw on January 6th were discretely and discreetly helping me. I can't reveal their names because I never betray a confidence.

One former member of Congress told me that Thomas communicated with Meadows. They called me late one night and revealed they were sure she was in the texts. I remember exactly what they said: "I know she is in there."

I also thought Ginni's husband, Supreme Court justice Clarence Thomas, could be nested in the logs. There were a series of messages from a "cthomas" email address that discussed strategies for having Republican state legislatures send alternate electors. If finding Ginni in the texts would be explosive, then identifying Clarence would have been positively nuclear. It would call the very independence of the judicial branch into question.

My hunches were half right.

The Supreme Court is supposed to be insulated from politics, but Ginni was an activist. She was involved in politics well before she married Clarence and continued to be an activist once they were hitched.

Ginni ran to be a national delegate to the Republican convention in 2020 and she helped set up a pro-Trump group called the Northern Virginia Deplorables that held flag-waving flash mobs and other events in the DC suburbs. Supreme Court spouses are typically low profile. Ginni's involvement with political groups had already led to questions about whether Clarence would need to recuse himself in cases with a political component. If Clarence had been in the logs, it would be a much bigger deal than all that.

When I began to suspect Ginni and Clarence had texted with Meadows, I put together a technical brief outlining how we might be able to cement the identifications. I sent it to the senior staff. The investigators approved my plan of attack. Then I got a call from Liz Cheney.

The Wyoming congresswoman wanted me to pull back. Cheney said she thought homing in on the Thomases was premature.

"I think we need to remove that briefing," Cheney said. "It's going to be a political sideshow."

Cheney was worried about the possibility that exposing one or both of the Thomases as an election denier and QAnon sympathizer could overshadow the committee's other work. The committee needed to show the American people that there was an organized, violent effort to reverse the election—and that there were indications it could have been directed by the White House. Thanks to their prominence, Ginni and Clarence would make a lot of headlines, but those headlines might overwhelm the other important work we were doing.

Sometimes I run hot. Liz Cheney and I are both type A personalities. The conversation did not go well. My point was simple: Data isn't political. It's not right or wrong. It's just data. Plus, there was no way to withdraw my technical analysis briefing to the team. The cat was out of the bag.

I'll admit that my temper escalated the tension in my rough call with Cheney. I've never been someone who likes being told what to do or where to go. That went double for my work on the committee. As a former intelligence officer and former congressman, I felt this investigation was the most important work I had done in my time on Capitol Hill. We had to get it right. It wasn't about me or Cheney. It was about following the data. There'd be no truth at the end of the tunnel if we didn't let the data light our way.

I also thought that, given Clarence's position and Ginni's prominence in conservative circles, the American public had to know what she had been up to. Some of the messages went beyond simply cheering Meadows on. It was legitimate for me to have concerns as to whether a Supreme Court justice had been involved in the legally questionable push to overturn the election. Was it possible that one of the country's nine top judges was on board with an authoritarian interpretation of the Constitution? The implications were overwhelming.

Cheney found it all improbable. I think she still had more faith in the institutional GOP than I did at that point. It made sense: Her father was Dick Cheney, a fixture in Republican politics for over fifty years. He served in four presidential administrations: as a staff assistant in Richard Nixon's White House, as Gerald Ford's chief of staff, as secretary of defense to George H. W. Bush (who appointed Clarence Thomas), and as vice president to the elder Bush's son George W. She grew up in the lap of the Republican Party. Cheney couldn't fathom that a conservative Supreme Court justice would be so far gone. While she had no misconceptions about Ginni Thomas, Cheney had trouble imagining Clarence would be stupid and reckless enough to involve himself in January 6th.

I could only be so mad at Cheney. After all, I wouldn't have been on the committee at all without her. We shared history and I knew she understood my technical and analytic acumen. We were together in this battle. She had shown tremendous appetite to take this all on and—as a Republican—admirable courage in doing so. When I took a deep breath and thought it over, I saw that she had a point about the political realities.

Also, we had almost no tools to take on the Thomases. The truth of the matter is, Supreme Court justices are appointed for life and, once in, there aren't a lot of regulations beyond what's self-imposed. It was basically up to Clarence to determine when he felt it necessary to recuse himself. If he had decided to bend the law for political reasons, it wasn't like people could vote him out at the next election. Shining a spotlight on Ginni could detract from the most important and urgent points we had to make to the public, and to no concrete end.

Cheney and I came to an understanding. I would check out my hunch about the Thomases and keep the members of Congress on the committee apprised. Our professional process guaranteed that the data we found could be used and integrated into the larger effort, but I assured Cheney we would triple-check our findings and route those findings to a select group of committee members. We needed to be sure about what we had and, if I was right, we would have to carefully analyze the possible consequences of our next steps before anything went public. Cheney was worried about leaks. This turned out to be a valid concern.

The email address that we thought might belong to Clarence wasn't his. Later on, we found out that the address belonged to someone else—a Republican politico and former senior staffer.

I hit the jackpot on the other phone number, however. It wasn't a UVA professor. It was Ginni Thomas.

When our team initially ran the number, the registration didn't come back to her. The analysis team utilizes a checklist of search options when encountering problematic identifications. For example, if the name being searched is a married woman and a search is initially unproductive, the next step is to check numbers and data under a maiden name. That's how we found Thomas. She was listed under her maiden name, Lamp.

Through the experience of uncovering hard-to-find numbers like Thomas's, we refined our methods. We also instituted a practice of returning to more difficult searches when we had a few minutes of downtime. Thomas reminded us to hone our procedures through continuous improvement and diligence. I guess I owe her for that. Thanks, Ginni.

Even though we had a solid identification in the digital sphere, I also turned to my human intelligence operation. I was 100 percent sure it was Thomas in those texts, but I wanted to be 100.1 percent sure. This was a big one.

I showed the number to a select few of my Republican sources. They confirmed it. The number was hers. My gut had been on point. But this was one situation where I really didn't want to be right.

* * *

Thomas's messages to Meadows were chilling. They suggested a total break from reality. Her first text landed on November 5, two days after the election. The results still had not been called. Thomas was already worried about fraud. Her text to Meadows was a long string of full-blast paranoia. I am not even including all of it here.

> "I hope this is true; never heard anything like this before; or even a hint of it. Possible??? TRUMP STING w CIA Director Steve Pieczenik The Biggest Election Story in History, QFS-BLOCKCHAIN 7 min video," she wrote.

After that introduction, she sent Meadows a link to a YouTube video.

> "The QFS blockchain watermarked ballots in over 12 states have been part of a huge Trump & military white hat sting operation in 12 key battleground states where 20,000+ natl guard were deployed;

Biden crime family & ballot fraud co-conspirators (elected officials, bureaucrats, social media censorship mongers, fake stream media reporters, etc) are being arrested & detained for ballot fraud right now & over coming days, & will be living in barges off GITMO to face military tribunals for sedition," Thomas wrote.

It was hard to read. A paranoid stream of consciousness with questionable punctuation and a trace of repressive violence. The message was head-scratching and disturbing at the same time.

The text logs did not include a response from Meadows.

Thanks to all of the time I had spent investigating the Far Right, I understood it as well as anyone possibly could. I still speak QAnon. Let me translate it for you.

The "QFS blockchain" was a conspiracy theory that allegedly originated with Steve Pieczenik. Rather than being CIA director, as Thomas's text suggested, Pieczenik is a former State Department consultant and a regular guest on Alex Jones's *Infowars*. In his prior appearances, Pieczenik had pushed the notion that the 2012 Sandy Hook Elementary shooting, which left twenty-six children and adults dead, was a "false flag" designed to give the government a pretext to take guns. I told you this shit was pervasive.

Those utterly false and offensive claims about Sandy Hook led to lawsuits from families of the dead children. (A judge has found Jones and his companies liable for defamation, but it has not yet been determined how much Jones will have to pay.) Now, after the 2020 election, Pieczenik was pumping out a new lie. He claimed that mail-in ballots were watermarked with "QFS blockchain encryption code" that would allow for fraud to be tracked by a government "sting operation." This was a variation on an internet theory that described QFS variously as a "quantum financial system" or "quantum blockchain." Like mass voter fraud, none of this nonsense is a real thing.

Pieczenik's claims were pseudoscientific deceptions. Thanks to Thomas, they had made it into the White House chief of staff's phone.

Quantum computing is a relatively new field that involves moving beyond the classical logic that runs all current computer systems and harnessing bits in quantum superpositions and the quantum correlations between them for added computing power. It's a developing technology that is a potential threat to the blockchain concept, which relies on classical assumptions about computing power for its security. So combining quantum computing with the blockchain, as Thomas does in this text, doesn't add up technologically. The idea of a nationwide election "sting" strained credulity for the same reason the allegations of massive fraud are hard to believe. Our federal government does not run elections. States have primary responsibility and administer votes through different local agencies and parties. Mail-in ballots are issued locally. Secretly altering the results or injecting watermarks to track ballots would require infiltrating all of the separate systems, states, and procedures—without leaving a trace. Pieczenik's claims were beyond far-fetched.

The fact that Thomas, the wife of a justice on the nation's highest court, was buying into this stuff was alarming. But the part that really shook me was her message's violent undertone. Thomas suggested the "military white hat" hacker operation would lead to "military tribunals" with Democrats being sent off to the terrorist detention facilities at Guantanamo Bay—a dark, authoritarian vision. The text clearly echoed QAnon and its talk of a coming "storm." Pieczenik and Jones were peddling a new variation of the old lie that was designed to gain traction among the Q adherents online.

On November 6, the day after she sent Meadows the unhinged "QFS-BLOCKCHAIN" video, Thomas sent another message. The vote count was ongoing, but it was starting to look bad for Trump. She did not want to see Trump admit defeat.

"Do not concede. It takes time for the army who is gathering for his back," she wrote.

The text logs did not contain a response from Meadows. Biden's victory would be declared the following day.

Three days later, Meadows had come down with COVID. Thomas offered her prayers and said she'd heard he was "working through" his illness. Then she went straight back to business. She exhorted him to "listen" to people who were out in the conservative media alleging mass election fraud and discussing various strategies for Trump to try to overturn the result. Her list included the conservative radio host Rush Limbaugh, who amplified the baseless conspiracy theory that antifa had stormed the Capitol in the immediate aftermath of January 6th, and Cleta Mitchell, one of the lawyers who worked to build a case for overturning the results.

> "Mark, I wanted to text you and tell you for days you are in my prayers!!" wrote Thomas. "Know the grassroots wants Truth to prevail over Lies!!! [. . .] Help This Great President stand firm, Mark!!! The Left tastes their power!!! [. . .] You are the leader, with him, who is standing for America's constitutional governance at the precipice. The majority knows Biden and the Left is attempting the greatest Heist of our History."

Meadows appreciated Thomas's support.

> "I will stand firm. We will fight until there is no fight left. Our country is too precious to give up on. Thanks for all you do," Meadows wrote.

Thomas's response might have been loaded with emojis. Either that or she was really, really fond of random question marks. To me, it looked like she regularly used both. It wasn't entirely clear, since the small emoji images had been turned to question marks on the text logs sheet.

> "Tearing up and praying for you guys!!!!!?????????????????? So proud to know you!!??????" answered Thomas.

This exchange showed another recurring element in the texts between Thomas and Meadows. The pair shared a religious fervor in their support for questioning the election. Like so many in the Far Right, they saw Trump's refusal to step aside as a heroic stand in an epic struggle between light and dark.

To Thomas, this was war. She made that clear in another message to Meadows on November 10, when she complained about insufficient support for Trump's stance from congressional Republicans. Thomas seemed to point to four congressmen—Louie Gohmert, Jim Jordan, Paul Gosar, and Chip Roy, who all helped with the election push—as outliers.

> "House and Senate guys are pathetic too . . . only 4 GOP House members seen out in street rallies with grassroots . . . Gohmert, Jordan, Gosar and Roy . . . where the heck are all those who benefited by Presidents coattails?!!!??" she wrote. "It is such a messaging war game/ information warfare being played to keep the truth from coming out. A Heist!"

Thomas knew she was a soldier in the information war. And while she fought, she had the privilege of access to the party's top tier, thanks to her high-level conservative connections. On November 13, she sent Meadows a message encouraging him to work with Sidney Powell, the lawyer who filed bogus lawsuits with half-baked affidavits and encouraged Trump to use EO 13848 to send troops into the streets. As Thomas pressed for Powell, she suggested that she had also brought this up with "Jared," a seeming reference to Jared Kushner.

> "Just forwarded to yr gmail an email I sent Jared this am. Sidney Powell & improved coordination now will help the cavalry come and Fraud exposed and America saved. ?? Don't let her and your assets be marginalized instead . . . help her be the lead and the face?!?" she wrote.

There was no response from Meadows in the logs turned over to the committee.

The next day, November 14, Thomas sent another message. This one had the name of her friend, Connie Hair, Gohmert's chief of staff, at the bottom. It seemed like something written the day before that Thomas may have copied and pasted to pass along. It referred to service in the armed forces by its author, and it was angry and militant. The text might've been prefaced by a single question mark from Thomas, and concluded with a longer string of them, to solicit Meadows's thoughts on what came between those interrogative bookends—or perhaps those question marks were actually emojis.

> "? The most important thing you can realize right now is that there are no rules in war. You destroy your enemy's ability to fight. This is what is happening right now—this war is psychological. PSYOP. It's what I did in the military. They are using every weapon they have to try to make us quit, to give up on our system of government and processes. They try to break our will to fight through demoralization, discouragement, division, chaos and gaslighting. It is fake, fraud and if people would take a deep breath and look at things through that filter we will see this through and win. The Constitu-

tion is on our side and it is worth fighting for. I believe in it. Our Founders and even those facing Omaha Beach have done MUCH more than we have since Election Day. I would suggest we all think in those terms because if we don't, and we allow this massive fraud to stand, we've lost our country anyway.-Connie Hair, Nov 13??????"

The logs did not include a response from Meadows.

The violent undertones in Thomas's earliest messages to Meadows were morphing into total declarations. In her mind, this was war.

Five days later, on November 19, she sent another message that apparently referenced her own experience when her husband, Clarence, had faced a sexual harassment allegation during his Supreme Court confirmation hearings in 1991. Thomas encouraged Meadows to embrace Powell and her Kraken lawsuits. This text was sent at 3:31 a.m. Thomas was up in the wee hours.

"Mark, (don't want to wake you!) The intense pressures you and our President are now experiencing are more intense than Anything Experienced (but I only felt a fraction of it in 1991). At stake: truth, evidence, facts and America. Or will lies win?!" wrote Thomas. "I know you all are feeling an unbelievable negative intensity if you drink in media or weak people/messages. Look at a calendar and set out the plan for getting truth, evidence out by dates certain. Sounds like Sidney and her team are getting inundated with evidence of fraud. Make a plan. Release the Kraken and save us from the left taking America down??"

Thomas went on to urge Meadows "to buck up your team on the inside." She feared looming "threats" to conservatives, including Trump's newly confirmed Supreme Court justice, Amy Coney Barrett, nicknamed "ACB" by some of her supporters. Thomas was rallying the troops in her high-stakes holy war.

> "Americans are praying for you all! Feel that and be the leaders God have made you into for this time!?????????? Ginni-You guys fold, the evil just moves fast down underneath you all. Lots of intensifying threats coming to ACB and others," she wrote. "So honor and respect you for helping this amazing President stand for all of us!!!!? This is Spiritual Warfare, as you must feel, Mark! It is about America continuing and this lonely leader and man!????????"

That was the message that included her name which, along with the text that had the 1991 reference, made me realize Ginni Thomas was indeed in the text logs.

Meadows must have been sleeping. He didn't write back until after seven in the morning.

> "Thanks so much," he said.

It looked like Thomas, who evidently hadn't slept much, "loved" that message less than an hour later.

On November 19, as Sidney Powell and Rudy Giuliani were giving the press conference where they blamed Trump's loss on the dead Venezuelan dictator Hugo Chávez, Thomas wrote in again.

> "Tears are flowing at what Rudy is doing right now!!!!?????????" she said.

Meadows, who had expressed misgivings about Powell in his conversations with others, seemed unsure about whether Thomas's tears were happy or sad. His response may have ended with one or two emojis, or two question marks.

"Glad to help??" he replied.

Thomas made clear she was impressed with Powell and Giuliani.

"Whoa!! Heroes!!!!" she wrote.

Based on the text logs, Meadows did not reply.

Three days later, after Powell had been cut from Trump's legal team, Thomas wrote in. She was concerned.

"Trying to understand the Sidney Powell distancing. . . ."

Meadows responded that Powell was not presenting any solid evidence.

"She doesn't have anything or at least she won't share it if she does,"
he said.

"Wow!" replied Thomas.

* * *

Although I had suspected it, I was taken aback when we definitively tied all these messages to Ginni Thomas. She seemed mentally unwell. It was an open secret around the Beltway that her views had gotten pretty extreme. What really shook me was the fact that, if Clarence agreed with or was even aware of his wife's efforts, all three branches of government would be tied to the Stop the Steal movement.

Thomas has always maintained that she keeps her work separate from her husband; she says Clarence agrees. However, friends and associates have described them as incredibly close. Also, I'm married. I know how things go between loving partners. I can't imagine a world where Christine wouldn't be weighing in on my work.

Analyst time. Was Thomas's claim that her perspective had no influence over her husband possible? Sure. Was it probable? Hell no.

In late 2020, as various Trump allies filed suits aimed at overturning the election, some tried to press their cases all the way to the Supreme Court. Trump was eager to have the land's highest justices rule in their favor.

"Whether it's a justice of the Supreme Court, or a number of justices of the Supreme Court—let's see if they have the courage to do what everybody in this country knows is right," Trump declared at a news conference on December 8, 2020.

Some of the cases the court was considering came from Powell, whom Thomas was advocating for behind the scenes. Another involved Louie Gohmert's staff, who hobnobbed with Thomas. The court ultimately didn't hear the election cases over Clarence Thomas's objection, which the justice made sure was publicly known by including his noted dissent in the final order. It was hard to imagine that Thomas wouldn't be pushing some of the same extreme views that she sent to Meadows on her husband. More than likely, he shared at least some of her demented outlook.

The Supreme Court also had the power to shape the January 6th investigation. When the House select committee sought Trump White House documents from the National Archives, the former president, citing executive privilege, fought to keep his records sealed. The court rebuffed Trump's request in January 2022. Clarence Thomas was the only one of the nine justices who ruled that the records should remain hidden. In February 2021, the justice also echoed conspiracy paranoia in a dissent where he expressed doubts about mail-in voting; he wrote, "We are fortunate that many of the cases we have seen alleged only improper rule changes, not fraud. But that observation provides only small comfort. An election free from strong evidence of systemic fraud is not alone sufficient for election confidence. Also important is the assurance that fraud will not go undetected." Clarence adopted the formal, robed version of his wife's text rantings.

By the time I discovered Ginni Thomas was in Meadows's messages, I knew her husband was trying to stop our committee's access to records. Clarence Thomas was in a position to rule on future elections and our response to the fringe militant movement—and his wife, a part of the far-right movement, seemed able to influence Clarence's thinking and eventual rulings. It was hard to sit with all that.

* * *

Even if you think it's a stretch to tie Ginni Thomas's conspiracy theorizing and advocacy for overturning the election to her husband, there is no question that there was a broader legal effort to keep Trump in power. And the wife of a Supreme Court justice was swimming deep in that pool.

One of the many right-wing groups she was involved in was the Council for National Policy; Thomas sits as a board member of its political advocacy arm, CNP Action. Members of the council's governing bodies promoted election-fraud conspiracies and leaned on state legislatures, state officials, and members of Congress to reject Biden electors. Other members of the council showed up in Meadows's texts. I am not naming them all here due to the ongoing investigation. The council's board of governors reportedly includes Cleta Mitchell, a lawyer who worked on Trump's election challenge suits and participated in his notorious phone call with Georgia secretary of state Brad Raffensberger. There are many others.

Later on, we would learn that, in addition to her twenty-one texts to Meadows, Thomas sent twenty-nine emails to Arizona lawmakers encouraging them to reject Biden electors. Those messages were not initially obtained by the committee. Emma Brown, a *Washington Post* reporter, revealed them after filing a public records request. Thomas sent an identical message to twenty of the lawmakers on November 9, two days after Biden had been declared the winner. "Please do your Constitutional duty!" its subject line blared, before seeking an "audit" of the vote. About a month later, on December 13, Thomas would send another blast to twenty-two lawmakers. It said they held the "Constitutional power and authority to protect the integrity of our elections."

"We need you to exercise that power now!" she wrote.

Of course, Thomas's email also included a YouTube link to a video about election conspiracies. Her case for turning over the election was firmly based in the digital fever swamps. It was also, like so many of the legal strategies that emerged in Trumpworld after the vote, legally dubious, at best.

By the letter of the law, the electoral college system allows so-called faithless electors. This is when an elector casts a vote for a presidential candidate that was not the choice of the majority of a state's voters. However, Arizona has a law specifically barring faithless electors, meaning its electors would go to Biden the moment the state's election result was certified. State law also specified that Arizona's canvassing had to be certified by the governor on the fourth Monday after the election— November 30, 2020.

As the deadline approached, Thomas was apparently working behind the scenes. On November 30, Republican state lawmakers held what they called a hearing at a downtown Phoenix hotel, where Rudy Giuliani and Jenna Ellis spent several hours presenting questionable voter fraud evidence. While it was happening, Arizona's Republican governor, Doug Ducey, gathered with state officials at the historic state Capitol about a mile and a half down the street and certified Joe Biden's victory. Trump personally got involved. He sent tweets that accused

Ducey of having "betrayed the people of Arizona" and of "rushing" the certification.

"What is going on with @dougducey? Republicans will long remember!" Trump wrote.

Ducey, who had been a staunch Trump ally, refused to cave. It was one of those moments where we only averted disaster because, thankfully, a key individual stood their ground. As troubled as I was by the direction of the Republican Party, it was heartening to see instances of people like Ducey, White House counsel Pat Cipollone, and Vice President Mike Pence upholding the values of our democracy. I can't imagine what would have happened if they weren't there—or rather, I don't want to.

As Ducey signed the results behind a desk, news cameras broadcast live. Suddenly, the soaring horns of "Hail to the Chief" blared from the cell phone in his pocket. Ducey was getting a call from the White House switchboard. He didn't pick up.

We are still learning about just how deeply Ginni Thomas was involved in trying to thwart the will of the American voters. Along with encouraging Meadows to go to war, advocating for Powell, and emailing the Arizona legislators, she was also corresponding with John Eastman, an attorney who wrote a memo detailing a six-part plan for Pence to overturn the election on January 6th. That blueprint began with Arizona's alternate electors. Eastman was a former clerk for Clarence Thomas, whose clerks are known for staying close—including to Ginni. It's a notoriously tight-knit network.

Ginni Thomas was not the only CNP Action member who showed up in Meadows's texts. One sent Meadows a text on December 5, 2020, that indicated they were helping Eastman with his work and that he was focused on filing a case with the Supreme Court.

"Mark, I was able to get John Eastman over the line. He's ready to file an original action in SCOTUS for the President. He needs to talk to you about two things. Can you call me so I can briefly give you the details?" the CNP member wrote.

This same CNP member also worked with Jenna Ellis. I am withholding their name due to the ongoing investigation.

Two Republican members of Congress, Utah senator Mike Lee and Texas congressman Chip Roy, also indicated they were in touch with Eastman in texts to Meadows.

I don't know exactly what Ginni Thomas discussed with Eastman. He is one of the individuals who battled the committee's efforts to obtain their records. Eastman lost that court fight in June 2022, after I left the investigation. We are all still learning about just how much Thomas was involved. And, of course, Meadows's texts are an incomplete record; we don't know if there are more messages with Thomas that he didn't turn over. The Arizona emails uncovered by the meticulous reporter were a lucky stroke. There could be a lot more out there.

Still, we already know enough to say that, like Sidney Powell, John Eastman, and Rudy Giuliani, Ginni Thomas was part of the loose coalition of lawyers and advocates who tried to fight the election in the courts.

The January 6th plot had a political arm, a media arm, a military arm, and a legal one.

* * *

America first learned about Ginni Thomas's texts with Meadows in March 2022. Reporters Bob Woodward and Robert Costa had obtained the messages and published an article. It was a leak.

The story was a blockbuster that dominated the news for days—Cheney was right about that prediction. I didn't like having that investigative thread go public before we'd had a full chance to pull on it. On the other hand, I was glad Americans were learning more about how folks with access to the highest levels of government were advancing wild conspiracy theories. People were stunned by Thomas's language and apparent disconnect from objective reality. The revelation of her texts was the first time many people were forced to confront the deranged language and fanaticism that I had realized was taking over the GOP.

On November 24, 2020, as a growing number of Republicans were acknowledging Trump's loss, Thomas seemed despondent in her texts to Meadows. She called it a coup and returned to the idea of good versus evil. She saw the world as a simple, tribal binary.

> "The fracturing now. The stabbing in the back of anyone daring to still say there seemed to be fraud. All the Rs congratulating Biden. Your/his loyalists can't take this. It is so evil," she wrote.

Meadows offered up his own apocalyptic assessment.

> "This is a fight of good verses evil. Evil always looks like the victor until the King of Kings triumphs. Do not grow weary in well doing," he replied. "The fight continues. I have staked my career on it. Well at least my time in DC on it."

Thomas thanked him and suggested it would be catastrophic "if globalists win." Then she said the thing that had become so painfully clear to me in recent years. For her and others like her, the Republican Party is no longer about ideals. It's about one leader. There is no party anymore. Only Trump.

> "This rotten GOP . . . just like Fox and the NFL, they are whistling past the graveyard if they think proceeding independent of DJT will work out," she wrote.

The woman who escaped Lifespring and knew she was still vulnerable to going overboard had found a new cult, a cult of personality.

After November 24, 2020, there was a relatively long gap without any texts between Thomas and Meadows. It's unclear whether they stopped their steady stream of messages or if there are texts unshared with the committee.

Thomas's very last message in the logs came on January 10, four days after the Capitol attack. In it, she was all over the map. Thomas was upset that Pence had not tried to reject the certification of Biden's win. She hinted at false flag January 6th denialism. And she questioned whether the country has a future.

> "We are living through what feels like the end of America. Most of us are disgusted with the VP and are in a listening mode to see where to fight with our teams," she wrote. "Those who attacked the Capitol are not representative of our great teams of patriots for DJT!!???????????? Amazing times. The end of Liberty???"

Sometimes I wonder the same thing, but for very different reasons.

EPILOGUE

The term "cult" is subjective.

Ginni Thomas was all in on Lifespring before she decided it was a destructive force. Other people say the program changed their lives for the better.

I had a negative, painful personal experience in the Mormon Church. In spite of this, I know others have gained incredible solace, faith, and support from Mormonism.

Something that one person sees as a cult can easily be another's lifesaver. Individual experiences are different and there's a lot of room for debate. Groups so destructive and irredeemable that they should inarguably be called cults are relatively rare. However, Donald Trump's QAnon-infused MAGA movement clearly fits into that category.

The core tenets of Trump's movement are lies. Trump and his acolytes have used these false doctrines to demonize their rivals and fuel a rage that has already led to shocking acts of violence. This anger is breaking up families. Shit, it almost got mine.

Trump certainly benefits, but his followers gain nothing from joining his movement. There's no charitable element. They are deceived and encouraged to turn on their fellow Americans. Grifters take their money at every turn. It's a tithing that never actually accrues any benefit or blessing. These are the hallmarks of the worst cults. Delusion, demonization, exploitation.

On June 5, 2022, I announced I was leaving the Republican Party. Despite everything, it was a painful, difficult decision. I had a healthy pour of whiskey that night.

Conservative values are a part of who I am. I believe in liberty, opportunity, and being damn careful with the taxpayers' hard-earned dollars. That's how we deliver on the American dream. I grew up idolizing Teddy Roosevelt and Ronald Reagan, and I was so proud to serve in Congress as a member of the party they once led. My service was the culmination of all the oaths to this country I had made in my military career. Since then, I feel like the GOP has left me.

If you are a true Republican, you can't support someone like Donald Trump. It's unconscionable to fall in line behind a man who uses lies and hate to raise money and accrue power. You can't belong to a party that, above all else, backs an individual with a tenuous grip on reality.

That's a fucking data judgment. Now, you've seen the evidence too. We've debunked the lies and tracked the grift. You can see the signals through all of Trump's noise. We know what he is.

Trump loves to question other peoples' Republican credentials. He calls them RINOs, short for "Republicans in Name Only." In reality, Trump is the biggest RINO of them all. He made a mockery of our values and took the party I once loved down a dark path.

So, where do I go next? That's hard to say. I thought telling this story was incredibly urgent and I drove hard over the past few months to get it down and share it with the world. Because of that, I haven't had a lot of time to rest or to think.

January 6th was an attempted coup. The good people at Merriam-Webster define a political coup as "the violent overthrow or alteration of an existing government by a small group." Trump and his band of allies were working to reverse an election and fundamentally change the character of our democracy. That's the definition of a coup.

It is particularly clear when you see all of the groups that were involved: the militants, the members of Congress, the lawyers. They were all working toward the same goal. There was coordination between the groups and they were communicating directly with the White House. This effort to overthrow the American order was organized and high-level. It was fueled by a perilous new ideology with insidious appeal. Religious nationalism, classic conspiracy myths, and high-tech distribution mechanisms have combined to forge a dangerous movement the likes of which this country has never seen.

I am tremendously proud of the work we did on the committee. We took on an enormous task under immense political pressure. It was especially hard for two members of my former party, Republicans Liz Cheney and Adam Kinzinger. As we worked, we took heat from our colleagues, friends, and even family. All of us faced real threats of violence. The members and hardworking staff on the committee showed tremendous courage. Standing with them was the honor of a lifetime.

This is history, and I was part of it. There's a burden that comes with that. This was not a story I could keep to myself.

I thought it was important for the world to know as much as possible about what we found. It is also crucial that the public gets a sense of what it was like behind the scenes of the committee—how carefully our data was compiled and vetted as well as the political and legal constraints we faced. It's vital for Americans to understand the limitations on the committee's power. There was so much we were prevented from finding. The committee is still fighting court cases and the clock is running out. It is up to the Justice Department to address the people who flouted our subpoenas and those who broke the law on January 6th. As phenomenal as the committee's work was, it is not going to solve the grave problems laid bare that day all by itself.

Along with sharing my experience working for the committee, I also thought it was worthwhile to tell a bit of my personal story. That part wasn't easy for me either. However, I believe that, in a divided country, dialogue is absolutely necessary. I know my family isn't the only one that's being divided by religion and politics.

We need to talk about all of these things. Nothing is going to get better if we are in denial. Or in our silos. Our Capitol was attacked. The country is hurting. Acknowledging the threat and trying to reconnect is part of how we might heal. Dialogue is a big part of how we can come back together. This book is my sincere attempt to pave the way for and contribute to that process.

There's one point Sidney Powell and Ginni Thomas are right about: this is a crucial turning point for the nation. If we're not careful, it could be the end of America as we know it.

Is there a road back? To be honest, I am not quite sure. What I do know is this: we are not going to be able to get our arms around our problems and get back on course unless we get serious. That starts with a frank conversation about what actually happened on January 6th.

We have a new enemy in this country, a domestic extremist movement that is growing online at fiber-optic speed. They are organized and militarized. The only way to defeat a military enemy is with military precision. The Far Right has honed its tactics, techniques, and procedures. We need to do the same.

QAnon and the MAGA movement have targeted our weak points. We need to shore them up.

Throughout this book, you have seen how extremists and exploiters have used ethical loopholes to thrive. Grifters and power-hungry politicians take advantage of weak campaign finance rules and insufficient transparency. Strong ethics regulations are the preventative medicine of a modern society. It's high time we take ours.

Once we harden our defenses, we need to go on the offensive. You don't win an information war by sitting back. The far-right media ecosystem is a primary driver of fantastical fanaticism. Some might say we need to shut it down and close off those who are spreading lies and anger. This idea has become known as deplatforming. It's the push that took Trump and so many of his followers off Twitter, Facebook, and YouTube.

As someone who values liberty, I have a bad, knee-jerk reaction to attempts to silence anyone, even if they are expressing damaging ideas. Free speech is one of the bedrock principles of our country. We can't lose sight of it while we defend our other values. Besides, restricting speech in one forum doesn't make it go away. It just migrates.

We need to be very careful about who we kick off the major public platforms. It could push them to go dark. They might turn to new places or build their own spaces. This is already happening. As the Far Right is squeezed out of the internet's main streets, they're turning to encrypted apps and the deep web. Retreating into the shadows, where they're harder to find.

In the military world, this is called an Intelligence Gain/Loss calculation or IGL. Shutting down the most violent and abhorrent content is important, but as we confront the far-right threat, we must also be mindful of this calculus and recognize that diminishing their platform might simultaneously decrease our window into their machinations. That's dangerous. If anything, we need to step up our awareness of their activities and our ability to know what's out there. And we need to be smart about drawing the line between keeping an eye on someone and saying they're beyond the pale.

Sunlight is a strong disinfectant. Rather than deplatforming far-right speech, we need to shed light on it—without ignoring the need to communicate our own positive vision for the country. QAnon has armies of digital warriors working for free. The truth needs volunteers to fight on its side.

I believe part of the reason the extreme MAGA movement was able to flourish is that so many of its core ideas and key players are absolutely, objectively nuts. Conspiracy theories about deep state kill teams, dead Venezuelan dictators, and the quantum blockchain are so crazy that they're tempting to ignore. But we can't dismiss them. Their appeal is real. Media, politicians, and the American people must engage. We need digital armies charging into the spaces where these dangerous ideologies are blooming. Once there, we have to push back with facts.

Far-right media isn't happening in a vacuum. As Fox News spews conspiracy theories and ignores every basic journalistic standard, major American companies have commercials on their airwaves—and businesses are running ads there because we're watching. These companies are funding the radicalization pipeline that led to the attack on our Capitol. It's not just Fox or the newer, more extreme right-wing cable channels, One America News and Newsmax. Large tech companies and major advertisers are also profiting off the fringe internet. We can't necessarily stop them. Free speech should always be paramount. But we can call it out. We can let them know we think it's unacceptable for them to do business with extremists. We can ensure that any company getting clicks or hosting fees from the Far Right is inextricably linked to them within the public square. And we can turn the channel.

While I do believe we need to aggressively and publicly confront the profiteers and bad actors in our political discourse, I am not calling for attacks and insults. There's way too much of that already. It's part of how we got so split and backed away into our respective corners. I have been guilty of firing off some of those shots myself, which I regret. I want us to come back. Dialogue needs to happen, but it needs to begin from a place of empathy. I hope this book can be something of a starting point for that conversation.

I have done my best to explain how extremist ideology functions and spreads. Its appeal is real. Good people can be taken in. I know this as well as anyone. I was almost there myself.

I'm not naive. The pull of the MAGA cult is strong. It has serious force behind it. We need to increase fact-based dialogue and connect with each other, but this threat isn't something we're going to be able to take on merely by holding hands and reconnecting. We can't cure the authoritarian illness plaguing the country with kumbaya. To fix this problem, talk needs to be combined with action.

I always say that crazy has more energy than sane. If someone has bought into a narrative that they're on the right side in a struggle against evil forces, it will be hard to win them back. This is strong stuff. Religious nationalism is weapons-grade propaganda, and extremists have the crazy energy to propagate it incessantly. At best, I think even an aggressive fact-based offensive could only turn around about 3 to 5 percent of the people who have gone down the digital disinformation rabbit hole. That won't be enough.

This battle won't be won quickly. The new information war is going to be a forever war. We will be dealing with these issues for a long time.

Government can be inefficient and slow. It can get bogged down by optics and politics. Lord knows I know that. They do need to kick into gear, but we can't wait for them to get started.

We need to get more serious about taking on far-right domestic terror. In the coming years, I hope we see aggressive public-private partnerships between law enforcement agencies and the brilliant academics and researchers who are focused on this space. All of our agencies need access to the cutting-edge data and programs for tracking deep-web activity that are being developed in the private sector. We need every bit of data we can get. The people who attacked our Capitol have powerful allies and resources at their disposal. US law enforcement needs to make sure it does too.

America was caught largely by surprise on January 6th. Now we have the data. We know what's out there and we know the stakes. Our tools for confronting this problem are better than ever. There's no excuse. We can't let January 6th happen again.

There is no more room for hesitation. The information war is on, and we are deep into the breach.

ACKNOWLEDGMENTS

To Christine, Lauren, Abby, Lilly, and my two wonderful granddaughters: without all of you, I couldn't do any of this.

Mom, I might not have taken the exact road you wanted me to, but without you I wouldn't be where I am today, and I wouldn't change a thing. I love you.

I know it's obligatory to thank my agent, editors, and all those who made this possible, but thanks are not enough for the herculean effort needed to put this book together in such a short time. I want to thank Sarah Crichton, the maestro at Holt, who oversaw the almost military-like effort needed to get this across the finish line. To Sarah's command staff, Tim Duggan, Conor Mintzer, and Pat Eisemann, I can't thank you enough for your expertise and care. I am also deeply grateful to Carolyn Levin for her wise counsel and to Luppe Luppen for his incredibly thorough fact-checking work. So many thanks to my friend and confidant throughout this process, my agent, Steve Ross. Steve was the igniter switch for this rocket called *The Breach*.

The introduction from Steve Kettmann to Steve Ross changed the course of my efforts in trying to inform the public on this most important challenge of defining the data and facts of QAnon and January 6th. Without the expert technical teams and professionals I hired to support the committee, we could not educate and show how data is the future in fighting this ever-expanding online information war. To Glenn, Mark, Mike, and the entire January 6th staff—you are the real heroes.

Like all Americans, I have the deepest gratitude for the dedicated law enforcement and staffers who protected our Capitol that day. Thank you.

Last, and certainly not least, without the remarkable efforts from and abilities of my good friend Hunter Walker, this sprint to the finish could not have been accomplished.

Denver Riggleman supported advanced intelligence analysis and technical development programs during his over two decades as an intelligence officer, NSA adviser, federal contractor, research and development technology lead, and successful CEO of support companies for the Department of Defense. A veteran of the Global War on Terror and multiple worldwide operations, he served with honor in the US Air Force for nine active-duty years. Riggleman is a former member of the House of Representatives from Virginia's Fifth Congressional District, which he represented as a Republican from 2019–2021, and the former senior technical advisor for the House Select Committee to Investigate the January 6th Attack on the United States Capitol. He is the CEO of Riggleman Information and Intelligence Group and co-owner of the award-winning Silverback Distillery. Riggleman currently lives in Virginia with his wife and family.

Hunter Walker is an investigative reporter and author from Brooklyn, New York. He spent the entirety of the Trump administration as a White House correspondent for Yahoo! News. Walker reported live from the Capitol on January 6th and went on to author a Substack newsletter dedicated to the attack. He has also written for a wide variety of magazines and websites, including *Rolling Stone*, the *New Yorker*, the *Atlantic*, NBC News, *Vanity Fair*'s Hive website, and *New York* magazine, among others.